WRESTLING *with* MOSES

WRESTLING *with*

MO

How Jane Jacobs Took On New York's

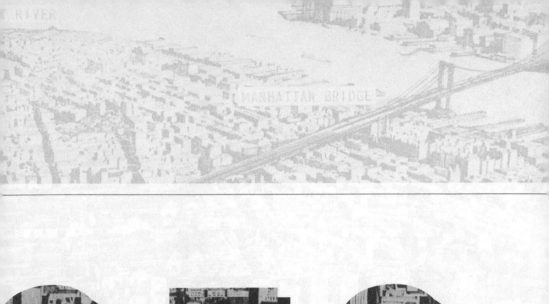

SES

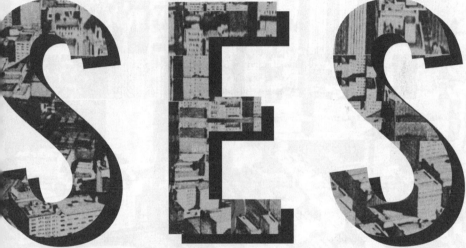

Master Builder and Transformed the American City

Anthony Flint

RANDOM HOUSE
NEW YORK

Published in the United States by Random House, an imprint of The Random
House Publishing Group, a division of Random House, Inc., New York.

RANDOM HOUSE and colophon are registered trademarks of Random House, Inc.

Library of Congress Cataloging-in-Publication Data

Flint, Anthony.
  Wrestling with Moses : how Jane Jacobs took on New York's master builder and
transformed the American city / Anthony Flint.
      p.   cm.
  ISBN 978-1-4000-6674-2 (alk. paper)
  eBook ISBN 978-1-58836-862-1
  1. Jacobs, Jane, 1916–2006.   2. Moses, Robert, 1888–1981.   3. City planners—
Biography.   4. City planners—New York (State)—New York—History—20th
century.   5. New York (N.Y.)—History—20th century.   I. Title.
  HT168.N5F55 2009
  711'.4092—dc22   2009002248

Printed in the United States of America on acid-free paper

www.atrandom.com

9 8 7 6 5 4 3 2

Book design by Liz Cosgrove

To my wife, Tina Ann Cassidy,
and all who love cities

CONTENTS

Anarchy and Order

The public hearing had already begun when she arrived. After stopping to add her name to the list of people requesting to speak, she headed toward the front of the auditorium, acknowledging the applause that rippled up from the crowd as she passed, a flash of white hair bobbing along the aisle, thick black glasses perched on an aquiline nose. She took a seat at the front of the hall.

The recipient of the applause was Jane Jacobs, a fifty-one-year-old author and activist, whose book *The Death and Life of Great American Cities* had made her synonymous with efforts to fight urban renewal projects that destroyed existing neighborhoods. On this pleasant spring evening, about two hundred residents of Manhattan's Lower East Side, Little Italy, Greenwich Village, and what would later be known as SoHo had gathered in a high-school auditorium for a public discussion of the proposed Lower Manhattan Expressway. They sat scattered in rows of fold-down seats, fanning themselves with pamphlets and craning to see the person who was speaking at a microphone in front of the stage.

The meeting had been called by officials from the New York State Transportation Department who believed the Lower Manhattan Express-

OPPOSITE: A master at the dais, Jane Jacobs famously turned her back on officials holding a hearing on the Lower Manhattan Expressway. *Fred McDarrah/Getty Images*

way would alleviate street traffic on clogged Manhattan streets and increase efficiency for drivers looking to cross from New Jersey to Long Island. The superhighway was to be elevated, providing ten wide lanes that would soar above the crowded city streets. But its foundation would cut through dense city blocks that had existed almost since the Dutch had settled Manhattan nearly four centuries before. Even the city officials knew that the price of this monument to progress would be steep: the government would have to evict twenty-two hundred families, demolish over four hundred buildings, and relocate more than eight hundred businesses to clear the way.

Though the ostensible purpose of the meeting was to collect opinions about the project, it had been hurriedly scheduled—to make sure testimony was gathered before legislation passed that required an even more extensive public approval process. For years, there had been clear opposition from the neighborhood's residents, who were now irritated that they had to state their case one more time. The manner in which the meeting was being conducted—the microphone faced toward the audience, not the officials the residents were nominally addressing—suggested that state officials were just going through the motions.

As a stenotypist moved her hands rhythmically over the key tabs of her machine off to the side, the officials frequently interrupted speakers to remind them of a time limit. When a man talking about the dangers of air pollution was told to speed it up, the audience began shouting questions to the officials: What changes had been made to the proposal? Was there anything better about the latest version of the roadway plan? The transportation men shrugged; they were only there to provide basic information and hear testimony, or rather bear witness to the fact that testimony was being given. The crowd began a chant: "We want Jane. We want Jane."

From the seat she'd taken near the front of the auditorium, Jane Jacobs made her way up the stairs and onto the stage. "It's interesting, the way the mike is set up," she observed tartly as she reached the microphone. She was calm, and her expression was matter-of-fact. "At a public hearing, you are supposed to address the officials, not the audience."

The chairman of the hearing, John Toth of the New York Department of Transportation, bounded down from the stage and turned the microphone around. But Jacobs turned it right back.

"Thank you, sir, but I'd rather speak to my friends," Jacobs said. "We've been talking to ourselves all evening as it is." The crowd roared with laughter.

After a pause, Jacobs continued. "What kind of administration could even consider destroying the homes of two thousand families at a time like this? With the amount of unemployment in the city, who would think of wiping out thousands of minority jobs? They must be insane." The expressway would destroy families and businesses, factories and historic buildings—in short, entire neighborhoods. Nobody wanted it, she said. But the government wasn't listening. It was as if the officials backing the project had parted from reality.

"The city is like an insane asylum run by the most far-out inmates. If the expressway is put through," she warned, "there will be anarchy." The officials in attendance were mere errand boys, and the residents had to make sure they would take a single message back to their bosses: that the people of lower Manhattan would not stand for this highway. But this message couldn't be mere words, she said; it had to be a physical demonstration, a defiant march. She called the crowd forward, and about fifty people, some carrying placards, moved up the stairs, with Jane leading the way.

Toth rose from his seat as the first of the protesters stepped onto the stage. "You can't come up here. Get off the stage!"

"We are going to march right across this stage and down the other side," Jacobs responded calmly, as if to a petulant child.

"Arrest this woman!" Toth frantically called to the police officers assigned to the hearing.

As Jacobs led the crowd onto the stage, the stenotypist gathered up her machine and clutched it to her chest, proclaiming that she was not an employee of the state, had nothing to do with the expressway, and had just purchased the brand-new equipment herself. With her free hand, she lunged out at the marchers to keep them away, and struck Jacobs. It was more jostle than shove, but a patrolman intervened.

"Why don't you just sit down here, Mrs. Jacobs," he said, gesturing to a folding chair at the rear of the stage. She went to the chair and stood behind it, resting her hands on its back.

As more and more marchers made their way to the stage and the stenotypist tried in vain to gather her handiwork, rolls of tape tumbled onto the floor. The defiant New Yorkers, seeing an opportunity, tramped on the unraveling streams and picked up clumps and tossed them in the air. Without the stenographic notes, the officials couldn't prove they had satisfied the requirement to gather public input. Jacobs had, in fact, discussed this with a few selected residents prior to the meeting: if the record was destroyed, it would be as though the hearing had never happened, delaying the project and buying more time. As Toth and the transportation men scurried to retrieve what they could, Jacobs climbed down from the stage and took to the microphone once again.

"Listen to this! There is no record! There is no hearing! We're through with this phony, fink hearing!"

As she led the crowd to the exit, a man in plainclothes who identified himself as the precinct captain took her arm and informed Jacobs she was under arrest.

"What are the charges?" Jacobs asked.

The captain said that Toth, the top official from the government, had directed him to arrest her for disrupting the hearing.

"I don't think that's very bright of him," Jacobs said.

"I don't think so either, but we have no choice," the captain said.

As the crowd huddled outside the auditorium in disbelief, Patrolman Joseph McGovern guided Jacobs into the backseat of an idling squad car. A lawyer who happened to be among the protesters called out an offer to represent Jacobs, and said he would follow her. The squad car eased away from the curb, heading south to turn around back toward the Seventh Precinct police station on Clinton Street, three blocks away. The demonstrators followed on foot.

At the station, a policeman led Jacobs to a holding room. From where she sat, she could hear another officer talking on the telephone, checking with the city's legal department to determine the offense with which she should be charged. The officer hung up and walked over to her. Jacobs had been even-keeled, even bemused, during the ride to the station, but she frowned as he told her she had probably committed a felony and would get at least six months in jail.

In the end, Jacobs was not accused that night of a felony. After about two hours in a holding room, she was charged with disorderly conduct, a crime unlikely to result in jail time, and released. At midnight, when Jacobs finally walked out of the precinct station, tired and disheveled, about twenty people were still waiting outside, grouped together in the cooler air and chanting, "We want Jane!"

The cops pleaded with Jacobs to calm them down, and, not wanting to continue the ruckus into the night, she asked them to be quiet. She made her way down the front steps of the station and out onto the empty street near the foot of the Williamsburg Bridge, the very spot where the Lower Manhattan Expressway would connect—if the government could ever get it through, that is.

A *New York Post* reporter stepped forward and asked her what had happened. Composing herself, she said she had done nothing wrong.

"I couldn't be arrested in a better cause," she said.

~~~

The morning after Jane Jacobs's arrest, Robert Moses rose before 7:00 a.m. and dressed, as he did each day, in an oxford dress shirt with cuff links, a well-tailored suit, and a dark tie. Though his black hair had thinned and turned to white and his dark eyes had grown slightly hooded, Moses was as dashing as he had been as a young man at Yale—six feet tall and olive skinned, his body toned by a lifetime of swimming. His driver arrived at precisely 7:30 a.m. to take him to his office on Randall's Island, a spit of land under the Triborough Bridge, a span that Moses had built thirty years before. He read the morning newspapers, which ran accounts of the raucous events at Seward Park High School.

Jane Jacobs, who had led the neighborhood opposition to the Lower Manhattan Expressway for so many years, had finally gotten what was coming to her, Moses thought. Maybe now this project—the final piece of his vision for a complete highway network throughout New York—could proceed without further interference.

Moses had first proposed the Lower Manhattan Expressway back in 1940, along with miles of roadways and bridges crisscrossing the metropolis. The other projects were up and running, but thus far Moses had been unable to push "Lomex," as it became known, through to completion. In the past, he had built bridges, highways, parks, and housing towers with astonishing speed, and his works had transformed New York. He was responsible for thirteen bridges, two tunnels, 637 miles of highways, 658 playgrounds, ten giant public swimming pools, seventeen state parks, and dozens of new or renovated city parks. He cleared three hundred acres of city land and constructed towers that contained 28,400 new apartments. He built Lincoln Center, the United Nations, Shea Stadium, Jones Beach, and the Central Park Zoo. He built the Triborough and Verrazano-Narrows bridges, the Long Island and Cross Bronx expressways, parkways down the side of Manhattan and north and east of the city, avenues, overpasses, causeways, and viaducts. Any New Yorker or visitor to the city has at one time or another driven down, walked through, sat in, or sailed into something that Moses created.

Like the pharaohs of Egypt building the pyramids, Moses reshaped New York through the exercise of shrewd and unfettered power. He was an independent actor, beholden to no one, and largely insulated from opposition, dissent, and outside influence—including the meddlesome wishes of voters. Working at the side of New York's governor Alfred Smith in the 1920s and serving briefly as New York secretary of state, Moses ran for governor of New York in 1934, losing badly. But he soon discovered that he could wield power much more effectively if he let others run for elective office, and instead angle to run the agencies that carried out the work of government. Over the course of his career he served as head of numerous agencies, including the Long Island parks agency, the New York City Parks Department, transportation and public works, the city agency in charge of housing and of urban renewal and reconstruction, chairman of the World's Fair, and chief of a special commission overseeing all the highways called arteries through and around New York. And there was the biggest power base of all: the Triborough Bridge and Tunnel Authority, sustained by federal funding and tolls, with its own budget. As chairman of the authority, in whose Randall's Island headquarters he sat that morning, Moses ran his own government, with its own seal, its own police, a fleet of cars, and even a yacht. Moses had written the legislation creating the authority, including his own job description, terms and bylaws, and the power to issue bonds and collect revenue from tolls. He was the most public figure in New York who had never been elected to anything, at one time holding twelve different city and state positions simultaneously—all of them appointments. He talked his way into these positions of power, rewrote rules and bylaws to strengthen and expand his responsibilities, earned the loyalty of workers and contractors who depended on him for their livelihoods, and made himself so indispensable that the chief executives with the power to fire him always declined to do so. He practiced bureaucratic politics with cunning and expertise, serving through the administrations of five New York City mayors and six governors.

By 1968, Moses was being feted at black-tie dinners, profiled in national newsmagazines, and awarded citations, medals, and honorary degrees. He had mingled with Queen Elizabeth and the pope, world leaders, presidents, governors, and mayors. It had been a great run, and Moses longed to finish it off with the Lower Manhattan Expressway. This last project would make all the other roads and bridges fit together in perfect harmony—the "loom across the weave," as he called it. Cars and trucks would be able to travel at high speeds not just around but through New York City, allowing it to maintain its dominance as a great economic power.

Only Jane Jacobs and her band of quirky crusaders stood in the way. Moses had waited out neighborhood opposition before—ignoring it, bargaining with activists or staring them down, or making sure the fine print of legislation rendered any opposition helpless. But somehow a woman from Pennsylvania coal country, with no college degree, had managed to stall this project for seven long years.

Settled at his cluttered desk on Randall's Island, Moses gazed out across the East River and New York's majestic skyline, and glanced over at the nearby model room, where cardboard creations of all his projects were collected under glass. The model of Lomex was outfitted with a Lucite handle, allowing him to lift the blocks of buildings in the highway's path and replace them with the smooth gray expanse of the Lower Manhattan Expressway.

In the lair of an empire he had so determinedly built over decades of public service for New York City, Robert Moses snapped up one of the black rotary telephones on his desk to find out more about what had happened that night. It was preposterous, he thought. Some busy housewife thought she was better equipped to plan a roadway network for New York that he knew would last for a century.

WRESTLING *with* MOSES

ONE

The Girl from Scranton

As the rattling subway train slowed to a stop, Jane Butzner looked up to see the name of the station, its colorful lettering standing out against the white-tile station walls as it flashed by again and again, finally readable: Christopher Street/Sheridan Square. As the doors opened, she watched as a crowd poured out, moving past pretty mosaics to the exit.

She had moved to New York from her hometown of Scranton, Pennsylvania, and had joined her sister, Betty, in a small apartment in Brooklyn a few months before. She was hunting for a job, but the morning's interview had concluded swiftly, so she'd decided to explore her new city. She darted out before the doors slid shut and made her way through the turnstile and up a set of stairs to the street. Without knowing it, Jane had alighted in the heart of Greenwich Village, the place she would call home for decades to come.

As she emerged, she immediately noticed that the streets ran off at odd angles in all directions. She saw storefronts with awnings shading cluttered sidewalks, kids chasing one another in front of a grocery, delivery trucks stopping and starting their way up the street. Walking north on

OPPOSITE: In 1947, Jane took a job writing for a State Department publication distributed in the Soviet Union; she would later be questioned about supposed communist sympathies. *John J. Burns Library, Boston College*

Seventh Avenue, she saw the skyscrapers of midtown in the distance and, when she turned around, the cluster of tall buildings in the financial district to the south. But in this spot most buildings were two or three stories, and few were higher than five or six. They were simple: no grand entrances, no soaring edifices. She gazed at shopwindows full of leather handbags and watches and jewelry, strolled past barbershops and cafés, and ran her fingers over the daily newspapers stacked high in front of shelves inside filled with candy and cigars. Everywhere she looked she saw people—people talking to one another, it seemed, every few feet, among them longshoremen headed to taverns at the end of their shifts, casually dressed women window-shopping, old men with hands clasped on canes sitting on the benches in a triangular park. Mothers sat on stoops watching over it all. Everyone looked, she thought, the way she felt: unpretentious, genuine, living their lives. This was home.

Arriving at her Brooklyn apartment that evening, Jane described the wonders of the neighborhood she had seen, concluding simply, "Betty, I found out where we have to live."

"Where is it?" Betty asked.

"I don't know, but you get in the subway and you get out at a place called Christopher Street."

Jane had moved to New York City in 1934. Armed with a high-school diploma, a recently acquired knowledge of shorthand, and the wisdom of a few months working in the newsroom of a Scranton newspaper, she hoped to break into journalism. She knew it wasn't going to be easy to succeed in a business dominated by men; her assignments in Scranton had been limited to covering weddings, social events, and the meetings of women's civic organizations with names like the Women of the Moose and the Ladies' Nest of Owls No. 3. It was the thick of the Great Depression, and any job was difficult to come by.

Her older sister, Betty, twenty-four, had warned her. Betty had come to New York a few years before with hopes of finding work as an interior designer, but was now grateful to have a job as a salesgirl in the home furnishings section of the Abraham & Straus department store. The headstrong Jane came to the big city anyway, joining her sister in the top floor of a six-floor walk-up in Brooklyn Heights, a neighborhood of Greek and

Gothic Revival mansions and Italianate brownstones at the edge of the East River, overlooking Manhattan.

Within weeks of arriving, Jane realized that breaking into journalism was going to take time and that, in the meantime, she'd need to support herself. She began poring over employment agency listings looking for any clerical position she could find, and soon settled into a routine. Each morning she would walk from her apartment building, across the Brooklyn Bridge, and into lower Manhattan, where most of her interviews took place. The rest of her day would be spent exploring the city; she would invest a nickel for a subway ride and get out at random stops. She had been to New York only once before, as a girl of twelve, and now, at eighteen, she was drinking in the sights and sounds of a metropolis that could not be more different from Scranton.

Greenwich Village seemed to capture all the promise of moving to New York City for the young bespectacled girl from eastern Pennsylvania. As soon as she could, Jane brought her sister to Greenwich Village. Betty shared her enthusiasm for the neighborhood, and they quickly found an apartment on Morton Street, just south of the Christopher Street subway station. Morton Street was a classic Greenwich Village lane, running four blocks from east to west from the Hudson River, bending at a forty-five-degree angle in glorious violation of the orderly street grid of the rest of Manhattan. It was lined with petite trees, front-yard gardens, iron fences, and stately rows of four- and five-story brownstones and town houses.

Their neighbors there ranged from truckers and railway workers to artists, painters, and poets, including Jackson Pollock, Willem de Kooning, and e. e. cummings. The White Horse Tavern, which for decades had been a gathering place for the bohemians of Greenwich Village, stood just around the corner on Hudson Street.

As excited as they were to be there, money was tight. After paying the rent, Jane and Betty had so little to spare that they resorted to mixing Pablum, a nutritious but notably bland cereal for infants, with milk for sustenance.

Their father's advice proved to be wise counsel in this time: that while the girls should pursue the careers of their dreams, they should also learn a practical skill to fall back on. The degree from the Powell secretarial and stenography school in Scranton gave Jane enough of an edge in the barren job market that after months of searching, she finally landed a job as a secretary for a candy manufacturing company. She would serve in similar clerical positions at a clock maker and a drapery hardware business in the years that followed. In her off time, she worked toward her dream career, honing her journalistic skills.

On those afternoons exploring the city after job interviews, and in her off-hours once she started working, she had begun writing down her observations of the city. In time she began to work them into articles. Early on she noticed that every few blocks of the city seemed to have a specialty trade—a little economy all their own. She sought to learn everything she could about these trades, striking up conversations with the shopkeepers and workers pushing racks of furs down the streets, and the leather makers in the deep back rooms into which she peered. Buckets of flowers on the sidewalk would prompt her to probe into the cut-flower trade; wandering through the diamond district on the Bowery on Manhattan's scrappy Lower East Side, she familiarized herself with the intricate system of jewelry auctions.

Immediately upon arriving home from work, she would toss her handbag on the sofa and settle in front of her manual typewriter in her room and write. After a while, she began to submit her pieces to popular magazines of the day. Much to her surprise, she arrived home one evening to find an envelope from an editor at *Vogue* who wanted to publish a story she had written on the fur district. The editors liked her plainspoken style and keen observations and wished to retain her as a freelance contributor. They proposed that she write four essays over the next two years, for which they would pay her $40 per article, a welcome addition to the $12 per week she was making as a secretary. Her career as a writer in New York City had officially begun.

Her early journalism reflected an eye for the detail and the drama beneath the quotidian. A 1937 piece on the flower market in lower Manhattan, titled "Flowers Come to Town," began with a typical flourish:

All the ingredients of a lavender-and-old-lace love story, with a rip-roaring, contrasting background, are in New York's wholesale flower district, centered around Twenty-Eighth Street and Sixth Avenue. Under the melodramatic roar of the "El," encircled by hash-houses and Turkish baths, are the shops of hard-boiled, stalwart men, who shyly admit that they are dottles for love, sentiment, and romance.

She went on to describe in detail the 5:00 a.m. arrival of orchids, garde-
nias, peonies, and lilacs from Connecticut, Long Island, and New Jersey
that were then meted out into buckets for sale by retailers. She considered the city's voracious demand for cut flowers and foliage—200 million
ferns, 150,000 roses a day from just one grower in a season. It made sense
when she thought about it: office reception areas, wedding receptions,
society functions, and funerals all needed flowers. It was a big market,
but the competition was fierce; she noted how the merchants adopted a
set of rules to maintain a level playing field, such as agreeing not to open
hampers in the flower market until 6:00 a.m., at the sound of a gong. She
was fascinated not only with the mores of the city but with the way systems seemed to self-organize to prosper.

In another article, Jane wrote about the diamond district, which in the
1930s was centered on the Bowery across from the entrance to the Manhattan Bridge, on the Lower East Side of Manhattan. She described how
the dealers in their beards and hats jotted down notes on the cut stones,
rings, necklaces, and lockets that pawnbrokers had sent for display at
auction, then made their bids with silent gestures or by squeezing the
auctioneer's arm. "Upstairs, in the small light rooms over the stores, dia-
monds are cut and polished and set or re-set, and silver is buffed. The
doors and vestibules to the rooms are barred and there is no superfluous
furniture, just the tools and tables where the skillful workmen sit with
leather hammocks to catch the chips and dust of diamond and metal,"
she wrote. "Silver is polished against a cloth-covered revolving wheel . . .
All the sweepings are carefully saved to be refined and the silver recov-
ered. The walls and ceilings are brushed and the old oilcloth coverings
and work clothes of the men are burned to extract the silver dust. Even
the water in which the workmen wash their hands is saved. A small room
where silver is polished may yield to a refiner hundreds of dollars worth of
metal a year." Outside, meanwhile, is the "lusty tumultuous life of the
lower East Side"—the rumble of the elevated subway, "Chinamen from
Mott Street," exotic aromas, and bums on the curbstones.

In those first years in New York, Jane worked forty hours a week, typing, filing, and taking dictation. All the while she continued to scout the
far reaches of the city, writing for *Vogue* as well as other periodicals. On
one outing she turned her attention to manhole covers, decoding their
cryptic inscriptions in order to map the underground rivers of electricity
and gas lines, the tributaries of brine to chill the storage areas of produce

markets, and the pipes carrying steam to heat skyscrapers. Her account of this subterranean maze, which showed how urban life was made possible by what was underneath, appeared in a New York magazine called *Cue,* which primarily published theater and restaurant listings. She also wrote feature stories for the Sunday *Herald Tribune*.

She began to range beyond purely urban subjects, writing about the way fishing boats operated in Chesapeake Bay, the pagan origins of Christmas, and the decorative buttons on military uniform sleeves (originally meant to keep soldiers from using them to wipe their noses). She even tried her hand at short stories, in one piece depicting the decapitation of James Madison in a creative rewriting of American history—"bump, bump, bump" went the founding father's head on the floor, she wrote. An editor at *Reader's Digest* deemed the piece "too gruesome for us," and apparently other editors reacted in a similar fashion. Jacobs experimented with science fiction, too, writing a story about fast-growing plants with fantastical intentions that similarly went unsold.

But writing about the city remained her passion. She often went up to the rooftop of her apartment building and watched the garbage trucks as they made their way through the city streets, picking the sidewalks clean. She would think, "What a complicated great place this is, and all these pieces of it that make it work." The more she investigated and explored neighborhoods, infrastructure, and business districts for her stories, the more she began to see the city as a living, breathing thing—complex, wondrous, and self-perpetuating.

~~~~

As she approached her fourth year in New York, Jane began to reconsider her opinion on higher education. It had become clear to her that she needed a boost to get a full-time job as a journalist. From a young age she had rebelled against what she viewed as the insipid curriculum of the Scranton schools, and scorned her teachers, whom she considered dimwitted. She was known to stick her tongue out when teachers' backs were turned and to challenge her teachers routinely. When a fourth-grade teacher claimed that cities formed only around rivers with waterfalls to provide electric power, Jane pointed out that Scranton had a waterfall but it had nothing to do with powering the city or the economy of the place. Another teacher asked her students to promise to brush their teeth every day. But Jane's father had just told her never to make a promise unless she was absolutely certain she could keep it. So she refused and urged her fellow students to do the same. The teacher kicked her out of the classroom, and Jane wandered along empty railroad tracks on her way home for lunch.

Now, in 1938, she used money from her parents to enroll at Columbia University's School of General Studies, more than a hundred blocks north of Greenwich Village, which had open enrollment for "nontraditional" students—those who had interrupted their education or needed to attend part-time. The school's lack of a set curriculum appealed to Jacobs.

At Columbia, she signed up for courses in any subject that interested her—chemistry, geography, geology, law, political science, psychology, and zoology. Before long she was enjoying school for the first time, feeding her curiosity about how the world worked. By 1940, with good grades and a pile of credits to her name, she was poised to earn a degree not from the School of General Studies, which was open to all, but from Barnard, Columbia University's distinguished college for women, the equivalent of Radcliffe at Harvard. To do so, however, she would have to take a few mandatory courses. Citing her lackluster high-school record, college officials told her she couldn't waive the requirements. Jane walked away in a huff and never looked back.

"Fortunately, my [high school] grades were so bad they wouldn't have me and I could continue to get an education," Jacobs said later—an education in the real world, that is. From that point on, Jacobs would scoff at academic credentials, rebuff universities seeking to give her honorary degrees, and refuse to be called an "expert" in print.

If she eschewed credentials, though, Jacobs was not averse to scholarly research and writing. While at Columbia, Jane spent long hours in the library, doing voluminous research for a paper on the creation of the U.S. Constitution. She concluded that the men of the Constitutional Convention of 1787 had deliberately designed the document as a flexible framework that would evolve over time, rather than a rigid set of rules.

"What they thought time would prove has given way to what we think time has proved," she wrote. "On September 17 the Constitution was signed, and the rest was up to the people."

The paper was published by Columbia University Press in 1941 and is well regarded by constitutional scholars to this day. Though her work on the Constitution foreshadowed her analysis of cities—that they are set in motion by planners and leaders, but their flourishing was up to the people who inhabit them—Jacobs never talked about her scholarly book and never cited it in her curricula vitae or biography, moving on from those Columbia days as quickly and thoroughly as possible.

After leaving Morningside Heights for good, Jacobs returned to the task of finding a full-time writing job. While she didn't succeed in quite the way she hoped, in 1940 she did break into the magazine business, taking a job as a secretary at the Chilton Company, the publisher of the *Iron Age,* a metals industry trade magazine. "They hired me because I could spell molybdenum," she later noted drily.

Jacobs was a natural for all aspects of journalism and magazine publishing—a stickler for details, an authority on proper writing style and grammar, highly organized, and good at coming up with story ideas—and her editorial skills quickly earned her promotion to associate editor. Within her broad assignment to track the ups and downs of the iron and steel industries as America went to war, she first turned to a subject with which she was familiar: the economic tumult in her hometown of Scranton and in surrounding Pennsylvania steel and coal-mining towns. The resulting article, published in 1943, revealed large numbers of unemployed workers and available housing in the Lackawanna and Wyoming valleys.

The piece, which Jacobs rewrote for the *New York Herald Tribune,* drew the attention of the executives at the Murray Corporation, makers of parts for the B-29 bomber and other warplanes, who ultimately decided to locate a plant in Scranton. She was pleased that her journalism could prompt such action, and she took a further step—signing up for a letter-writing campaign to a Pennsylvania state senator and the War Production Board to urge wartime manufacturing and materials production in the Scranton area. The effort and the article won Jacobs her first invitation to speak in public, at a rally by the Labor Party, an upstart political organization formed by labor leaders and liberals who supported Franklin Delano Roosevelt's New Deal policies. Party leaders were urging the government to make better use of the employment base in northwestern Pennsylvania, and Jacobs's findings lent legitimacy to their movement. Shortly after that appearance, Jacobs learned that her hometown newspaper, the *Scrantonian,* was preparing a newspaper article about her. She had gone from writing to being written about. "Ex-Scranton Girl Helps Home City," the headline trumpeted. "Miss Butzner's Story in Iron Age Brought Nationwide Publicity."

But all was not well at *Iron Age*. The editor was a man who did not appreciate women in the workplace, and the assertive and ambitious Jacobs had annoyed him from the start. He began developing strategies to drive her out, like sending her on a night of business entertainment that turned out to be a stag party and paying her far less than her male counterparts. When Jacobs discovered this, she began a campaign for equal pay—and for the right of the publishing company's employees to join a union. Jacobs was developing her own sense of right and wrong, and there were few shades of gray.

The atmosphere in the *Iron Age* offices soon became contentious and uncomfortable. Once again scouring the want ads, she discovered an intriguing position available at the Office of War Information: helping to write feature articles for overseas distribution. There she could write about topics beyond iron and steel, in a more professional environment working for the federal government.

She got the job and reported to the State Department's offices at Columbus Circle, upgrading her appearance with neat calf-length skirts, blazers, and white blouses tied at the neck and her hair done up in a cascading bun in Andrews Sisters style. It was steady work, and she was being paid to write and work with words. She felt that she was moving on and up in the world of journalism and that a life as an established writer—membership in an exclusive club in a place like New York City—was within reach.

A romantic life was another matter. Being a single working woman in New York City in wartime was not at all uncommon, and Jacobs seemed to be content in her independence. But everything changed one evening in 1944, when her sister, Betty, threw a party at their new apartment on the corner of Washington Place and Sixth Avenue in Greenwich Village, a block from Washington Square Park. In her new job at a company responsible for making warplanes, Betty had met an architect named Robert Hyde Jacobs, who was doing design and engineering work on planes, and invited him to the Village. Lean, curly haired, and bespectacled, he walked through the door and saw Jane in her green woolen dress, chatting with other partygoers and stealing a glance at the latest arrival to the party. Their eyes met, and after Betty introduced them, they began talking as if there were no other guests at the party.

They smoked cigarettes, and Jane looked him over as he talked. There was something rakish about him, with his round wire-rimmed glasses and that lock of hair tumbling down his forehead. He looked like one of the dashing World War I–era poets, like Yeats. Bob told her that he'd been an art teacher at City College, and even dabbled in acting, performing minor roles in amateur productions. But that was all in the past. Now he was a full-time architect and designer. Like Jane, Bob had gone to Columbia, but had attended the architecture school. He was excited about the profession, and the way he talked about design was compelling. He wanted to create spaces that functioned well for people. His mind was equal parts blueprints and intuition, and she was smitten. "Cupid really shot that arrow," she later said.

For his part, Bob was taken with Jane's keen powers of observation and her obvious intelligence. They agreed to see each other in the days ahead, went for walks through the streets and parks of Greenwich Village, and decided they were meant for each other. They married a month later. The engagement was that long, Jacobs said, only because she needed to schedule a time to meet Robert's parents in Alpine, New Jersey.

The wedding was in the living room of the Butzner family home at 1712 Monroe Avenue in Scranton, with no best man and no maid of honor, and only immediate family in attendance. Jacobs chose simple decorations of roses, lilacs, and irises from the garden. One important man was missing: Jane's father, Dr. John Decker Butzner, who had died in 1937, in his fifties. Dr. Butzner had been homeschooled, and encouraged his children to take the initiative to go their own way. At the age of nine, Jane was writing poems, and had two published in the local newspaper. She won third prize in the *American Girl* poetry contest for this tribute to walking in the rain:

> The little wisps that curl and rise
> Like stems of phantom water lilies; gleams
> Of jewel-weed gilding waters of the streams
> Yes, I shall love as long as waters flow
> The willow trees and I we know; we know.

Independent thinking, tinged with defiance, was a family tradition. Jane's ancestors had been hard-charging soldiers in the Revolutionary and Civil wars. Among her proud possessions was a scrapbook tracing the campaign of her grandfather James Boyd Robison, who ran for Congress in 1872 as a candidate for the Greenback-Labor Party, a progressive workers' movement. She also treasured the memoirs of her great-aunt Hannah Breece, a schoolteacher who devoted herself to educating Alaska natives, traveling around by dogsled and kayak, wearing a poncho made of bear intestines. Breece was a role model for overcoming assumptions about what women could or couldn't do; Jane's mother, Bess Robison Butzner, was Jane's rock-solid friend and lifelong correspondent, a schoolteacher and a nurse who met Dr. Butzner while both were working in a hospital in Philadelphia.

Through school, Jane's sharp mind and her penchant for challenging authority—her parents raised her to pay attention to ethics but never blindly conform—made her a bit of a loner and slightly quirky. Like many adolescents, she made up imaginary friends to talk to. But hers were Thomas Jefferson and Ben Franklin. Franklin "was interested in lofty things, but also in nitty-gritty, down-to-earth details, such as why the alley we were walking through wasn't paved, and who would pave it if it were paved. He was interested in everything, so he was a very satisfying companion." She explained traffic lights to him, and women's clothes, and the city's system of trash bins and collection. Another imaginary friend was a Saxon chieftain named Cerdic, plucked from the pages of an English historical novel.

Growing up in the house on Monroe Avenue, Jane could walk or bicycle to the places she needed to go. Theirs was a safe and benign neighborhood of old trees and intact sidewalks despite being rippled by frost heaves. Scranton stoked her curiosity about cities, and how they thrive and fail. It was one of Pennsylvania's top half-dozen cities, with a population of 100,000 in the 1920s, and in the center of rich anthracite-mining country that produced a wealthy class and fine Victorian homes. It had earned the moniker the Electric City because of its enthusiastic deployment of electrified streetcar lines. In Scranton, Jacobs saw a downtown, with its short blocks and courthouse square, that functioned efficiently and was lively.

It was nice to be back at the house she grew up in and to have the wedding there, but Jacobs was eager to start her new life. The newlyweds traveled to northern Pennsylvania and then upstate New York for their honeymoon, which they spent bicycling on country roads. As the Allies prepared to invade Normandy, the couple returned to Greenwich Village, and Bob was welcomed on a temporary basis to share the apartment at 82 Washington Place with the sisters. On the weekends there were parties, as Jane's brothers, Jim and John, came down to enjoy Greenwich Village. One night, John, an officer in the army, met his future wife, Viola, nicknamed Pete. Jane and Bob conspired to leave the couple alone on the rooftop. Jacobs would correspond with them throughout her life, scribbling "Dear John and Pete" on newspaper clippings.

It took Jane and Bob a while to find a home to call their own. In 1947, walking the streets of Greenwich Village together, the Jacobses spotted 555 Hudson Street. Sandwiched between two buildings on a run-down block between Eleventh and Perry streets, on the fringe of the quaint residential neighborhood southwest of Washington Square Park, the three-story building had a storefront on the ground floor—a convenience store that had been vacated, with a faded Canada Dry sign still out front. It was next door to a Laundromat, which also had apartments above it. At a time when many couples were beginning to buy houses in new suburban developments, the Jacobses saw potential in the place and had the $7,000 saved up to purchase the entire building.

It was no small matter to turn a dilapidated building into a home to raise a family, but renovating 555 Hudson Street became a labor of love for Bob and Jane. They lived on the top two floors while they installed a kitchen on the ground floor, then a dining room, and then a living room that extended out through new French doors to a fenced-in, postage-stamp backyard. They cleared the debris out back and created a garden oasis—standard procedure today for city dwellers with ground-floor space in the back, but more of a novelty then; most people didn't think a comfortable outdoor space could be fashioned out of a gritty urban lot.

As true urban pioneers—fixing up a building decades before young professionals followed suit, moving into lofts and derelict houses in similar up-and-coming neighborhoods throughout Manhattan—the Jacobses had settled into a neighborhood that was both cosmopolitan and edgy. The stately town homes to the northeast, around Washington Square Park, housed the city's elite families. Closer to the Hudson River, to the west, the Irish Catholic longshoremen and working-class blacks and Puerto Ricans occupied the apartments and walk-ups, while the bars and emerging jazz clubs on Hudson and over on Bleecker Street were hangouts for bohemians and beatniks.

The clutter and chaos of Greenwich Village extended into 555 Hudson Street, which friends described as deeply untidy, with little potted spider plants and ashtrays on makeshift shelves and dishes constantly stacked in the sink. Jane and Bob often worked on jigsaw puzzles together, by agreement looking at the box cover only once; they framed the toughest ones and hung them on the apartment's walls. They were frugal. Weekends in the country were spent at Bob's uncle's apple farm in upstate New York, picking the fruit. Bob cut Jane's hair, and Jane wore simple sandals made for her by a Village shoemaker and owned a single oversized costume-jewelry necklace, which she wore over and over. When the couple started their family—James, whom they would always call Jim, was born in April 1948, and Edward, known from birth as Ned, followed in June 1950—Jane became quite domestic, baking cookies and preparing holiday feasts, though piles of pots and pans seemed to be a permanent condition.

Though she loved to cook, Jacobs was never a stay-at-home mom for long. After the war ended, the Office of War Information was folded into the State Department's Overseas Information Agency, and Jacobs stayed with the organization, writing and editing pamphlets that touted American culture, history, geography, and science overseas. She ended up doing the most work for a slick, eighty-page *Life*-like magazine called *America Illustrated* (*Amerika Illiustrirovannoye*, in Russian), which had been distributed by the Office of War Information in the Soviet Union during World War II as a way to build goodwill and understanding with an ally. Now, as the cold war dawned, it was being expanded and more lavishly produced in order to promote American values and culture, thereby combating communism, the rationale went. The glossy pictures of Arizona deserts, TVA dams, Radio City Music Hall, the white steeples of New England churches, and the U.S. Senate in session made for a slick package, and the magazine was popular in Moscow and beyond.

Having left Grumman after the war to work for an architectural firm, Bob was developing a specialty in the design of medical facilities, while Jane rode her bicycle each day from Greenwich Village to the State Department's publications branch in the heart of Times Square. Each day, as she worked, sitting in a swivel chair at a long metal table alongside her co-workers, Jane deepened her interest in urban planning and architecture as she took on assignments about America's built environment. Albeit for the Soviet audience, she wrote about Washington, D.C., and Philadelphia, about planning, housing, architecture, and, significantly, Washington Square in Greenwich Village. She also wrote straightforward accounts of "urban redevelopment" in the United States, which, after the passage of the federal Housing Act of 1949, was known as urban renewal: the government program of bulldozing city blocks to build new housing and commercial enterprises. Though the articles were not critical of the practice, Jane had begun her education on the implementation of these new policies.

While at *Amerika,* Jacobs grew curious about the U.S.S.R.; she proposed a freelance article on Siberia, and posed—while pregnant—for a photo spread in *Amerika* on American maternity clothes. In the late 1940s she and Bob unsuccessfully applied for visas to travel there at the consulates in New York and Washington. At about the same time, Jane had become intrigued by the writings of Saul Alinsky, the champion of the poor and the powerless in the Chicago slum that was the basis for Upton Sinclair's novel *The Jungle.* Alinsky, regarded as the father of grassroots community organizing and later an inspiration to labor leaders such as Cesar Chavez, organized the neighborhood on the southwest side of Chicago known as the stockyards, so that it had a voice in City Hall, and among businesses and employers. Jacobs admired Alinsky's tactical view that community action emerges from the bottom up. Alinsky had inspired dozens of community organizations across the country similar to the one he founded in Chicago, and Jane came to share his belief that being for progressive ideals meant translating theory into action, not just talking or writing about problems and injustices.

Amid deepening suspicion of communism and socialism after World War II, however, Alinsky was a dangerous person to admire. Alinsky represented an antigovernment rhetoric and a singular challenge to authority of all kinds. He was never considered a threat for violence the way members of the Weather Underground would come to be—he once tried to stage a "flush in" by flushing all the toilets at O'Hare Airport—but he was serious about giving "power to the people," a favorite phrase of his, in ways that the government could interpret as inciting to riot.

In 1949, Jacobs received a letter from the Loyalty Security Board, the State Department's agency for rooting out Communist Party activity among government workers. The initial standard questionnaire was brief and sought information about the Jacobses' applications for visas to the Soviet Union, her subscription to the *Daily Worker,* and her *Iron Age* supervisor's description of her as a "troublemaker." She answered the questions one by one—that she was interested in Russia and hoped to write an article on Siberia, that she subscribed to many journals and magazines, and that her boss at *Iron Age* was a chauvinist who paid men more than women and who resented her for getting promoted from a secretarial position.

The response was evidently insufficient, and the board sent another, more detailed interrogatory in 1952. America was in the grip of the second "red scare," fueled by the Berlin blockade, the execution of the Rosenbergs, the Korean War, and Senator Joseph McCarthy.

Jacobs, unable to contain her indignation, sat down at her manual typewriter and wrote several single-spaced pages to the government that was questioning her: "Upon first reading the questions submitted to me, I was under the impression that possibly I was to be charged with belonging to the [public workers'] union and to registering in the American Labor Party. But since neither of these has been declared illegal for government workers, I concluded, upon further thought, that I am probably suspected of being a secret Communist sympathizer or a person susceptible to Communist influence." She said she was shocked and dismayed that government workers could be questioned about their associations, what they read, and their political beliefs. But she wanted to be clear: "I was brought up to believe there is no virtue in conforming meekly to the dominant opinion of the moment. I was brought up to believe that simple conformity results in stagnation for a society, and that American progress has been largely owing to the opportunity for experimentation, the leeway given initiative, and to a gusto and a freedom for chewing over odd ideas."

Jacobs boldly acknowledged that while the Soviet Union was clearly a threat to America, another lay at home in "the current fear of radical ideas and of people who propound them . . . I believe I have the right to criticize my government and my Congress." Several pages of explanations of her membership in the United Public Workers of America and the American Labor Party followed. While she confessed to an evening of going door-to-door against a Republican congressman, Jacobs denied being a member or affiliate of the Communist Party and said she abhorred the Soviet system as political tyranny. "I believe in control from below and support from above," she asserted.

Jacobs had no reason to believe the interrogatory was anything more than routine, and didn't give much thought to whether her lengthy response risked drawing even more attention to her. Instead, she saw the interrogation as an opportunity to express her beliefs in free expression, civil liberties, and the freedom, in a democracy, to challenge established systems. The persistence of the government in issuing the second interrogatory did, however, suggest to her that centralized authority could not be trusted, but only confronted with equal brutishness.

She also did not worry about being fired as a federal employee, because she was already making plans to move on. Jane was not interested in leaving New York, and when the State Department announced it would relocate the overseas pamphlet and magazine work to offices in Washington, D.C., she plunged into a search for a new job. Though she briefly considered a position at *Natural History* magazine, her interest in architecture, planning, and design had been piqued by a magazine to which Bob had recently subscribed—*Architectural Forum.* She would flip through it as soon as it arrived; to Jane, it was the perfect combination of style and substance. This was the magazine she wanted to write for.

~~~~

Among the more erudite magazines published by Henry Luce's Time Inc., *Architectural Forum* ran features on star designers such as Frank Lloyd Wright and big spreads by the photographer Walker Evans. Its editor was Douglas Haskell, a Yugoslavian-born writer who would become one of the country's most respected architecture critics. In the spring of 1952, Jacobs talked her way into Haskell's office at Rockefeller Center— a bustling complex of media companies—to apply for a position as a writer. Haskell admired her gumption and wasn't worried about her lack of formal training; never trained as an architect himself, he believed it was an advantage to write without being influenced by any scholarly point of view.

Haskell hired her for a trial assignment on a building in Herald Square and, after a few weeks, made her an associate editor, responsible for covering hospitals and schools. Her husband, who had graduated in 1941 from Columbia University's School of Architecture, tutored her on the technical aspects of architecture and design.

"I was utterly baffled at first," Jacobs said, "being supposed to make sense out of great, indigestible rolls of working drawings and plans, but my husband came to my rescue and every night for months he gave me lessons in reading drawings, learning what to watch for as unusual, and discovering what other information I needed to have." The whirlwind education was typical of the close partnership that was their marriage.

"I had no credentials . . . so I set myself up as my own expert," she said.

Over the next eight years, Jacobs wrote on a wide range of subjects—from a hospital complex in Lima, Peru, that organized its maternity ward to encourage the natural process of birth, to the layout of a health center in California that similarly seemed to have a positive effect on patients. A common theme was starting to emerge: how buildings could be designed to serve the primary function of making human beings feel comfortable. Since working on hospital and medical center projects, Bob had been drawn into the practice of designing environments that would promote good health, making him an excellent coach for these articles.

Two years into Jane's tenure, she was given an assignment that would be a turning point in her career—an update on urban renewal plans in Philadelphia. Rather than the new suburban development that was attracting attention at the time, Haskell wanted to focus on what was happening to cities. By the mid-1950s, cities across the country had fallen into dire straits, losing population and jobs to the booming suburbs. For decades, big cities had been seen as crowded, congested, unhealthy places of slums and tenements. The condition had prompted a prominent succession of planners, architects, and intellectuals to rethink human settlement—to make it more orderly and efficient. The city was a problem to be solved; great thinkers were coming up with modern ideas, and planners and policy makers were implementing what was universally regarded as solutions.

The man at the helm in Philadelphia was Edmund Bacon, who held the same czar-like position as Robert Moses in New York. He targeted the run-down neighborhoods in and around the center city for massive redevelopment schemes, with housing towers and commercial centers replacing the dilapidated buildings and scattered vacant lots. Haskell wanted someone to travel to Philadelphia and gauge the success of his grand revitalization plans. Largely because the staff was shorthanded, he chose Jacobs.

Going to meet the great Ed Bacon, Jacobs confessed she was "not what you would call a city-planning expert." But she knew Philadelphia was a grand experiment at the time, and Ed Bacon was very fashionable. She took the train from New York and met Bacon, who escorted her to a section of the downtown area the city was working on. "First he took me to a street where loads of people were hanging around on the street, on the stoops, having a good time of it, and he said, well, this is the next street we're going to get rid of. That was the 'before' street," she said.

"Then he showed me the 'after' street, all fixed up, and there was just one person on it, a bored little boy kicking a tire in the gutter. It was so grim that I would have been kicking a tire, too. But Mr. Bacon thought it had a beautiful vista."

She turned to him and asked, "Where are the people?"

Bacon sidestepped the question. He emphasized the need for order in cluttered and messy downtown neighborhoods, and the importance of having a "view corridor," a clear sight line revealing the order of the new metropolis. They walked to the next block, where people were sitting on stoops, talking, running errands, and darting in and out of their homes, and Bacon told her it was an example of what cities needed to eradicate. She stepped back and looked at him in astonishment. Apparently, Bacon didn't see the neighborhood vibrating with life that she did.

Back in the offices of *Architectural Forum,* Jacobs shared her growing misgivings about urban renewal with her co-workers. It was just the sort of edgy analysis Haskell had asked for, but others in the office were reluctant to question the prevailing wisdom of planners like Bacon. He was trying to save Philadelphia, they said. Planners across the country, including the biggest of them all, Robert Moses in New York, were dedicated to the economic salvation of American cities; challenging them was misguided, even unpatriotic.

The urban renewal movement had decades of theory behind it. At the end of the nineteenth century, as cities came to be viewed as congested, unhealthy places, a parade of planners began to come forward with ideas for a better way to arrange human settlement in the twentieth century. Among the first was the British-born Ebenezer Howard, who published a treatise in 1902 proposing the garden city—a town of no more than thirty thousand people, located outside the urban core, surrounded by greenbelts, and with carefully planned access to nearby workplaces. At the time, the common idea was that the antidote to the cities' ailments was to spread people out. In Scotland, Patrick Geddes believed that people should naturally settle along a spectrum, depending on their needs, from a dense urban center to the countryside. Accommodating these different growth patterns required a broad framework that came to be known as regional planning—a focus not just on the city but on the outskirts and beyond. Lewis Mumford, the architecture critic for the *New Yorker,* took inspiration from Geddes and similarly advised that growing populations be dispersed across a larger region—centered on major cities, but not limited to their confines. Benton MacKaye, founder of the Wilderness Society and originator of the Appalachian Trail, sought to bring people out of the city and into nature. For Frank Lloyd Wright, the vision of the "horizontal city" included freestanding homes on individual plots, taking advantage of new technology—the automobile—to make better use of America's abundant lands.

Perhaps the most influential thinker on modern architecture and city planning in the twentieth century was Charles-Édouard Jeanneret-Gris, who called himself Le Corbusier. His 1923 book *Towards a New Architecture* suggested a radical simplification of previous styles, a major departure from the past, and an embrace of the streamlined, contemporary building protocol. As a founding member of the Congrès International d'Architecture Moderne, or International Congress of Modern Architecture, he essentially led the intellectual movement that brought modernism and what would become known as the International Style to the United States. The movement, which urged a clean break with the Victorian past and the traditional, classical buildings of nineteenth-century Europe, embraced new construction methods and emphasized elegance and simplicity: less is more, and form follows function. An early example was Le Corbusier's Villa Savoye, a sleek white box on stilts with horizontal windows and an open interior plan. The German architect Mies van der Rohe was another leader in the movement and designed the Seagram Building on Park Avenue in 1958—a black and bronze skyscraper with a steel and glass "curtain wall," rising up without ornamentation from a clean pedestal at street level.

Just as he streamlined form in his architecture, Le Corbusier had a grand vision for streamlining the city. His concept of the Ville Contemporaine and later the Ville Radieuse, or "Radiant City," called for razing older sections of the city that had been built up willy-nilly over time, to be replaced by dozens of cruciform high-rise towers in open plazas that could accommodate millions. In 1925 he came up with a plan to bulldoze most of the center of Paris in order to make way for this scheme. All functions of life, like shopping or work, were to be strictly separated into distinct zones; it was the mix of uses—the belching factory close to the tenement house—that made conditions so unhealthy in the first place, he argued. Highways would be necessary to connect the various elements, and they would be elevated, directly serving buildings above the ground floors.

Jacobs was not entirely opposed to modernism as an architectural movement, and admired both the Seagram Building and the work of the Philadelphia-based architect Louis Kahn, who created a series of heavy buildings that visually told the story of the materials used in construction. She even described his Trenton Bath House as a "marvelous creation." But she was not caught up in the promise and inevitability of the movement, as many of her colleagues were. For her, examples of good modernism were rare; new theories and sketches and renderings were one thing, but what happened in real life was another. Too much was getting lost in translation as modernism became official policy in cities across the country. By the 1950s, what had begun as an intellectually rigorous and aesthetically elegant movement guided by master architects had resulted in the ubiquitous strip malls, low-slung school buildings, and glass office boxes that populate the suburbs to this day. Cities mimicked suburban modernism in turn, bulldozing cluttered blocks to make way for wide-open plazas and drab housing towers. As urban renewal cleared out the clutter and brought in light and air, Jacobs began to see that the fine-grained street life of the city was being lost.

In Philadelphia, Jacobs sensed this rush to substitute superblocks of boxy, streamlined towers for human-scaled collections of buildings that functioned well. Her skepticism was confirmed for good one day in 1955, when a burly Episcopal minister named William Kirk made his way into the offices of *Architectural Forum* and demanded to talk to editors about the massive clearance and redevelopment taking place in East Harlem. He found a willing listener in Jacobs, who was reminded of her experience in Philadelphia. Kirk, born in Pennsylvania coal country like Jacobs, was head of the Union Settlement Association, a community services agency that was originally started to help Italian immigrants and after World War II offered education, recreation, nutrition, and arts programs for a growing black and Latino population in East Harlem.

City planners working under the influence of Le Corbusier and others believed that the only way to help the poor in the area was to bulldoze the cluttered blocks of tenements and shops and start over. The federal policy to implement this approach was the urban renewal program known as Title I, a process where older buildings were condemned and cleared away so that private developers could build anew. In Harlem, developers used Title I to build Lenox Terrace, wiping out three city blocks to make way for a superblock of eight twenty-story cruciform towers, with more than seventeen hundred new apartments; a sister project, Delano Village, leveled stores, churches, the Savoy Ballroom, and the original Cotton Club. Other projects, including Lincoln Towers and Park West Village, had much the same effect. The urban renewal manual made it plain that leaving any part of the slum intact would amount to slum preservation. The housing towers and integrated stores on the ground floors required a clean slate.

The problem, Kirk told Jacobs, was that nobody was following up on the work to see if the new projects were better than what they had replaced. Jacobs, back from a brief maternity leave—she had given birth to her third and final child, Mary, in 1955—listened intently. The residents in the new housing towers, Kirk said, were not at all comfortable in their new surroundings. He invited her to come to East Harlem and see for herself.

She met him in a part of the city that was unfamiliar, off the northeast corner of Central Park above 110th Street. She was amazed by what she saw. One block there were bodegas and laundries and social clubs and cigar-rolling shops. On the next, there was only a desolate patch of worn ground with a tall, drab housing tower in the center. Except for some suspicious-looking figures hanging out by battered playground equipment, it exhibited no sign of life whatsoever. It was like a bloodletting, Kirk suggested—the planners were draining all the life from these neighborhoods. Families that were able to relocate into the new buildings found them strange and uncomfortable. The big grocery stores on the ground floors of towers, or the auditoriums built as entertainment centers on the second floors, were just no substitute for the bodegas or the Savoy. To find out why, Jacobs and Kirk talked to people on the street.

"I can remember the people in East Harlem hating a patch of green grass," Jane later said. "I couldn't understand why until one of them told me that the tobacco store had been torn down, the corner newsstand was gone, but someone had decided the people needed a patch of green grass and put it there." The planners had simply acted on what they thought was best, without regard for what the people in the area wanted, or what worked best for them.

In this moment, the virtue of the seeming disorder of city neighborhoods crystallized for Jacobs. "By showing me East Harlem, [Kirk] showed me a way of seeing other neighborhoods, and downtowns too," she said. Her equally powerful epiphany was that planners were arrogant and self-impressed, forcing big changes on communities without bothering to evaluate their effects. As these ideas began to swirl in Jacobs's head, little did she know that she'd soon get to address her grievances to a highly influential audience.

~~~~

A few months later, in the spring of 1956, Haskell, Jacobs's boss at *Architectural Forum,* was forced to back out of a speech he was scheduled to give due to illness. The talk was for the Conference on Urban Design at Harvard University's Graduate School of Design, an institution that had embraced modernism and contemporary planning like no other. Haskell asked Jacobs to go in his place. Though she had only spoken publicly once before and suffered from stage fright, she reluctantly agreed. There might be a way, she thought, to incorporate her observations from East Harlem, with Kirk, into a broader critique.

On the day of the speech, in April 1956, her apprehension grew with each step she took from Harvard Square through the redbrick, iron, and granite gates into Harvard Yard, past the steps of Widener Library and the soaring white steeple of Memorial Church, and to the entrance of the architecture school. The campus represented everything she had spurned: credential-obsessed academia, and the modernist movement that was driving urban renewal. Harvard was in the full throes of the modernist movement, largely due to the influence of Walter Gropius, a professor at the design school and one of the leaders of the Bauhaus movement, which, like the International Style, emphasized simplicity and function. The campus itself was on the brink of a modernist overhaul, including a new home for the design school, a building by the architect of the World Trade Center, Minoru Yamasaki, and Le Corbusier's only building in North America, a curving concrete structure built roughly in the shape of a piano, and located near the faculty club. Modernism had gained momentum from the 1930s and swept across the country in the 1950s, and Mies van der Rohe created the modernist campus of the Illinois Institute of Technology.

The attendees at the conference were a bit intimidating—including Edmund Bacon, whom Jane had met in Philadelphia; José Louis Sert, the dean of the design school; the landscape architect Hideo Sasaki; and Victor Gruen, the designer of the housing towers in parks that rose up on the bulldozed West End in Boston. They were the leading lights of architec-

ture and planning in the United States, and most of them were propo-
nents of modernism and believers in urban renewal.

Anticipating a less-than-friendly reception, she began.

"Sometimes you learn more about a phenomenon when it isn't there,
like water when the well runs dry—or like neighborhood stores which are
not being built in our redeveloped city areas," she said.

"In New York's East Harlem, for instance, 1,110 stores have already
vanished in the course of re-housing 50,000 people. Planners and architects are apt to think, in an orderly way, of stores as a straightforward matter of supplies and services . . . but stores in city neighborhoods are much
more complicated creatures, which have evolved a much more complicated function. Although they are mere holes in the wall, they help make
an urban neighborhood a community instead of a mere dormitory."

She continued. Hardware stores, candy shops, diners, barbershops—
the eclectic diversity and mix of uses were all being eradicated in urban
renewal projects and replaced with monolithic housing and giant supermarkets where the planners thought residents would surely go. But in
East Harlem and new housing developments such as Stuyvesant Town,
built under Moses, the people flocked to the closest mom-and-pop stores
that had been left untouched, blocks away.

"Do you see what this means?" she implored. "This is a ludicrous situation, and it ought to give planners the shivers."

Not yet ready to dismiss urban renewal as an entirely hopeless enterprise, Jacobs suggested that future designs mimic the mix and jumble of
older urban neighborhoods, and create parks and open spaces that not
only let in light and air but also served as functional social spaces that
were "at least as vital as the slum sidewalk." Planners must "respect—in
the deepest sense—strips of chaos that have a weird wisdom of their own
not yet encompassed in our concept of urban order.

"We are greatly misled by talk about bringing the suburb into the city,"
she concluded. "The city has its own peculiar virtues and we will do it no
service by trying to beat it into some inadequate imitation of the non-city."

Jacobs had told the leaders of planning and urban design they were
getting it wrong—destroying everything that was vital about the city and
replacing it with development that looked good on the drafting table but
in reality was no improvement at all—and she fully expected to be
greeted with grim-faced silence, or, at best, polite applause. But the audience erupted in a roar. One man applauding was Lewis Mumford, who

introduced himself after the speech and for the next several years encouraged Jacobs to share her critiques with new audiences, submit articles to the *Saturday Evening Post,* and "keep hammering."

A reporter for the *Harvard Crimson,* the school's student newspaper, led the story on the conference with "the failure of most universities to prepare students in the public relations of urban design," and noted only in the last line of the story that "Jane Jacobs, staff member of *Architectural Forum,* discussed the need for small 'holes in the wall' as informal centers of an urban area." Although the speech was not widely covered and there was no rejoinder from modernists or advocates of urban renewal, word spread quickly among scholars and others in planning and urban design—many of whom were not pleased with what Jacobs had had to say, or with her audacity in having said it.

Back in New York, William H. "Holly" Whyte Jr., a writer and editor at *Fortune* magazine, had heard about the speech and was about to give Jacobs her biggest break yet. Whyte was curious about how people behaved in physical surroundings. A Princeton man who fought at Guadalcanal in a marine unit making intelligence maps, he had joined *Fortune* after the war, and one of his first assignments was to examine the way returning GIs lived the middle-class life in a planned suburban town called Park Forest in Illinois. He spent months there, observing the men making their way in corporate careers, leaving housewives at home in a tranquil and sometimes listless community. The story for *Fortune* would morph into the landmark book *The Organization Man,* published in 1956, and Whyte would go on to become a leading authority on the design of parks and public spaces.

Whyte was friendly with Haskell and knew of Jacobs already, being at another Henry Luce magazine. He was in the process of putting together a series on the modern metropolis and was casting about for writers. He put in a call to meet her. When the two met and Whyte asked Jacobs to write an article based on the Harvard speech, she initially declined, saying she didn't have enough authority to submit something to *Fortune.* But when another writer tapped for the job fell ill and Whyte called on Jacobs for a second time, she agreed.

In "Downtown Is for People," published in *Fortune* in 1958, Jacobs laid out her critique: downtown redevelopment efforts across the United States were completely misguided, and showed no understanding of how

people actually behaved in cities. "These projects will not revitalize downtown; they will deaden it," she wrote. "They will be stable and symmetrical and orderly. They will be clean, impressive, and monumental. They
will have all the attributes of a well-kept, dignified cemetery."

The reader response was unusually strong, and Whyte proudly pen-
ciled the comment "Look at what your girl did" on copies he sent to
Haskell of letters from academics, city planners, and even mayors. In Jacobs, Whyte saw things he admired: a fresh look at an established system
and a bold journalistic challenge. Whyte, in turn, had given Jacobs a shot
at a crucial turning point in her career; for this, she was always grateful—
though never publicly. She thanked him only in a private inscription in
the book she would ultimately write.

~~~~~

D owntown Is for People" officially established Jacobs as a critic of contemporary planning; it also served as the opening salvo in her battle
with Robert Moses. In the article, Jacobs cited several examples of what
she saw as destructive and dysfunctional urban renewal. She critiqued
downtown redevelopment schemes in Pittsburgh, Cleveland, New Orleans,
Nashville, and San Francisco. But she also singled out a favorite Moses
project—Lincoln Center—for withering criticism.

Lincoln Center, which would require the bulldozing of eighteen
blocks on Manhattan's Upper West Side, had been designed as a world-
class performing arts center and Manhattan campus for Fordham University, as well as other cultural and educational institutions. It epitomized
the Moses approach—out with the old, in with contemporary architecture and wide-open plazas. In the critique, Jacobs hit all her big themes.
Moses and his team of designers didn't understand how streets actually
worked—how they were a unifying force that gave places life. They were
concocting grand schemes at their drafting tables, without understanding
how people actually behaved in the built environment. Moses was so in-
tent on making big projects happen—at great cost, given the demolition
and eviction of residents and businesses—that he didn't seem to care
whether the new places were pleasant or functional.

"This cultural superblock is intended to be very grand and the focus of
the whole music and dance world of New York," Jane wrote. "But its
streets will be able to give it no support whatever." The Metropolitan

Opera House will turn its back on the street where concertgoers disembark from taxis. Jacobs later called Lincoln Center an example of "built-in rigor mortis."

At the time, Lincoln Center was a popular project, and Moses was a popular man. Jacobs's colleagues at *Architectural Forum* were aghast at her criticism; the magazine had lavished praise on Moses's previous projects, especially his grand public swimming pools.

"My God, who was this crazy dame?" said C. D. Jackson, the publisher of *Fortune,* who called a luncheon with the magazine's editors to give Jacobs a chance to defend her critique. "Of all things to attack, how could we give aid and comfort to critics of Lincoln Center?"

But Jacobs stood firm. Millions were being invested in Lincoln Center, she said, and it was a journalistic obligation to examine whether the project was being done properly. The whole approach to redeveloping cities was fatally flawed, and Moses was leading the way.

Few dared to challenge Moses in the 1950s, even in writing, but for Jacobs the battle would soon move beyond the realm of print. While Jacobs was writing "Downtown Is for People," Moses had been pushing forward with a plan to build a roadway through Washington Square Park, the very park where Jacobs brought her own children to play. Moses wanted to provide better access to his massive urban renewal project just south of the cherished greensward. The collision course was set.

TWO

The Master Builder

On the rain-soaked morning of December 12, 1936, as Jane Jacobs emerged from the apartment on Morton Street and into the cozy chaos of Greenwich Village, Robert Moses stood two miles uptown, christening a much more orderly kind of city. His driver had picked him up at his home on the Upper East Side and cut across to the northwest tip of Manhattan, to the banks of the Hudson River. There Moses stepped out of the black Packard limousine onto the deck of a bridge he had built.

At eight hundred feet high, the Henry Hudson Bridge was the tallest arched span in the world, vaulting over a shipping canal that separated the island of Manhattan from the rest of New York State, its steel latticework painted forest green to blend in with the wooded hillsides. Through the mist and the pelting rain, Moses could barely see the cliffs of New Jersey across the Hudson River to his left. The weather was not ideal for a grand opening, but nothing could spoil the moment. It was the final ribbon cutting of a furiously busy year—a year of red, white, and blue bunting, the silver blades of ceremonial shovels, bands and banners, and the staccato flash of press cameras.

First there was the progress on the West Side Highway, which had

OPPOSITE: By 1938, Robert Moses had transformed New York's landscape with new bridges, tunnels, highways, parks, and other public spaces. Here he stands proudly in front of a map of his accomplishments. *MTA Bridges and Tunnels Special Archive*

been extended from Seventy-second Street to the new bridge on which he stood. He had charged an army of construction workers with the implementation of his West Side Improvement project, submerging railway tracks in a tunnel so the roadway could run along the shore of Riverside Park, which was itself being refurbished and expanded from a new boat basin at Seventy-ninth Street to Harlem. Moses had also opened ten new swimming pool complexes over the summer, at a pace of one a week. He had created a system of large new state parks in the orbit of the city, beginning with the elegant and wildly popular Jones Beach, and completed extensive renovations at Jacob Riis Park and Rockaway Beach on Long Island's southern shore. In July, he cut the ribbon at Orchard Beach in the Bronx, a crescent beach he created by dumping barge loads of white sand from Long Island. He had also restored and expanded the city's existing public spaces, among them Sara Delano Roosevelt Park on the Lower East Side, Bryant Park behind the New York Public Library, Prospect Park in Brooklyn, and Central Park, where he had built Tavern on the Green and a zoo.

That summer, Moses had opened his greatest achievement yet: the Triborough Bridge, a twenty-two-lane art deco masterpiece of concrete, cables, and steel that linked the previously isolated boroughs of the Bronx, Queens, and Manhattan. Plans had been in place for a bridge over the East River as early as 1916, but the project stalled after the stock market crash of 1929. Moses, who wanted to facilitate travel to the Long Island parks he had opened, was able to revive it, creating the independent Triborough Bridge and Tunnel Authority, which had the power to borrow money to construct the bridge and charge a twenty-five-cent toll to pay for it. Moses had hired a new architect who gave the bridge a more modern design while cutting costs. Described in a promotional pamphlet as the "hanging highway in the sky" to link "three mighty boroughs . . . [saving] time and money for 10 million motorists," the Triborough Bridge was an instant success, smoothing the delivery of goods, people, and services to New York City, upstate New York, Long Island, and Connecticut. It was a landmark project for Moses, a smash hit with the public and the press.

"The Triborough is not just a bridge nor yet a crossing. It is a great artery, connecting three boroughs of the city, and reaching out at its borders into adjacent counties and states," Moses had said at the opening ceremony, as President Roosevelt christened the span by riding in a motorcade of dozens of sedans and motorcycles. "It is not merely a road for automobiles and trucks, but a general city improvement, reclaiming dead areas and providing for residence along its borders, esplanades, play facilities, landscaping and access to the great new parks."

Though he had by no means completed his last project—the Cross Bronx Expressway, the Whitestone, Throgs Neck, and Verrazano-Narrows bridges, Lincoln Center, Shea Stadium, and the United Nations were still to come—on that day of the grand opening of the Henry Hudson Bridge, Moses was already the nation's most prolific builder of public works. With his parks, zoos, playgrounds, pools, roadways, bridges, and tunnels, he had changed the way millions of New Yorkers spent their leisure time and got around. As Jane Jacobs was in lower Manhattan writing about the quirky charms of the city, Robert Moses was all over the metropolis, seeking to transform it.

Smartly dressed in a suit, oxford shirt, and necktie, Moses surveyed the watery deck of the Henry Hudson. The celebration would have to move inside to the station house beside the tollbooths. But the symbolism would be fitting nonetheless. The complex at the entrance of the bridge housed the uniformed attendants, who would collect a dime per car, a method perfected by Moses that would pay for the construction costs in short order.

Mayor Fiorello La Guardia arrived at the bridge and greeted Moses warmly. La Guardia, whose nickname was the Little Flower, had been elected as the city's first Italian-American mayor in 1933 and had tapped Moses to be his city parks commissioner. Moses was grateful for the appointment and knew La Guardia relished a gala opening; he had combined the Henry Hudson event with a celebration of the mayor's fifty-fourth birthday, the previous day.

A full foot shorter and a good deal less muscular than his appointee, La Guardia looked at Moses with a mix of wariness and admiration. Here was a man who held several appointed jobs at once, but had never been elected to anything. In addition to the parks job, La Guardia had named Moses the city's representative on the bridge- and road-building authorities established by the state. Moses was chair and sole member of the Henry Hudson Parkway Authority and Marine Parkway Authority, which together were merged into the New York City Parkway Authority, and chairman of the Triborough Bridge and Tunnel Authority, the quasi-public, independent authority for which Moses wrote the enabling legislation. Moses was also chairman of a new state parks agency and commissioner of the Long Island state parks. At one point Moses had held twelve appointed positions at the same time. His knack for getting named to powerful jobs led some colleagues and elected officials to refer to him as "commissioner for life." When the jobs were at newly created agencies, he managed to write the legislation that spelled out the job descriptions himself, always taking special care to make it difficult to be fired.

As the dignitaries gathered for the start of the ceremony, however, La Guardia could not help but feel grateful for Moses's guile. The fact that the Henry Hudson had been built at all was testament to his value as a champion of public works. A high-speed thoroughfare at the tip of Manhattan had been planned many years before—as early as 1901—but no politician had been able to muster the financing or navigate neighborhood politics to get construction started. Moses, by then an expert in both arenas, pieced together city, state, and federal funding, and had the bridge abutments in place the morning the money was in the bank.

Previously, cars and trucks had been forced to inch across the ship canal that led from the Hudson to the Harlem River on the clogged Broadway Bridge, well below the new bridge, through a neighborhood known by the Dutch name of Spuyten Duyvil. Residents there had wanted a more modest span, arguing that a towering arched structure would spoil the last great wild area in Manhattan, Fort Tryon and Inwood Hill parks, but Moses had dispatched the neighborhood forces with carefully modulated responses. A lower corridor would require a drawbridge, leading to traffic jams every time a ship passed, he knew. Further, he could receive federal funding from the Civil Works Administration if the route went through Inwood Hill Park, as it could then technically be considered a parks access road. As an inducement to neighborhood residents, he promised playgrounds and parks in the area of the Henry Hudson, though, as it turned out, the playground would be accessible only by a steep set of stairs, particularly unsuited for mothers with strollers.

The Henry Hudson Bridge had followed what was emerging as Moses's formula for steamrolling projects through: secure the funding, personally work the legislators, court the press to publicize benefits, and build quickly before the opposition can mobilize.

Moses had identified very real benefits of the bridge, which in any fair estimation far outweighed the concerns of a few residents. Now it would be possible to drive easily to Bronxville, Westchester County, and points north in New York State. What's more, the bridge was part of a system that eased the flow of traffic all across the metropolitan area, connecting Manhattan to the rest of the world across the vast waterways that surrounded it. About a mile down the road, the George Washington Bridge to New Jersey had opened in 1931. The West Side Highway took traffic down to midtown and all the way to the lower end of Manhattan, Wall Street, and a new tunnel to Brooklyn. The Triborough opened up destinations to the east—Queens and Long Island—and Westchester County and Connecticut. Motorists hungrily took to these new routes; in its second year of operation, six million cars traveled on the Henry Hudson Bridge. For La Guardia, the modern infrastructure was critical for revitalizing the city's economy, and Moses was the man making it happen.

On that day in 1936, Robert Moses controlled virtually every batch of concrete poured, every shovel in the ground, and every land transaction linked to the development of roads and parks in and around New York City. He employed thousands of workers and doled out millions in construction, engineering, and consulting contracts. He devoted every possible moment to executing his plans for New York, at breakfast, in his limousine, or at intermission at the theater in the evening; only Sundays were reserved for time with his wife, Mary, and two young daughters. "He was always burning up with ideas, just burning up with them," said a friend. "Everything he saw walking around the city made him think of some way that it could be done better." Behind the scenes, Moses worked with legislators and councilmen, negotiated contracts, sketched out architectural details, and carved out special time to work with the press— limousine tours of projects for reporters, lavish dinners with editors, and leaks and scoops to favored writers, timed to get out in front of controversies. The Henry Hudson bridge and parkway system was no exception; Moses had arranged guided tours for the press to follow the grand opening.

After the ceremony, Moses and a chief engineer bundled into his car and drove up and down the new parkway and across the bridge. Moses was already calculating the torrent of dimes that would be collected. But in the coming days, he would be praised in the press not for his fiscal prudence but for the grandeur of what he had accomplished: "the most beautiful drive in the world," a "masterpiece," and a "motorist's dream" that allowed drivers to go from lower Manhattan to Poughkeepsie without stopping for a traffic light. One scribe said the span was worthy of the praise that the poet William Wordsworth bestowed on Westminster Bridge crossing the Thames:

> Earth has not anything to show more fair:
> Dull would he be of soul who could pass by
> A sight so touching in its majesty:
> This city now doth, like a garment, wear
> The beauty of the morning; silent, bare,
> Ships, towers, domes, theatres, and temples lie
> Open unto the fields, and to the sky;
> All bright and glittering in the smokeless air.

Another ribbon cutting, another triumph.

~~~~~

From an early age, Robert Moses possessed a singular drive, ambition, and confidence befitting a privileged upbringing. Born December 18, 1888, in New Haven, Connecticut, Moses was the second son of Emanuel Moses, a German-Jewish immigrant who fled the anti-Semitism of nineteenth-century Bavaria and founded an extremely successful department store. His mother, Isabella Silverman Cohen, was an energetic and strong-willed society woman in the well-to-do circles of the German-Jewish diaspora known as "our crowd." The Moses family lived on Dwight Street in New Haven, but at the urging of Bella, as she was known, they moved to New York in 1897, into a five-story brownstone on East Forty-sixth Street left to her by her father. From the age of nine, Moses slept in a custom-made bed and ate dinner expertly prepared by a cook and placed in front of him by servants in a dining room of chandeliers and fine china. The family took summer trips to Europe or retreated to an estate in the Adirondacks. Robert was driven at all times by a chauffeur, a practice he would continue for the rest of his life, never learning to drive a car.

While other young men in such surroundings might become listless and pampered, Moses quickly developed a hard-charging style that would stand him in good stead in his intellectual and professional life. In this he took after the women of the Moses family, in particular his grandmother and mother. While Emanuel Moses was reserved and passive, Bella was stubborn and arrogant. His grandmother Cohen was known to cut to the front of ticket lines, elbowing people out of her way.

Handsome and charming, Moses excelled in his years at prep school. He quickly joined the ranks of the popular boys while developing a reputation among teachers as nothing less than brilliant. A good athlete, he chose sports—swimming and track—that emphasized individual achievement over teamwork.

In 1905, at the age of sixteen—he had completed preparatory school a year before most of his peers—Moses entered Yale University. He would quickly learn that his religion—the freshman directory identified him as "Hebrew"—would prevent him from breaking into Yale's major social clubs and student associations. Instead, he aimed for a lower tier of organizations, like the *Yale Courant,* an alternative to the more prestigious *Yale Literary Magazine.* As a sophomore, he joined the swimming team, where he proved himself a strong competitor.

His intellectual interests ranged widely in his Yale years, and he impressed his fellow students with his voracious appetite for knowledge, as he often stayed up most of the night reading. One Yale friend recalled seeing a stack of books on his desk, none of which had anything to do with the courses he was taking. He became president of the Kit Kat Club, made up of literary scholars and admirers of Samuel Johnson, and with a classmate published an anthology of student poetry.

Like Jacobs, Moses tried his hand at poetry, mimicking a grandiose, Victorian style:

To-morrow!
But the morrow sure
To-morrow!
The lashes slumber lure;
Ah! Shall we greet the dawning day,
Perchance in vain we longing say,
To-morrow!

Headstrong and confident, if something of a loner, Moses made his presence felt on campus, writing strongly worded editorials for the *Yale Daily News* urging a diversion of funding from football to so-called minor sports, including swimming. But it wasn't long before he overstepped. He came up with an idea for raising funds for the swimming team that the captain disagreed with, and retorted that if the captain didn't go along with his scheme, he'd quit. Much to his surprise, his resignation was accepted on the spot. The confrontation would leave a lasting impression on Moses; he did not like feeling powerless. He would not rejoin the swimming team, despite intense lobbying efforts enlisting everyone from teammates to the pool custodian.

In the end, he received recognition at Yale in other ways. By his senior year he had become a well-known figure in literary and arts circles, conversant in Latin, and able to quote long stretches of verse. He left behind the single rooms he used for the first two years and started bunking with roommates, whom he invited home for weekends in New York. He made new friends and was elected to Senior Council, a student government body controlled by fraternity men. In 1909, Moses graduated Phi Beta Kappa, and took his place in the yearbook photograph in dignified necktie and three-piece suit.

Though he told friends he wanted to go into public service, he sought to remain in academia for a little while longer. He wanted to be a Rhodes scholar, but at the time the program was available only every other year, and not in the year he graduated from Yale, so the family paid for him to attend Wadham College at Oxford University.

Moses relished the time in England. "The Oxford education . . . confers on the average undergraduate independence of mind," he wrote in an article for the *Yale Alumni Weekly*. The ambitious American became captain of the swimming and water polo teams, as well as of the Oxford Union debating club. He received a master's degree from Oxford in jurisprudence and political science and wrote a thesis on the ideal system for structuring government jobs, a topic that became a focus of his postgraduate education. He envisioned a civil service system where people were hired and promoted based on merit and performance, rather than on political ties and patronage—though he insisted that the most important jobs in government should go to the most educated.

After some time in Lucerne and Berlin, in 1912 he returned to the United States, where he was often mistaken for British as a result of the accent he now affected—and two years later earned his Ph.D. in political science from Columbia University, at the age of twenty-five. He clearly

valued the authority and prestige conferred by the degree, never object-
ing when he was introduced as "Dr. Moses." His blue-chip credentials
were complete—Yale, Oxford, and Columbia.

Eager to plunge into the inner workings of government, Moses attended a training school at the Municipal Research Bureau in New York.
The bureau was the research and advisory arm for the nationwide progressive movement, which sought to rid local governments of patronage,
corruption, and waste. Moses, impatient to make an impact on the organization, soon volunteered to work for the bureau for no salary, which his
family wealth allowed him to do in a number of jobs throughout his career. From these early days, he was more interested in accruing power
than in making money. Perhaps because of his second-class status at Yale,
he was determined, once he entered the arena of politics and government, to get to a position of influence quickly. His impatience led him to
be critical of the Municipal Research Bureau's style, and its preference
for careful study over bold action.

Moses would also find love at the lower Manhattan offices of the bureau. In the winter of 1914, he befriended a secretary from Wisconsin,
Mary Louise Sims, granddaughter of a Methodist minister, and asked her
out for a date. In Sims, Moses saw a smart and hardworking woman who,
with fair skin and blond hair, seemed to exude wholesomeness. By the
summer of 1914, when Moses, then twenty-five, went to the family com-
pound at Lake Placid in upstate New York, he was talking of Mary and little else. The next year he brought her to meet the family, and they married
later that year. Like Robert and Jane Jacobs, Robert and Mary Moses
would remain married for a half century.

Working at the Municipal Research Bureau, Moses found that his expertise in government organization and civil service was much in demand. John Purroy Mitchel, a young prosecutor whose gambling and
conspiracy investigations had produced a series of resignations in government, had been elected mayor in 1914. At thirty-four, the "boy mayor," the
youngest chief executive New York had ever seen, set out to reform city
government, which at the time was controlled by the infamous Tammany
Hall machine—the system of sweetheart deals, kickbacks for government
contracts, and buying votes with patronage that epitomized turn-of-the-
century municipal corruption.

When Mitchel looked to the bureau for help in restructuring the city's
system of hiring and promotion, Moses was ready with his dissertation.

He proposed a merit-based system with an elaborate flowchart of evalua-
tions and quantitative measures of performance, revolutionary ideas for
the time. Predictably, those who had cushy sinecures through Tammany
Hall connections reacted fiercely, booing and hissing in the back of the
room at hearings where Moses presented the new system. Moses, lugging
a bulging leather briefcase and wearing the same white Brooks Brothers
suit day after day, calmly talked through the heckling. It was a fleeting
moment in the spotlight, however. In 1917, Mitchel was defeated by a
candidate from the Tammany Hall machine, and the new administration
was not interested in Moses's ideas. His first major initiative in government came to an ignominious end.

By that time, the United States had plunged into World War I, and
Moses managed to find work at the Emergency Fleet Corporation, a government organization set up to speed construction of shipyards. But he
was fired after less than a year for writing a sharply worded report on in-
efficiencies in the procurement process. Moses, who had moved to an
apartment on the Upper West Side, found himself jobless. His mother
continued to send him money, but he wanted to be more self-sufficient to
raise his two young daughters, Barbara and Jane, in the lifestyle to which
he had become accustomed. He had visions of a bigger family—he
wanted a son—though those plans ended when doctors informed Mary
she could not have any more children.

~~~

In the fall of 1918, Moses received a telephone call that would set him
on his path. Belle Moskowitz, a fiery, forty-year-old reformer close to
New York's incoming governor, Alfred E. Smith, offered Moses a job running a new commission charged with reorganizing the state's government
from top to bottom. Moses eagerly accepted and went to work, drawing
on his blueprint for reorganizing New York City's civil service. Over the
course of several months, he demanded extensive revisions from his staff,
and the initial document was aggressive and ambitious. At Moskowitz's
suggestion, Moses softened the blueprint's language so that it would have
a better chance of approval by the government establishment.

The final 419-page report, which called for consolidating 175 state
agencies, bureaus, and commissions into 16 departments, extending the
governor's term from two to four years, and giving the chief executive
more power to appoint and remove officials, reflected Moses's belief in

consolidating power so that government could act more quickly and decisively. Like his proposal to restructure civil service in municipal government, the state government reorganization was beaten back. Smith was voted out in 1920, and again Moses was out of a job. But Moses and Smith remained friends, often taking long walks together in lower Manhattan, discussing politics and government. The two men—remarkable colleagues given the difference of their backgrounds, Moses the Oxford scholar, Smith the cigar-chomping Irishman—plotted a comeback. When Smith was reelected in 1922, Moses returned to Albany, the state capital, as part of the governor's inner circle. Though he had no official title, Moses quickly established himself as the governor's most trusted aide. He helped write legislation, and lawmakers knew he was speaking for the governor when he stopped them for chats in the halls of the statehouse.

"Bob Moses is the most efficient administrator I have ever met in public life," Smith observed of his apprentice. "He was the best bill drafter in Albany . . . I know he went to Yale and Oxford, but he didn't get that keen mind of his from any college. He was a hard worker. He worked on trains, anywhere and any time. When everyone else was ready for bed he would go back to work."

After being elected to his second term as governor, Smith put Moses in charge of several important projects, including a reorganization of the state's prison system and the institution of railroad grade crossings, and was so impressed with the work that he offered Moses virtually any state job he wanted. There was one thing he would like to be in charge of, Moses told Smith. He would like to run all of New York's parks.

The idea had come to him on a hike around Long Island. In his spare time, Moses often ventured out from a bungalow he and Mary rented in Babylon to the beaches and estuaries east of New York City, where he discovered vast acres of state- and city-owned land and beachfront in the region. There was no easy way for the public to gain access to these largely wild areas, he realized, and no formal system for the state to maintain, develop, or acquire new land. The disarray was particularly acute on Long Island, but Moses learned that the problem was statewide and proposed a new agency to Smith that would turn the large tracts of unused land into a huge, integrated park system, accessible by the public, by car, on a network of new parkways.

"You want to give the people a fur coat when what they need is red flannel underwear," Smith told Moses. The governor was dubious at the sheer breadth and cost of the plan—a $15 million bond issue to acquire hundreds of acres and build extensive amenities. But Moses took Smith on a tour of Long Island, the Catskills, and the Adirondacks, convincing him of the potential to create a world-class parks system. Moving earth, building grand public works, and laying down roads were thrilling for Moses, but he knew what Smith would find valuable about the idea: parks were good politics. Voters loved them. Millions of ordinary New Yorkers sought places to escape to on the weekends, but they had no dazzling destinations and no way of getting anywhere.

Moses won Smith over, and the governor pushed the state legislature to pass the plan in 1924. Smith named Moses president of the newly created New York State Council of Parks and chairman of the Long Island State Park Commission.

Thus empowered and funded, Moses leased an office in Manhattan and furnished it lavishly. He hired secretaries and staff, including a driver, and acquired the finest black Packard limousine available. Meanwhile, he was building an additional parks headquarters on the estate grounds of the financier and diplomat August Belmont in the town of North Babylon, Long Island. He worked from early in the morning until midnight, often including Saturdays, and his team was expected to do the same. Soon the black sedans of the parks commission began appearing at the edge of farmers' fields at all hours, as surveyors mapped out the ambitious new parks system and the network of roadways that would provide access to it.

In Moses's vision, these were not just any roadways but landscaped parkways or "ribbon parks"—two lanes in each direction, sweeping and carving through the wooded countryside—with no traffic lights, no left-turn lanes, and no commercial development except for service areas with a strictly uniform appearance. Cars—and only cars, as Moses made sure that all bridges over the parkways were too low for buses—could zip along the motorways at forty miles per hour, their progress uninterrupted.

To Moses's chagrin, the people of Long Island did not greet his plans warmly. Farmers shooed away members of Moses's team with shotguns, and town managers rose up in rebellion against this unprecedented incursion by the state. Above all, the plans stirred the ire of the wealthy landowners who had settled in the pastoral countryside east of Brooklyn and Queens, including some of the wealthiest families in America, Morgans and Vanderbilts and Winthrops and Carnegies. Several of Moses's parkland expansion schemes and two major east-west routes, the Southern State Parkway and the Northern State Parkway, would nip off corners of estates and run through country-club grounds.

Moses plowed ahead. "If we want your land, we can take it," he told one farming family. Instead of negotiating with the wealthier residents, Moses simply cited the enabling legislation for the parks agency, which he himself had written. The estate owners dispatched their lawyers, but Moses prevailed in the lawsuits; he had the law of New York State behind him, and it allowed him to "appropriate" needed land. By 1927, any meaningful resistance had been toppled, and earthmovers, graders, and pavers began their work, bringing the first segments of the network of parks and roadways that Moses had envisioned to life.

Moses was satisfied with the victory, but he knew his power could come to an end if Smith was defeated again. When John Mitchel failed to win reelection in 1917, Moses had seen how his proposals to reform government disappeared. The key, he decided, was to raise the public's expectations and get projects rolling, so that elected officials would not dare to try to stop them. Involving ordinary citizens in the process was the first thing to go; public participation, he had already learned, only slowed things down. Great public works could not be achieved by committee. "There will be squawking no matter what we do," he said. "We must face at once the demands of those impatient for new facilities and the anguished cries and curses of those who want to be left alone."

From the 1920s on, Moses sought to rope himself off from dissenting views, and even mere questions, about his projects. The Long Island experience had taught him how to dispatch with sophisticated and organized opposition—and he discovered that opposition from the powerful and the wealthy could actually be useful. When one member of a country club testified at a hearing that he feared Long Island would be "overrun with rabble from the city," Smith responded: "Rabble? That's me you're talking about." Moses wasted no time portraying the estate owners and country clubbers as selfish elitists, standing in the way of access to recreation for the people. "A Few Rich Golfers Accused of Blocking Plan for State Park," read the front-page headline in the *New York Times* on January 8, 1925. "We were bested by every sort of social or political influence," Moses said, but when one opponent said "undesirable people" would come to the parks, "there was no further need for us to make any argument. That [man] won our case." Moses began to view controversy as an essential part of getting things done.

In those early years, Moses strove to model himself after Baron Haussmann, who created the grand boulevards and civic monuments of nineteenth-century Paris under Napoleon III. The man who transformed Paris "has been described as a talker, an ogre for work, despotic, insolvent, full of initiative and daring, and caring not a straw for legality. Everything about him was on a grand scale," Moses later wrote admiringly. His "dictatorial talents enabled him to accomplish a vast amount in a very short time, but they also made him many enemies, for he was in the habit of riding roughshod over all opposition."

In the democratic twentieth-century United States, Moses did not have a dictator to back him, and thus developed strategies designed to make his projects inevitable, protecting them from democratic resistance. Along with writing his own legislation and running aggressive public-relations campaigns, one of his principal tactics in defeating opposition was simple: act fast. Plowing ahead with land acquisition and laying asphalt, he learned that once projects were started, they gained a momentum all their own. The opposition had a tough time arguing against something that was already half-done or built, and courts would never make him tear something down that public funds had already paid to build. A fellow state commissioner once filed suit after Moses failed to use union labor in constructing bathhouses. The court rebuked Moses for violating state law, but the structures, already completed, were left standing. "Once you sink that first stake, they'll never make you pull it up," he told a friend.

Moses's success building parks and parkways was accompanied by other achievements; his perseverance was paying off. The state legislature, under pressure from Smith, had finally passed the Moses-authored plan to reorganize state government in 1926, six years after its debut. A year later, Smith rewarded his most trusted aide by nominating Moses to be secretary of state. In what was his first salaried position in the state government hierarchy, Moses threw himself into the job, using the perch to push a wide range of initiatives. He built hospitals, prisons, and parkways, projects about which Smith would boast during his campaign for president in 1928.

Moses's tenure as secretary of state was short-lived. In 1928, Smith lost in the presidential campaign to Herbert Hoover, and a rising star named Franklin Delano Roosevelt was elected governor of New York. FDR and Moses detested each other. A few years before, when Roosevelt was in private legal practice, stricken by polio, and readying for his run for governor, he had asked Moses to hire his loyal adviser, Louis Howe, at the new state parks agency. The suggestion was that Moses should provide Howe with a position in which he would do little actual work. Moses refused. After Roosevelt was elected governor—despite a plea from Smith to keep Moses as secretary of state—the future president readied his own choice for the position. Moses learned that he would be the only member of the state cabinet not to be reappointed, and resigned before Roosevelt could make the announcement.

But Roosevelt recognized that Moses had momentum developing the parks system, a popular project with the public and especially the press. Though he would have liked to rid New York state government of Moses entirely, Roosevelt allowed him to continue the parks work. The strategy Moses had crafted on Long Island had worked perfectly. If the public supported his projects, he could stay on no matter who the chief executive was.

The vision for the parks system on Long Island had been audacious from the beginning. By the end of the 1920s, Moses was thinking even bigger. While exploring the southern coast of Long Island, he discovered miles of new land that had been created by shifting currents, waves, and sand deposits. The barrier beach known as Fire Island was accessible only by boat. Sketching plans on the back of an envelope, Moses set out to transform a nearby sandbar into a signature public recreation area with bathhouses, restaurants, and a water tank hidden inside a soaring Venetian bell tower—all just a short trip from downtown Manhattan. He pushed his team of engineers and architects to make every detail and finish the finest possible, insisting on sandstone and brick for the bathhouses, huge parking lots, a theater, and "wholesome" games like shuffleboard. The two Jones Beach bathhouses, faced with an especially expensive brick that Moses had admired on an East Side hotel, cost a million dollars each to build. The design was a mix of Moorish, Gothic, and modern styles, complete with mosaics, elegant signs, fountains, railings, and trash cans that all evoked a maritime theme. Moses was involved in the smallest details, including a suggestion for shelves at just the right waist-high level for diaper-changing mothers.

Moses was able to secure the necessary state funding for Jones Beach by articulating his early philosophy—that the public, albeit primarily white and middle-class, deserved the best and would treat public facilities with respect. When Jones Beach was "made as attractive as if it were a private club of rich men, but sufficiently large to prevent overcrowding, something happens. The crowds are well-dispersed, quiet, respectable and leisurely. The atmosphere is that of a great public club and the patrons behave like club members," he wrote. Jones Beach opened in 1930 and was wildly popular, with millions flocking there every summer. The project's success helped keep Moses afloat during another period of political tumult.

When Roosevelt ran for president in 1932, his ally and lieutenant governor, Herbert H. Lehman, became governor of New York. Lehman viewed Moses with more tolerance than affection, but recognized his talents for securing funding and building public works—hugely important at a time when the federal government was ramping up spending to counter the Depression. Lehman appointed Moses chairman of the Emergency Public Works Commission and let him put men to work on big projects throughout the state. It was during this time that Moses would realize the importance of having projects planned and ready to go, in order to be first in line when the federal government announced new funding programs. He had such financing in mind as he rushed to secure the corridor for the Henry Hudson Bridge, and was eager to show Washington another project worthy of federal largesse: the Triborough Bridge.

New York City engineers drafted plans for a span connecting Manhattan, the Bronx, and Queens—hopscotching over Ward's and Randall's islands at the tip of the East River—beginning in 1916, originally calling for the bridge to be clad in ornate granite and pairs of Gothic arches between steel suspension towers. The project was shelved after the stock market crash of 1929, however, and Moses stepped in by enlisting a new engineer, Othmar Ammann, to streamline the design and give it a more modern appearance. Federal funding was the key for getting it built, but Moses knew that Washington would be more likely to support the project if there was a long-term entity to bolster the financing and maintenance of the bridge. He proposed the independent Triborough Bridge Authority, signed into law by Governor Lehman on April 7, 1933, to handle the finances of construction and operation. The authority was given the power to issue bonds, for additional funding that was needed to complement the federal aid, and could expect a steady stream of independent revenue from tolls it would collect on the bridge.

The result was a self-contained entity that operated outside the checks-and-balances system of city and state government. The Triborough Bridge and Tunnel Authority would become the base of the Moses empire; he wrote the legislation creating it and served first as a member of the board and then as chairman. The authority had its own seal, as elaborate as the city's or the state's, and it adorned the sleeves of a fifty-plus-man police force, as well as official correspondence, license plates, and places of prominence on the structures themselves—as if to announce there was a new form of government in town, rebuilding and reshaping Gotham.

From the moment he took charge of the state parks agency, Moses recognized the importance of hiring teams of men who were bright and hardworking—but at the same time never so independent that they questioned his authority. The Triborough Bridge Authority allowed him to cultivate loyalty by doling out perks such as houses and consulting contracts for associates, even going so far as to put the spouses of key staff members on the payroll. He brought in the best and the brightest in architecture and engineering, such as Ammann, the brilliant Swiss-born engineer and designer of the George Washington Bridge, which opened in 1931, and Aymar Embury, designer of the Central Park Zoo and the McCarren Pool in Brooklyn, who favored the sleek and modern style known as art deco. When Moses called for a new administration building to serve as Triborough headquarters on Randall's Island—supplanting institutions for the sick and the poor, which he hastily relocated—he turned to Embury for a beefy limestone-facade structure befitting his new base of power.

With money continuing to flow in from Washington, the authority soon ran at a surplus, allowing Moses to hire armies of union workers and consultants, real estate developers, insurance companies, and investment bankers who essentially owed him their livelihoods. He was steadily building a moat around himself that he hoped would allow him to operate with complete independence from city and state government.

When La Guardia was elected mayor of New York in 1933, Moses seized on a new opportunity to expand his influence. The new mayor wanted physical development to be the hallmark of his administration and tapped Moses as a top lieutenant to carry out that goal. La Guardia helped Moses gain complete control over the Triborough authority, making him chief executive officer and chairman, and also named him city parks commissioner. Just as he had consolidated disparate bureaus for the new state parks agency during Alfred Smith's tenure as mayor, Moses wrote legislation unifying the parks departments of the city's five boroughs into a single organization. Then he launched an ambitious construction and restoration campaign for New York City's public spaces. The line of architects applying for jobs in the new city program of public works was two blocks long in front of Parks Department headquarters on Fifth Avenue.

With the same zeal he had demonstrated at the state level, Moses revamped the city parks network by taking control of unused city and state land throughout the city and turning it into parks and playgrounds, sprucing up dilapidated facilities to the delight of local neighborhoods. In those early years of the La Guardia administration, Moses had close to two thousand projects going at once, ranging from park bench repairs to new golf courses to the new Central Park Zoo—the opening of which he had to miss because he caught the flu, nearly collapsed, and was ordered to stay in bed. His staff worried he was working so hard he sometimes never seemed to eat or sleep. He wore his suits until they were threadbare and his shoes until they went to tatters, counting on Mary to notice and replace them.

If the dedication to work nearly exhausted him, the payoff was clearly evident. Even the most cynical New Yorker was grateful for the citywide spruce-up that included thirty-eight thousand gallons of fresh paint, seventy miles of new fencing, walkways, and bridle paths, hundreds of drinking fountains, comfort stations, tennis courts, golf courses, and thirty-four new playgrounds. The trees were pruned, weeds removed, statues burnished. The achievements "seem little short of miraculous," a 1934 *New York Times* editorial gushed. "It is almost as if Mr. Moses rubbed a lamp, or murmured some incantation over an old jar, and made the jinn leap out and do his bidding."

The success was intoxicating, and in 1934 Moses decided to run for governor. As it turned out, he was a better political insider than candidate. On the stump, he berated the press, refused to pose for traditional cam-

paign photographs, had little patience for courting campaign contribu-
tors, and delivered speeches that came off as lectures. Running as a Republican, Moses conducted an intensely negative campaign against the
incumbent governor, Lehman, a popular and mild-mannered New Deal
Democrat backed by Roosevelt. Though their families had grown up
close to each other, and Lehman had kept Moses on running public
works projects, Moses called Lehman weak, stupid, corrupt, and a liar.
The attacks backfired among voters, and Moses lost by a record margin.
He telephoned Lehman early on election night with congratulations, took
his campaign workers out for a big dinner at Sardi's, and tried to put the
whole experience behind him by the morning.

Having offended Lehman and his staff during the campaign, Moses
was again in danger of losing his appointed positions. Advisers to both
Lehman and La Guardia urged their bosses to fire Moses. Through a top
aide, President Roosevelt pressured La Guardia to get rid of Moses once
and for all, and drafted a White House directive cutting off federal funds
for the city if Moses remained in place. La Guardia hesitated, siding with
the man who was delivering the parks renovations so popular with the
public. Now a deft manipulator of the press, Moses leaked the plot to the
press, and Roosevelt was portrayed as engaging in petty politics. Remarkably, Lehman, too, opted to keep Moses on, putting aside the attacks of
the campaign; with so many public works projects under way, Moses was
too important to lose. The master builder remained in power.

Outmaneuvering the president of the United States only made Moses
more cocksure. His thirst for power kept growing, and his exercise of it
grew less and less judicious. If a member of a commission or council was
recalcitrant with a vote, he would have his team investigate for blackmail
fodder—a drinking problem or an affair—though he himself was dogged
by rumors of infidelities. Throughout the 1930s, Moses developed a well-
earned reputation for vindictiveness. He razed the Casino, an elaborate
banquet facility in Central Park, because Mayor Jimmy Walker, who had
used it for lavish private parties, had crossed his beloved friend Alfred
Smith. He demolished the Columbia Yacht Club at the foot of West Eighty-
sixth Street after he felt the commodore running the club had been rude to
him. When Roosevelt killed his plans for a new, six-lane bridge from Battery Park to Brooklyn, Moses reluctantly agreed to build the Brooklyn-
Battery Tunnel instead—but insisted that the portal had to be right at the
spot of the historic Castle Clinton and the aquarium it housed, requiring its

destruction. In every case, Moses operated outside the jurisdiction of city government; on more than one occasion, La Guardia resorted to dispatching police to make sure Moses didn't tear things down.

Though fiery rhetoric had not served him well in his bid for governor, as city commissioner and head of an independent authority Moses felt free to lob bombs at will. He reserved special vituperation for architecture and planning professionals, even as he embraced many aspects of contemporary design. He had a lively private correspondence with Frank Lloyd Wright, and supported the construction of the Guggenheim Museum, though in public he castigated the star architect as someone who "was regarded in Russia as our greatest builder." Lewis Mumford, the urban theorist and architectural critic for the *New Yorker,* was, according to Moses, "an outspoken revolutionary" who only wrote articles and never built anything, part of a crowd of leftist urban theorists. Moses's references to communism were intentional. Before Jane Jacobs was defending herself in the State Department interrogatory, and as Joseph McCarthy prepared to bring red-baiting to an art form, Moses had an intuitive sense of how to undermine others while promoting his own agenda: he questioned their patriotism.

Moses was nothing if not mercurial, punishing those he perceived as enemies and rewarding loyal friends and those he took under his wing. When security guards caught a fourteen-year-old boy named David Oats who had sneaked onto the grounds of the 1964 World's Fair in Queens, they brought him before Moses himself for a lecture. But instead, Moses was charmed by the trespasser, caked in mud as he was, and asked him if he would like to pursue his interest in the fair. Moses brought him into the planning process; Oats went on to lead the World's Fair Association and became a fervent defender of Flushing Meadows Corona Park. Moses left him priceless World's Fair memorabilia in his will. Other friends received good treatment for life. He gave Alfred Smith his own key to the Central Park Zoo so the retired governor, a lover of animals, could enter at any time to walk through the menagerie. Moses always remembered a favor, just as he never forgot a slight. His staff lived in fear of angry outbursts, he swore and used ethnic slurs, and on one occasion he physically assaulted a political rival. The dials of his personality—charm, anger, gratitude, vindictiveness—were turned all the way up.

A lover of theater, the opera, and big bands like those led by Guy Lombardo, a close friend, Moses also possessed a flair for entertainment. He relished the opportunity to flaunt his showmanship at New York's World's Fair in 1939. La Guardia put him in charge of the project, and Moses quickly identified a site—an ash heap in the northern section of Queens, which he transformed into Flushing Meadows Corona Park, later home to Shea Stadium and the World's Fair of 1964. The World's Fair had become an important event for cities, producing the Eiffel Tower in Paris, the Crystal Palace in London, and the Beaux Arts exhibition known as the White City in Chicago. The fair had become an opportunity to show off a vision of the future, and Moses settled on a theme: "the world of tomorrow." He brought in General Motors to put on Futurama, a model of the twentieth-century city knit together by highways. Some forty-five million visitors were dazzled by the promise of such a modern metropolis.

That the centerpiece of the World's Fair was an exhibit on cars and highways was no accident. Moses was convinced that middle-class families would remain in New York if they could get around by car, and pushed ahead with plans for a comprehensive roadway network for the metropolitan area. He viewed mass transit—crowded streetcars, buses, and subways—as a hallmark of the past. Cities built the first subway systems around the turn of the century, and for nearly four decades moving people en masse was an efficient way to provide transportation in places of great density. But for Moses, the automobile provided mobility and convenience that transit could never match. He was strictly a planner for cars and trucks and never incorporated transit in his plans—even when it would have been simple to put a rail line down the median of his highways, as other cities, including Chicago, were planning to do. "Cities are created by and for traffic," he declared.

And so Moses charged on, determined to make it easier for traffic to flow in and around New York City. The Marine Parkway Gil Hodges Memorial Bridge, at the time the world's longest span for vehicles, opened in 1937, providing access to Rockaway and Jacob Riis on the southern shore of Long Island. The Henry Hudson got a second deck in 1938. The Bronx-Whitestone Bridge connecting Queens and the Bronx opened in 1939. The new roadway network in Brooklyn, Queens, and out onto Long Island was taking shape, as the Grand Central, Interborough, Belt, Laurelton, Cross Island, and Whitestone parkways were all in final stages of construction. When traffic jams clogged the system, Moses simply proposed widening and extending the highways even more.

The elevated Gowanus Parkway, his last parkway project before a re-newed campaign of expressways following World War II, gave a taste of what was in store for the urban neighborhoods in the path of progress. Moses had insisted on putting the four-lane parkway along Third Avenue in Brooklyn, where an elevated subway line already ran. Knowing that a dark, damp overpass would be far worse than the El, residents pleaded for the roadway to instead cut through an industrial area one block over. But Moses would not agree to move the corridor he had planned. He had made the calculations and knew best where the roadway should be, just as he had in the case of the Henry Hudson Bridge at Spuyten Duyvil. Fiddling around with the right-of-way would only lead to costly delays. Thus, the Gowanus soared through, rattling windows on either side, and left the avenue in darkness. The neighborhood would, as a result, succumb to blight, closed storefronts, and crime.

Moses believed that some pain was necessary in modernizing an old, cluttered city like New York. Yes, some people had to be moved, and yes, the process could be viewed as ruthless, but he considered his methods more disciplined than inflexible. "You can draw any kind of picture you like on a clean slate and indulge your every whim in the wilderness in laying out a New Delhi, Canberra, or Brasilia," he said, "but when you operate in an overbuilt metropolis, you have to hack your way with a meat ax."

~~~

Beginning in the 1940s, Moses turned to a new project: housing. In 1942, the New York state legislature passed the Redevelopment Companies Law, which allowed the city to clear land using eminent domain, the constitutionally enshrined power of government to seize private property for public use. Under the new law, once land was taken, it was to be turned over to private developers to invest in large-scale housing projects. The idea was to enlist the private sector to build affordable housing that would help the city retain its middle-class population, who were increasingly departing for the suburbs. The Metropolitan Life Insurance Company was the first to take the plunge, building Stuyvesant Town, a complex of thirty-five new buildings on more than sixty acres on the Lower East Side, housing twenty-four thousand people.

Stuyvesant Town was for Moses the first big opportunity to design large-scale housing in New York City, and Moses convinced La Guardia to let him manage the project. Though continually riddled with controversy because of its whites-only covenant, a clause demanded by Metropolitan

Life, and the outright eviction of most of the low-income residents who lived at the site prior to rebuilding, Stuyvesant Town nevertheless achieved the stated goal of the city—more affordable places for the middle class to live—and Moses had his entrée into the area of housing.

New York's Redevelopment Companies Law was only the first step. Moses and many others in government believed that a more systematic effort was necessary, to fund an even more massive redevelopment of the city encompassing several blocks at a time. The vision was to clear away slums and build not only housing but new commercial, civic, and cultural projects as well. A friend and fellow Yale man, Senator Robert Taft, gave Moses advance notice that Congress, worried about the decline of the nation's cities, was about to pass the Housing Act of 1949, which included a program known as Title I, in which cities could take property by eminent domain and turn it over to private developers for redevelopment. Moses had seen how New Deal money for parks and projects like the Triborough Bridge was a godsend, and was similarly ready with several proposed projects so New York City could be first in line for the new millions for public housing under Title I. The policy that would come to be known as urban renewal allowed Moses to work at a much grander scale.

The motivation behind urban renewal was the prevailing view, after World War II, that major cities were in decline, marked by unhealthy, crowded conditions, traffic congestion, and an eroding manufacturing base. New York, Boston, Philadelphia, Chicago, and other cities found themselves losing population to the suburbs and became increasingly fearful of turning into economic backwaters. Moses and other planners of the time proposed the solution: new infrastructure, including highways and parking garages, to provide better access to downtowns; cultural and civic attractions; and the massive construction of affordable housing to retain working- and middle-class families.

The problem, of course, was that cities had already been developed over the previous hundred years. There was no blank canvas for Moses and other urban planners to create this new vision of the modern city. They needed to tear down existing neighborhoods and start over and, to do so, set out to designate those neighborhoods as blighted slums. The modernist movement in urban planning and architecture provided the rationale—that close-knit, dense urban street grids must be replaced with fewer and taller buildings surrounded by open space to let in light and air. The cluttered, medieval-style cities of Europe had outlived their usefulness; modern times and new economic realities demanded a new approach to human settlement. Moses and the modernists believed that cities weren't static places and that centuries-old block and building layouts needed to be revisited and revised.

Moses was in a strong position to lead urban renewal in New York City. He convinced William O'Dwyer, who succeeded La Guardia as mayor in 1946, to name him to the new post of "construction coordinator," giving him free-ranging power over redevelopment efforts. Moses was also named chairman of the Emergency Committee on Housing, which had urgency in its title that Moses would eagerly exploit to push projects and secure funding. In 1946, he became chairman of the Committee on Slum Clearance, which ultimately allowed him to channel federal funds to New York for urban renewal—easily outrunning other planning czars in Boston and Philadelphia. New York over the next twelve years would receive close to $70 million in Title I funds, far outperforming Chicago, which received the second-largest amount of funding at about $30 million. In his industry, Moses was the pacesetter, and no one came close to keeping up.

In the same way that Moses wanted to break the logjam of traffic congestion with smooth, wide-open highways and bridges and tunnels, he viewed the problem of housing as a kind of engineering challenge. While he claimed he was not a big fan of modern architecture—he preferred a more traditional style to appeal to broad public tastes, such as the neoclassical style he employed at Jones Beach—the emerging modernist formula for urban design provided a handy vehicle for maximizing the number of housing units. The model had been established by Le Corbusier—towering slabs with open space at their bases, which would serve as a kind of communal front yard for the low-income families who would inhabit the developments. For the housing campaign using Title I funding, Moses relied on private developers to undertake design and construction, some of whom produced fine examples of modernist architecture, the dominant style of the time. But in other cases, particularly for low-income housing, the architects hired by the private-sector developers, who were seeking to cut costs, produced complexes that were monotonous and plain. Urban renewal and housing in New York City soon took the form of big rectangular structures and cruciform, X-shaped towers on what became known as superblocks—the cold and uninviting environments that Jane Jacobs observed in East Harlem and that stymied the basic functions of city life. Increasingly, Moses abandoned the attention to fine details that characterized Jones Beach and the swimming pools and bathhouses, instead focusing on the number of new apartments— just as his later expressways, built with the single goal of the swift flow of traffic, possessed none of the charm of his wooden-guardrailed parkways. Swept up in the power he had amassed, he pursued the singular goal of building more housing, with less attention to how the projects actually functioned.

There were other problems. The private developers that Moses used were interested in building profitable luxury housing, along with the more modest apartments, to be occupied by teachers and nurses and municipal employees working in the city. But invariably, even the ostensible affordable housing in many projects was still out of reach for the people living in the "blighted" neighborhoods that had been cleared away. Under the guidelines of Title I, evicted residents were supposed to be guaranteed relocation, but thousands of low-income and minority families fell through the cracks and could not navigate the bureaucratic procedures to move into new homes. Critics began to refer to urban renewal as "Negro removal." And many of those lucky enough to move into the new apartments soon found that living conditions were not up to the standards that had been promised. The downside of handing over operations to private developers became apparent, as tenant complaints about basic functions were ignored.

To head off what he perceived to be a growing unease about urban renewal and the new housing construction, Moses cranked up the public-relations machine that had proved so useful in getting his parkways built on Long Island. He instructed a staffer to create pamphlets with plans and renderings that make "the statement that we mean business, that the procedure will be entirely fair and orderly, and that hardships will be, so far as humanly possible, avoided."

In 1951, he produced a glossy brochure with Mondrian-like graphics on the cover, detailing seven major clearance projects in the works and plans for many more. From Harlem to Greenwich Village, and Morningside Heights to Brooklyn Heights, the promise was for modern city living to replace old and tattered neighborhoods.

"Five minutes from Wall Street and Times Square, in the heart of Manhattan, is rising a dream of the future that genius, skill and inspiration have made today's reality," read a brochure for the Washington

Square Southeast urban renewal project. "It is Washington Square Village—destined to be a spacious new concept of city living to New York and the world."

The vision extended well beyond housing. Moses set out to reinvent all the major features of the city—with new cultural and civic institutions, universities, and commercial development. Throughout the mid-1940s and early 1950s, he used urban renewal to create some of his best-known redevelopment projects. He laid plans for Lincoln Center, the performing arts complex on the Upper West Side, to be built in alliance with powerful nonprofit institutions such as the Juilliard School, the Metropolitan Opera, and Fordham University. The design competition for the complex attracted some of the biggest names in modernist architecture. A few blocks south, Moses transformed Columbus Circle, creating the New York Coliseum, a bulky civic center at the Paris-like monument and traffic circle at the southwest corner of Central Park. At the same time, Moses used his various positions heading city agencies to lead the effort to locate the new United Nations headquarters in New York, initially favoring a site at Flushing Meadows in Queens, but ultimately bringing about the modernist tower and plaza complex over the FDR Drive at Forty-second Street. Inspired by Le Corbusier, the big vertical rectangle was dark green glass on its east and west faces and white marble on its north and south ends, and featured a sweeping General Assembly building and park at its base. Almost immediately, it would become one of the city's iconic structures.

As this massive redevelopment of New York City plowed ahead, Moses was lauded by the business community, academia, and the press as a visionary master builder; the future of New York as an economic power was at stake, and Moses, more than anyone, was dedicated to the city's salvation. While mayors came and went, his prominence was a constant. Vincent Richard Impellitteri, who came into power when O'Dwyer was forced to resign due to allegations of corruption, deferred to Moses more than any of his predecessors had.

With so many major projects built or under construction, Moses was feted almost weekly at black-tie dinners, where he accepted awards and gave rousing speeches on the future of New York—speeches that, of course, highlighted his many accomplishments. He attended elaborate parties at the Jones Beach pavilion with his friend the bandleader Guy Lombardo, held court over lunches catered in his multiple offices by on-call chefs, and was a favored guest at major civic events. In his free time he went swimming in the ocean and angled for bluefish in Great South Bay on his broad-bottomed small motorboat, which Mary had named the *Bob*. Life was good.

By the mid-1950s—twenty years after his triumphant year opening the pools and playgrounds, the Triborough and the Henry Hudson bridges— Moses was on a winning streak with no end in sight. Federal funding for urban renewal continued to pour in, allowing him to transform whole sections of New York City. Elected officials and businessmen alike understood that any major initiative in New York City required the approval of Robert Moses.

Even the most shrewd and powerful men of the city could not prevail over Moses. Walter O'Malley, owner of the Brooklyn Dodgers, had for several years pressured Moses to help him condemn land at the corner of Atlantic and Flatbush avenues, near the entrance to a Long Island Rail Road station, for a new home for the Dodgers. Thanks to suburbanization and the roads that Moses had built, Dodgers fans were fleeing the city for burgeoning Long Island developments such as Levittown and weren't coming back to the Dodgers' home stadium, Ebbets Field, which had no access to the LIRR and only seven hundred parking spaces. Attendance had dropped precipitously, and the stadium was deteriorating. O'Malley proposed a new, privately financed domed facility, but he needed the city to help him clear the proposed site, then occupied by a meat market and some industrial and storage buildings. Moses refused at every turn, saying he could not "dress up" the stadium site as a Title I project—although he had massaged the standards of the program in many other instances. Moses wanted to build a new baseball stadium, but not in Brooklyn— rather, in Queens, in Flushing Meadows Corona Park and the World's Fair grounds, the site of what would ultimately become Shea Stadium. O'Malley's idea wasn't his idea, and Moses wasn't about to budge.

Robert Wagner, the newly elected mayor, worried that the Dodgers would leave New York, called a meeting with O'Malley and Moses, which took place on the porch at Gracie Mansion in 1955. In the meeting, recorded by a crew from CBS News, Moses accused O'Malley of being a fat-cat sports team owner who was blackmailing the city. O'Malley, Moses said, was essentially saying he would pick up his marbles and go home. Though Moses was as responsible for the impasse as O'Malley, he knew the characterization would strike a chord with the public. During the World Series against the Yankees that year, O'Malley announced he would take the team to Los Angeles, and O'Malley is reviled to this day for moving the Dodgers out of Brooklyn.

Moses was at the height of his power. Virtually untouchable in his government post, and highly skilled at outmaneuvering and crushing his opponents, he seemed invincible. O'Malley, a well-connected Irish businessman and strategic thinker, couldn't find a way around him. Mayors, from La Guardia to O'Dwyer to Impellitteri and ultimately Wagner, bent to his wishes. Governors tiptoed around him, and even presidents couldn't outfox him. The president of the United States couldn't get him fired. By 1956, nobody—certainly not mere citizens—tangled with Robert Moses and won.

Certainly not a bunch of mothers.

THREE

The Battle of Washington Square Park

Jane Jacobs left the offices of *Architectural Forum,* took the elevator to the lobby of Rockefeller Center, and pulled out her bicycle for the ride home to Greenwich Village. She pedaled across Forty-second Street and all the bustle of midtown Manhattan, past the Empire State Building and the big Macy's department store at Herald Square, her handbag in a basket on the front handlebars. As she entered Chelsea, below Twenty-third Street, and then the Village, the buildings became lower, and the streets went from smooth pavement to rough cobblestones. She dismounted at Hudson Street and walked the bike up to No. 555.

Flipping through the mail, she came across an envelope that read, "Save Washington Square Park." She'd read in the newspaper that the park was under threat. The parks commissioner, Robert Moses, planned to put a roadway through it, cutting it in half—and Moses had a reputation for getting things done.

The letter inside, from a citizens' committee to save Washington Square Park, described the proposal. In its current form, Fifth Avenue, New York's grand boulevard, stretched from Harlem all the way to Washington Square Park, but then ended abruptly at the park's signature arch.

OPPOSITE: Robert Moses sought to extend Fifth Avenue with this roadway through Washington Square Park. *New York City Parks Photo Archive*

A carriageway there allowed city buses to turn around and swing back up Fifth Avenue, which was a two-way street in those days. The Moses proposal was to extend Fifth Avenue straight through the park, Jane read. It would punch through to the south side and continue on into lower Manhattan as Fifth Avenue South.

The Fifth Avenue extension was a critical piece of Moses's larger vision for Greenwich Village, one of a dozen areas in the city he had targeted for urban renewal—essentially wiping out sections of the old, cluttered neighborhood and putting in new, modern construction and wider streets. As chairman of the mayor's Committee on Slum Clearance—a position he held simultaneously with that of parks commissioner—Moses was in the process of razing ten city blocks between the park and Houston Street to the south.

That area was a typical Greenwich Village neighborhood of five- and six-story buildings predominantly housing immigrants and low-income families, warehouses, and struggling manufacturers such as hatmakers. After World War II, the area had become threadbare and unkempt, with shabby building fronts and deteriorating interior conditions. Moses had designated it as a blighted slum, initiating an urban renewal plan that called for massive demolition to make room for giant towers containing some four thousand apartments, including rooms that could be rented for a low rate of $65 a month. The buildings, known as superblocks, would be set in open space, obliterating the existing network of small streets. In the first phase of the project, in which Moses would build a new housing complex called Washington Square Village, 130 buildings would be smashed by wrecking balls, and 150 families would have to pack up their belongings, leave their homes, and either apply for the new housing if they could afford it or find new places to live on their own.

The roadway through Washington Square Park would be not only a new gateway to Washington Square Village but part of Moses's larger effort to replace the crazy quilt of streets in the area, which had their origins in the days of Dutch and English settlement, to accommodate the automobile age. An extended Fifth Avenue would speed the flow of traffic in the area all the way to yet another roadway Moses had proposed: the Lower Manhattan Expressway, a crosstown highway that would provide speedy east-west travel between the Hudson and the East rivers. It all worked together as a package: a modern road network and massive redevelopment. The project was all the more important because its success would signal to other neighborhoods the way of the future. Washington Square Park was in the way.

Jacobs, who had researched urban renewal for her articles in *Amerika* magazine, knew there was federal muscle behind the Moses plans. The federal Housing Act of 1949 provided millions in federal funding, as a kind of Marshall Plan for cities, and the superblocks of regimented housing towers were already replacing old neighborhoods in New York City— from Harlem to the Lower East Side—and in Boston, Philadelphia, Chicago, and St. Louis as well. Now Washington Square Park was being drawn into the transformation.

Like her Greenwich Village neighbors, Jacobs loved the park. It was, as Henry James had put it, a place of "established repose," an oasis amid the concrete, bricks, and asphalt of the city. Ten years earlier, she had lived just a block west of the park, at 82 Washington Place, a stately apartment building that had been home to Richard Wright and Willa Cather, who described the park's charms in "Coming, Aphrodite!": the fountain gave off "a mist of rainbow water . . . Plump robins were hopping about on the soil; the grass was newly cut and blindingly green. Looking up the Avenue through the Arch, one could see the young poplars with their bright, sticky leaves." In those days, Jacobs would emerge from the big building and look to the right and see the comforting sight of the trees and the fountain and the statue of Giuseppe Garibaldi, the Italian national hero. After she moved a few blocks over to 555 Hudson Street and started her family with Robert, she began to appreciate the park as a mother. Through the early 1950s, she brought her sons to the play areas or strolled around with them under the dappled canopy of trees.

As Jacobs knew from her research on the area for articles for *Amerika,* many before her had been fiercely protective of the space. In the late nineteenth century, a group of residents in the homes around the park fought off a proposal to locate a sizable armory there. Later, the neighbors rose up in rebellion when the city had the audacity to propose an iron fence around its perimeter.

Though it had its formal elements, like the arch and the neat rows of homes with their identical stoops on the north side, Washington Square Park was never just a showpiece, meant to be seen but not touched. The people of Greenwich Village liked its worn-in, comfortable character. It needed no dressing up, as it was a place steeped in history. Henry James, Edith Wharton, Walt Whitman, Edgar Allan Poe, Stephen Crane, and

Willa Cather were drawn there. Then the artists Willem de Kooning, Edward Hopper, and Jackson Pollock frequented its grounds, and later the beat writer Jack Kerouac and the folksingers Bob Dylan, Joan Baez, and Peter, Paul, and Mary. A young man named Ed Koch, later the mayor of New York, would come down to strum a guitar by the fountain. Home to protests, marches, riots, and demonstrations, the park had come to symbolize free speech, political empowerment, and civil disobedience. Downtown businessmen marched through it, clamoring for new silver and gold currency standards; women held a solemn vigil there after the Triangle Shirtwaist Factory fire killed 145 workers in 1911. It was a park where New Yorkers both turned their faces to the sunshine and looked inward to their conscience.

Some of New York's most august institutions were located all around the park—Macy's and Brooks Brothers, social clubs like the Century Association, opera and theater that was the precursor to Broadway, the *New York Times* before it moved to Times Square, grand mansions and town homes before there was such a thing as the Upper East Side, and the Metropolitan Museum of Art and the Whitney Museum before they were moved uptown. The incubation of one of the world's great cities occurred within a walk of this park.

But most of all, Washington Square Park was a place to be outside and to run around amid green grass and trees, in the middle of a city that could feel very paved and gray. In the 1950s, hundreds of thousands of Americans were leaving cities for the suburbs, preferring a house with a backyard, a place to throw a football or set up a swing set. But for most city dwellers, their only backyard, the only place they could let their kids be outside, was the neighborhood park. For anyone within walking distance in Greenwich Village, Washington Square Park was that place. It was the model for Central Park—the basic idea that people living all around a big park should be able to walk to it and stroll around a green space in the city, as a matter of public health and sanity—and as such, as vital a piece of urban infrastructure as any bridge or expressway.

Now one man was threatening it all—the history, the stewardship, the respite—and Jacobs was furious. She talked it over with her husband, who was equally dismayed at how the roadway would split the park down the middle. Moses had promised there would be extensive new landscaping on either side of the roadway, but there was no getting around the fact that green space and playgrounds would be replaced with the harsh formality of bituminous stone curbing. Bob's sense for design, as a trained architect, led him to believe the park would become wasted, unused, or derelict space. Nobody would want to go there to be beside a highway. "Moses' temple to urination," he remarked, and Jane laughed.

Not content to merely send in the form letter the save-the-park committee had provided, Jacobs wrote a note in longhand dated June 1, 1955, to Mayor Robert Wagner and the Manhattan borough president, Hulan Jack:

> I have heard with alarm and almost with disbelief, the plans to run a sunken highway through the center of Washington Square. My husband and I are among the citizens who truly believe in New York—to the extent that we have bought a home in the heart of the city and remodeled it with a lot of hard work (transforming it from a slum property) and are raising our three children here. It is very discouraging to do our best to make the city more habitable, and then to learn that the city itself is thinking up schemes to make it uninhabitable. I have learned of the alternate plan of the Washington Square Park Committee to close the park to all vehicular traffic. Now that is the plan that the city officials, if they believe in New York as a decent place to live and not just to rush through, should be for. I hope you will do your best to save Washington Square from the highway.
>
> Respectfully,
> Jane Jacobs
> (Mrs. R. H. Jacobs Jr.)

Jacobs also filled out the form letter for the Washington Square Park Committee, checking off her opposition to a four-lane roadway and supporting closing the park to all traffic except for a bus turnaround. In that moment, Jacobs began her journey not just as a writer about cities or as a mother of young kids, but as a New York City activist.

For such a contested piece of real estate, Washington Square Park is simple—almost ordinary—in appearance. It is dotted by buttonwood and elm trees with muscular, drooping branches and peeling bark, including an English elm in the northwest corner believed to be the oldest in

New York City. Benches bend along the gentle curve of the walkways. The arch, a sturdy structure reminiscent of the Arc de Triomphe in Paris, was added in the middle of the northern border to honor George Washington's centennial as the nation's first president. A fountain, built in 1856, was in a quirk of the layout set slightly off to the side, rather than being directly in line with the terminus of Fifth Avenue. Around the fountain were playgrounds and walkways, places to let a dog run around, and spots for musicians and street performers. But it had no special gardens like the Tuileries in Paris, no uncommon flowers or plants. The playgrounds were unremarkable. Still, the park felt comfortable and safe. It was cozy and well framed, lined with brownstones, town houses, churches, and university buildings. Arriving at the base of Fifth Avenue was "as if the wine of life had been poured for you, in advance, into some pleasant old punch bowl," wrote Henry James, author of the nineteenth-century novel that invokes the park's name.

A casual observer might think the whole area was carefully planned. Its basic parameters were the result of intentional urban design, based on the London residential square model from the eighteenth century. But Washington Square Park has a tumultuous history that suggests a kind of accidental public space.

It started, like everything in Manhattan, as a pristine natural area. Before the Dutch arrived, there were peat bogs, pine barrens, eelgrass meadows, and estuaries. Washington Square Park was a mushy bowl between the jagged hills of northern Manhattan and the bedrock close to the surface around modern-day Wall Street. A trout stream ran through it—called Minetta Creek, a snaking waterway through the reeds and cattails—and still does to this day, under the streets, nurturing the greenery above. The Lenape people, the Native American tribe that inhabited New York, hunted waterfowl even as the first fur traders from the Dutch West India Company settled on the southernmost tip of the island. Only after African slaves started arriving did the city begin its inexorable march northward, as farmland was needed to sustain the colony of New Amsterdam. The homes built in what is now Greenwich Village, referred to by the Dutch as Noortwyck, were first abandoned due to conflicts with the Lenape, but reclaimed when the Dutch freed numerous slaves and gave them land for farming and for raising livestock. Although the Dutch and then the English would later take the land away from them, freed African slaves were the vanguard that led to the permanent settlement of Green-wich Village all around Washington Square Park.

After the British took over in 1664, and renamed the city in honor of the Duke of York, the center of commerce remained in lower Manhattan, but English military officers built large homes to the north, in the countryside that reminded them of Greenwich, England. The name stuck, and the area was the city's first pastoral retreat. Wealthy Americans took over after the Revolutionary War, settling into country estates amid the fields and fresh breezes. The spot that became Washington Square Park remained undeveloped, but it wasn't a park from the beginning. It was a graveyard.

At the end of the eighteenth century, the city was in the grip of a yellow fever epidemic, and officials needed a place to bury the poor people dying monthly by the dozens. When the site of Washington Square Park was designated as a burial ground, surrounding estate owners, including Alexander Hamilton, tried to fight off the proposal. Despite their protests, the public cemetery was established in 1801 and adorned with a fence, trees, and other plantings. It is believed that some twenty thousand bodies remain under the park, and bones and skeleton-filled underground chambers have periodically turned up during construction and utility excavations.

The area was also used as a public gallows—leading the big English elm at the northwestern corner to be called the "hanging elm," though no records exist of an execution from its limbs—and a dueling ground. It would have remained as such were it not for Philip Hone, a wealthy military hero from the War of 1812 who became mayor of New York in 1826. Hone sought to model the area after the successful squares of London's West End, around which property values had soared. He launched a campaign for a military parade ground at the site, winning approval in time for a fiftieth anniversary celebration of the signing of the Declaration of Independence, when the square was officially renamed in honor of George Washington. Afterward, Hone expanded the park from about six acres to its current size of ten. Upscale residential development reminiscent of London and Philadelphia, which was already building neat lines of Greek Revival redbrick homes around places like Rittenhouse Square, started going up all around Washington Square Park.

From 1830 to the turn of the century, the neighborhood around the park was the most desirable in New York; this was where the Taylors, Griswolds, and Johnstons all flocked, aristocratic families that had lineage going back to the *Mayflower*. Later, it was the Vanderbilts and Astors, whose lavish parties and costume balls prompted Mark Twain to call the materialistic post–Civil War era the "Gilded Age." All the while, a community of the arts and letters grew up around the square. Edgar Allan Poe had an apartment nearby and read "The Raven" in a rich benefactor's parlor; Winslow Homer bathed canvases in brooding darkness and glowing light in a studio around the corner.

In 1870, under the direction of Tammany Hall's leader, William "Boss" Tweed, the city embarked on a major campaign to overhaul all its existing parks, after a building spree that included Bryant Park behind the New York Public Library, Prospect Park in Brooklyn, and the 843-acre Central Park designed by the landscape architect Frederick Law Olmsted. Smaller, older public spaces deserved a face-lift, City Hall decreed, and a Viennese landscape designer named Ignatz Anton Pilat was commissioned to give Washington Square Park new gardens and gaslight lampposts. Pilat, who replaced straight lined walkways with Olmsted's signature curves, trying to evoke the expansive countryside in the middle of the city, also added the carriageway that would be the precursor to Moses's road.

Though the park was by this time no longer officially a parade ground, military officials in the National Guard still sought to make a piece of the park their own. In 1878, they proposed the construction of an armory—the giant storage facilities for weaponry and supplies and mustering places for soldiers that were going up in cities all across the country. Wealthy residents including Thomas Eggleston and Samuel Ruggles, who was instrumental in creating Gramercy Park a few blocks to the east, successfully petitioned against the plan. Ruggles formed the first citizen-based organization to keep the city's park safe from development, the Public Parks Protective Association, and in 1878 the New York state legislature passed a law keeping Washington Square Park for use "in perpetuity for the public as a public park, and for no other purpose or use whatsoever." The tradition of stewardship began.

The park got its signature arch at the end of the nineteenth century. City officials were planning the centennial of George Washington's presidency, and William Rhinelander Stewart, a neighborhood resident and a scion of one of New York's Knickerbocker families, led a fund-raising campaign to build an arch in honor of the founding father. McKim, Mead

& White, the Beaux Arts architects of Columbia University's campus and Pennsylvania Station, designed a classical Roman monument of bright Tuckahoe marble seventy-seven feet high, bathed in electric light, with intricate inlaid panels in the vaulting underside of the arch, two statues of Washington topped by elaborate medallions on each soaring column, and an eagle set in the middle of its sturdy and ornamented cornice. Positioned at the foot of Fifth Avenue exactly in the middle of the north side of the park, the arch reflected the grandeur of London and Paris and was instantly a postcard image of New York and Greenwich Village.

The monumental city, however, was also the city of the desperately poor, and Washington Square Park was no exception. Despite the grand designs and the staggering wealth of the estate owners all around, the park was never the exclusive front yard for the well-off. Nor was it ever gated off as a private space, as Gramercy Park would become. Starting early in the nineteenth century, tramps and prostitutes were as common a sight there as promenading swells. Its central location also made it a popular spot for agitated New Yorkers of all kinds to hold protests, vigils, and demonstrations. In 1834, stonecutters unhappy with New York University's decision to use prison labor for the marble fixtures for its campus buildings fanned out around the park smashing windows and marble mantels. Fifteen years later it was the Astor Place Opera House riot, pitting English against Irish. Then came the draft riots of 1863, when predominantly Irish laborers roamed the streets around the park, cutting telegraph lines and beating and killing black men. Suffragettes and veterans of the Spanish-American War marched through. There was no such thing as trespassing there. It was a place to which people of all classes and political persuasions came to express themselves.

At the turn of the twentieth century, Greenwich Village became a magnet for rebellious artists, painters, writers, and social commentators. Walt Whitman and the newspaper pioneer Horace Greeley were in the vanguard, hanging out at the nearby beer hall Pfaff's. Stephen Crane, Theodore Dreiser, the journalist Lincoln Steffens, Marcel Duchamp, Man Ray, and an invasion of artists and intellectuals followed, crowding into flats in three- and four-story redbrick buildings, setting up studios around the square, playing chess in clubs, reading poetry at cafés and bars like the Brevoort and the Golden Swan, and dining at restaurants reminiscent of the Left Bank in Paris—the Pepper Pot, Polly's, the Red Lion, the Russian Tea Room, and Samovar. Intellectuals banded together and started theater houses for the plays of Eugene O'Neill, another Village resident, and ran bookstores out of ground-floor space filled with both James Joyce and local literary journals produced a few blocks away. Poetry readings, the tango, player pianos, fashion shows, masquerade balls, and lectures and symposia filled the days and nights of Greenwich Village around Washington Square Park—a rival in many ways to Paris before and after World War I, as a capital of culture and new thinking.

> Let's settle down in Washington Square,
> We'll find a nice old studio, there.
> . . .
> We'll be democratic, dear,
> When we settle in our attic, dear,
> In Washington Square.

So went the 1920 Cole Porter song "Washington Square." The park became the leading character in poems, short stories, paintings, plays, and films. "Nobody questions your morals, and nobody asks for the rent. There's no one to pry if we're tight, you and I, or demand how our evenings are spent," wrote the dashing Harvard-trained writer and poet Jack Reed, whose associates included Walter Lippmann and Lincoln Steffens. Sympathetic landlords put up with missed payments by the struggling artists and writers; one boardinghouse on the south side of the square was home to so many it was dubbed the House of Genius.

The Village continued its spirit of rebellion through the Roaring Twenties and Prohibition and was, naturally, the site of several infamous speakeasies. In the Great Depression, the liberal political leanings of Greenwich Village lurched toward radicalism. Independent journals like the *Masses* began publishing there, supporting workers and antiwar sentiment, drawing the attention of federal investigators for communist sympathies. Meanwhile, contemporary artistic movements including abstract expressionism were flourishing; the painters Jackson Pollock, Willem de Kooning, and Edward Hopper began their march to fame. The Whitney Museum of American Art on Eighth Street gave the art a place to be viewed; the theaters and cafés let people hear new plays and poems. Soon there were more artists than immigrants in Greenwich Village, painting, fashioning stained glass, or sculpting clay and marble.

At the same time the starving artists were doubling up in cold-water flats, upper-middle-class families and professionals flocked to the neighborhood, and real estate boomed around Washington Square Park. Highrise apartment towers began going up at the base of Fifth Avenue, towering over the north side of the park. New subway lines were being built nearby. New York University moved ahead relentlessly with plans for massive new campus buildings lining the square. And Greenwich Village became a tourist attraction, with busloads of visitors coming to gawk at the crazy, creative lifestyle of the bohemians and soak up the atmosphere at the jazz clubs and Left Bank–caliber restaurants.

Into the 1950s, as the beat writer Jack Kerouac, the poet Allen Ginsberg, the jazz musicians Charlie Parker and Thelonious Monk, and folksingers like David Sear all came to inhabit the cafés and clubs and studios and apartments of Greenwich Village, Washington Square Park shed the formality of the Henry James era and became a comfortable old living room, like the inner chambers of cafés on MacDougal Street. The street furniture got vandalized, the lawns turned brown, and the fountain basin leaked.

As an urban historian, Jane Jacobs appreciated the extraordinary evolution from cemetery, gallows, and dueling ground to a setting for Victorian promenades and classic Beaux Arts monumentality, to an outdoor rendezvous for Pete Seeger, Woody Guthrie, and Bob Dylan, and on into the age of Aquarius. Hoop dresses to black jeans: that was the power of a place that was unplanned and organic. It was everything that was proper and respectable and aristocratic about New York City life—and at the same time it represented rebellion against the establishment, authority, and order.

~~~~~

The man from Oxford and Yale didn't quite see it that way. This park needed a shave and a haircut, and to find a steady job. It needed to knock it off with the poetry readings and start serving a practical function for the city again—as a crossroads for the modern city.

The space that the residents of Greenwich Village viewed as comfortable and unpretentious was to Moses another city park that had fallen into disrepair. The plantings had withered, and the benches were broken or sagging. Moses cited this decline as a rationale for major changes. Like so much of the city, Washington Square Park needed to be upgraded and modernized. Sketching out his plans on yellow legal pads, Moses, as parks commissioner, first proposed a complete redesign in 1935, allowing vehicles to go around a new, oval-shaped layout in a giant traffic circle. The four corners of the park were to be rounded off, shrinking the ten acres of open space; the fountain was to be torn up and replaced by a central strip of gardens and pools.

The development around the park after the turn of the century had spawned several neighborhood groups—the Greenwich Village Association, the Washington Square Association, and the Fifth Avenue Association (the latter two having merged in 1926 to form the Joint Committee for the Saving of Washington Square)—which pleaded for building preservation and zoning changes that would slow down the large-scale development. In reaction to Moses's 1935 redesign, they consolidated their efforts into the single Save Washington Square Park Committee.

Moses quickly recognized he needed to deal with the neighborhood opposition, just as he had done with the Long Island estate owners attempting to block his parkways there. His strategy was similar: portraying the opponents as not-in-my-backyard elitists, standing in the way of progress. But he took his tactics one step further—threatening to withhold all improvements if the Greenwich Village residents would not cooperate. He declined an invitation to appear before the Greenwich Village Association to explain his plans, instead dashing off a sarcastic letter to the group:

> You will be glad to hear that the reconstruction of Washington Square Park is going to be left to posterity, and that contrary to what appears to be prevailing local opinion, we have not decided on any drastic changes—although we have been studying the future of this square from every point of view. We plan only to restore and improve the square now, without changing its present base character and design. There are all sorts of people around Washington Square, and they are full of ideas. There is no other section in the city where there are so many ideas per person, and where ideas are so tenaciously maintained. Reconciling points of views . . . is too much for me. The filling in of Orchard Beach in the Bronx, the development of Jones Beach or of Marine Park in Brooklyn, and the building of the Triborough and Henry Hudson bridges, are child's play in comparison.

In 1939, Moses returned with a new plan, essentially the same proposal for a one-way roadway around the park, snipping off all four corners and adding a lily pond in a long strip in the center. Henry Curran, a resident and former deputy mayor, said that the oval Moses was proposing to replace the rectangle of Washington Square Park looked like a "bathmat." The name stuck, much to the parks commissioner's dismay. In the face of growing opposition, Moses again warned the residents that if his scheme did not go through, Washington Square Park would sink to the bottom of the city's list for improvements of any kind. The neighborhood would lose out on millions in New Deal funding and labor that would go someplace else.

The threat had an immediate effect. John W. Morgan, president of the Washington Square Association, initially opposed the "bathmat" scheme, but others in the organization supported it as an acceptable trade-off for badly needed upgrades—and for redeveloping the area south of the park, which by the 1930s had become tawdry. The group grudgingly supported Moses's vision, by one vote. But a faction splintered off and collected thousands of signatures against it. Outraged by what they viewed as a cave-in, the members of the Volunteer Committee for the Improvement of Washington Square Park argued that the park would be turned into a speedway, endangering students and mothers with children.

A group of New York University students protested any changes to the layout of the park, claiming that pedestrian safety would be threatened. They were also worried about university tradition: the statue of the Italian patriot Garibaldi was the site for hazing freshmen and sophomores. The students and the Greenwich Village residents who remained opposed to Moses combined to create a powerful lobbying force directed at the Board of Estimate, New York's powerful governing body of the time, which needed to approve the redesign. One member of the board, the Manhattan borough president, Stanley Isaacs, who had tangled with Moses over the Brooklyn-Battery Bridge, announced that there was insufficient neighborhood support, and the bathmat plan was put on the shelf.

With the onset of World War II, many of Moses's public works ground to a halt, and the master builder backed off on the Village and its park— but not before taking several parting shots, which clearly reflected an impatience with not getting his way.

"It seems a shame you should suffer because of some stuffy, arrogant and selfish people living around the square," he told eleven-year-old Naomi Landy of Perry Street, one of the "Children of Greenwich Village" who wrote an open letter to city newspapers pleading for playground improvements.

> The trouble is that our plans were blocked by stupid and selfish people in the neighborhood who don't want to give you a place to play, but insist on keeping Washington Square as it was years ago, with lawns and grass and the kind of landscaping which goes with big estates or small villages. These people want the square to be quiet and artistic, and they object to the noise of children playing and to other activities which we proposed.
>
> Under these circumstances we moved our . . . men and material to other crowded parts of the city where playgrounds are badly needed and . . . people welcome them and don't put obstacles in our way.

His comments had a ring of truth. The residents were effectively claiming ownership of a public space, and they did seem to oppose change of any kind. While Washington Square Park was on the back burner, Moses crafted a new approach. Once he had a plan, he rarely let it go. After the war he returned his focus to the area with the urban renewal plans for south of the park, holding secret meetings with top New York University officials for redevelopment under urban renewal. He also kept up the criticism of residents who sought to keep the neighborhood just the way it was, like an artillery commander softening up the invasion landing. Moses demonstrated both his annoyance at not getting his way and a rhetorical flair for beating down the opposition.

He wrote to a distinguished resident who called for historic preservation in 1950:

> I realize that in the process of rebuilding south of Washington Square there would be cries of anguish from those who are honestly convinced that the Sistine Madonna was painted in the basement of one of the old buildings there not presently occupied by a cabaret or speakeasy, that Michelangelo's David was fashioned in a garret in the same neighborhood, that Poe's Raven, Don Marquis' Archie the Cockroach, and Malory's Morte D'Arthur were penned

in barber shops, spaghetti works and shoeshine parlors in the purlieus of Greenwich Village, and that anyone who lays hands on these sacred landmarks will be executed if he has not already been struck down by a bolt from heaven.

Transforming Washington Square Park was an endurance test, and Moses was confident he would outlast the naysayers, as he had many times before. The urban renewal plans south of the park were moving ahead, and Moses promised the development teams that the new development would have a Fifth Avenue address. The developers, after all, were the ones who would make his urban renewal vision a reality.

His final chess move appeared on the front pages in 1952: the carriageway would be replaced with a north-south roadway of four lanes, two in each direction. The fountain would be eliminated. A roller rink would be installed on one side of the roadway and a new playground on the other. The model was Riverside Park, a long strip of green that ran along the Hudson on the West Side and was elegantly integrated with the off-ramps and free-flowing traffic lanes of the West Side Highway. Once and for all, traffic would be able to get through Washington Square Park. Fifth Avenue would be the address of the model new metropolis spawned by urban renewal, and resistance would be shown to be futile.

~~~~~

When Jane Jacobs had moved from the State Department to her new job at *Architectural Forum* in 1952, she had no particular plans to get involved in neighborhood politics. She was busy with her job, and with raising her two sons and, later, her infant daughter, Mary. But after she received the flyer from the Committee to Save Washington Square Park and wrote the mayor and the Manhattan borough president, she looked again at the letter for the name of the person organizing the opposition. It was a woman named Shirley Hayes, and Jacobs dashed off a note to her as well. "Thanks for your good work," Jacobs wrote on the lower left side of a form to join the committee. "I've written the mayor and the borough president each, the attached letter. Please keep me informed of any other effective action that can be taken."

Hayes, a mother of four who lived on East Eleventh Street, a short walk from Washington Square Park, welcomed Jacobs to the fight. Jacobs was impressed as she learned more about the woman who was so energetically organizing the neighborhood, typing up letters, recruiting volunteers, and scheduling evening meetings. Born in 1912 in Chicago and trained as a painter and an actress, Shirley Zak Hayes moved to New York to pursue her dream of making it on Broadway. A handsome blonde with a Marilyn Monroe hairstyle, Hayes met her husband, James, when both appeared in a production of *Hamlet*. They married, James took a job in advertising, and the couple chose to live in Greenwich Village and raise their four sons there. As a mother, Hayes grew to love the Village and Washington Square Park. She became increasingly upset at the big apartment buildings going up all over, and equally dismayed by Moses's urban renewal project south of Washington Square. The park roadway plan, she was convinced, would destroy the neighborhood for good. "There is no justification for sacrificing this famous park and Greenwich Village's residential neighborhood to either Mr. Moses' commitments . . . or to this piecemeal and destructive approach to solving the city's impossible traffic patterns," she said. "A few women got together to say no, no, no."

After the Moses proposal of 1952, Hayes founded the Washington Square Park Committee, a combination of three dozen community groups, church groups, and parent-teacher organizations from local schools. She befriended another concerned mother and neighborhood activist, Edith Lyons, and together they launched a grassroots effort to give a voice to a neighborhood they believed was under siege.

A prolific letter writer and an aggressive coalition builder, Hayes identified the most influential officials at City Hall and pressed them to listen to the views of the neighborhood. Her relentless pleas earned her a position on the Manhattan borough president's Greenwich Village Community Planning Board, and in that position she demanded that the board come up with alternative plans for the park. At the same time, Hayes sought out as many residents, shopkeepers, and clergymen as she could find to join the effort. She wrote to her Greenwich Village neighbor Eleanor Roosevelt in 1953. She wrote to the Reverend Rosco Thornton Foust, rector of the Church of the Ascension, Sister Corona at St. Joseph's, and the rabbi at the Village Temple, imploring them to mention park meetings in their sermons. She deployed neighbors to stand on corners and make traffic counts, so she had her own documentation of the number of vehicles passing through the neighborhood, instead of relying on the data compiled by Moses's traffic engineers. She circulated petitions against the roadway plan and within a matter of weeks had four thousand signatures. She wrote dozens of letters to newspaper reporters. The correspondence piled high at the offices of the Manhattan borough president, occupied in 1952 by Robert Wagner, soon to be mayor. Moses, sensing that Hayes could lead an uprising, wrote to her personally in 1953, assuring her that her views were being considered.

From the day the Moses plan appeared in the newspapers, Hayes did not limit her fight to derailing the proposal. She was not interested in negotiating for a less harmful roadway. She sought no less than to block any roadway, and any car traffic whatsoever, through the park. There would be no deals and no compromise. Jacobs took note of this tactic as she waded into the Washington Square Park battle herself.

Her early involvement, following her letters to City Hall and the note to Hayes in 1955, was more as a foot soldier than a leader. The first time she was mentioned in a newspaper article it was inaccurately, as Mrs. James Jacobs. Jacobs helped drop off petitions at stores around her house and struck up conversations with shopkeepers and customers about goings-on in the neighborhood. Jacobs also went to local rallies and her first meetings of the Board of Estimate, the governing body that had the final say on any changes to Washington Square Park. She soon realized that to be effective, citizen activism required a more concerted effort— something akin to a full-time job. Merely following the twists and turns of the roadway battle was difficult, as seemingly definitive action at City Hall was followed by new Moses maneuvers that kept the plan alive.

The Greenwich Village residents had secured a victory in May 1952, when the Manhattan borough president, Robert Wagner, ordered the roadway plan withdrawn for further study. Then, in 1954, the City Planning Commission approved the next steps for urban renewal south of the park, making Moses more determined than ever to create a grand gateway through the park leading to the huge new campus of housing. In 1955, Moses made what he viewed as a major concession: submerging the four-lane roadway and building a pedestrian overpass across it. Depressing the roadway, he thought, might make it less objectionable, without building a full-blown tunnel, an idea promoted by Anthony Dapolito, a neighborhood baker who would later become known as the mayor of Greenwich Village. Boring beneath the surface was a common strategy for moving traffic through urban environments, and one that had already been used in New York near Grand Central Station. But it would be expensive to dig under the park and build a platform of public space above. A gentle dip and a pedestrian overpass were as far as Moses was willing to go.

The neighborhood lashed out against the submerged-roadway plan, calling it no better than the original four-lane proposal. By 1957, Hayes and Lyons were flooding City Hall with thousands of notes from residents in opposition to any new roadway and any car traffic through the park. Wagner's successor as borough president, Hulan Jack, who initially teamed up with Moses to promote the submerged-roadway plan, backed off, and proposed a more diminutive, thirty-six-foot-wide, two-lane roadway.

Though Jack was a useful ally, he was clearly getting too soft with the residents, Moses thought. In a condescending letter that he began with the salutation "Dear Hulan," Moses described the plan as "ridiculously narrow" and totally unworkable. He made it clear that no more compromises were to be made with the rabble-rousers. Four lanes, forty-eight feet wide, with a mall in the middle to be planted with trees, submerged if necessary but otherwise on the surface. No more modifications.

Determined not to let the neighborhood get the upper hand, Moses did his best to keep the residents off balance, delaying key hearings until the last minute, then quickly scheduling them in the hope of minimizing attendance. After twenty years of trying to redesign Washington Square Park, he had lost his patience, and he pushed harder than ever to deliver on his promise for a continuous Fifth Avenue. Shirley Hayes and Edith Lyons had marshaled an impressive effort, but the plan, thanks to Moses, was still under active consideration by the city. It would not die easily. Greenwich Village needed to step up its efforts to defeat it.

The turning point came in 1958, when Raymond S. Rubinow, an eccentric consultant who lived not on Washington Square but on Gramercy Park several blocks away, volunteered his services. Rubinow, a friend of Jacobs's, had just started a career helping businesses like Sears and Welch's grape juice create foundations to fund social and civic causes. An economist—his Russian-born father was credited with establishing the concept of social security—Rubinow had become obsessed with preserving New York City's old neighborhoods and historic buildings, and devoted himself to such causes as saving Carnegie Hall from the wrecking ball. He took control of the organization that Hayes had built, and one of his first moves was to give Jacobs a greater role, as a strategist and additional liaison to the community and the media. After consulting with her,

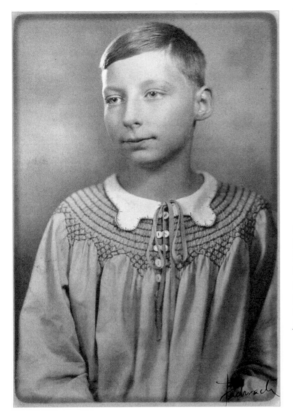

Growing up in Scranton, Pennsylvania, Jane Butzner became known for her sharp wit and her fearless challenging of teachers, both belied by the gentle mien on display in this early photograph. *Courtesy of Jim Jacobs*

Jane and Robert Jacobs camping at Montauk. Jane met Bob at a party in 1944; they would marry only weeks later. *John J. Burns Library, Boston College*

Urban pioneers Bob and Jane Jacobs, here assisted by first son Jim, renovated 555 Hudson Street in Greenwich Village, turning a dilapidated house into a cozy home. The house would become the unofficial headquarters for neighborhood activism in the fight against urban renewal and also provide the second-floor perch from which Jacobs made many of her most important observations on the functioning of city life. *Courtesy of Jim Jacobs*

By 1956, Jacobs was a staff member of *Architectural Forum*. That year she attended an urban design conference sponsored by the University of Pennsylvania, mingling with the leading theorists and designers of the day, including I. M. Pei (far right), Ian McHarg and Louis Kahn (third and sixth from left), and Chadbourne Gilpatric from the Rockefeller Foundation (talking to Jacobs). She was the only woman who wasn't there as the wife of a participant. *Grady Clay/courtesy of the Penn Institute for Urban Research/University of Pennsylvania*

A Jew among bluebloods at Yale University just before World War I, Moses, seated at far left, worked his way onto the Senior Council and the *Yale Courant*, where he soon awed colleagues with his knowledge of literature and his intellectual prowess. *MTA Bridges and Tunnels Special Archive*

Moses held many positions but wielded the most power as chairman of the Triborough Bridge and Tunnel Authority, an independent organization with its own seal, its own fleet of vehicles, and hundreds of employees. Headquarters was by the bridge on Randall's Island, isolated from other government offices in the middle of the East River. *MTA Bridges and Tunnels Special Archive*

An early riser known for his prodigious work ethic, Moses early in his career mastered the art of drafting and then pushing through legislation designed to increase his power and financing. *MTA Bridges and Tunnels Special Archive*

Moses sought the extension of Fifth Avenue through Washington Square Park as the gateway to a signature redevelopment project, Washington Square Village. Moses pushed the towers-in-a-park layout, inspired by the modernist architect Le Corbusier, as the model for urban renewal and new housing construction in New York City, leading to the showdown over the proposed redevelopment of Jacobs's very own neighborhood in Greenwich Village. *MTA Bridges and Tunnels Special Archive*

As she became a famous activist and writer, Jacobs continued to relish her family life. Here she is baking for her husband and sons at 555 Hudson Street. *Courtesy of Jim Jacobs*

Greenwich Village in the 1950s and 1960s was a haven for writers, poets, artists, and musicians, including Bob Dylan, and Jacobs, here at the White Horse Tavern, became part of the avant-garde, both as an author and critic of urban planning and in her citizen activism. *Cervin Robinson*

The elite promenaded there in the days of Henry James, then mothers with strollers, protest marchers, and folksingers in the beatnik era—Washington Square Park has served as an outdoor living room, respite, and gathering place. Here a young Ed Koch, future mayor of New York, strums a guitar near the fountain. *Alvin Thayer/La Guardia and Wagner Archives/La Guardia Community College/CUNY*

Jacobs encouraged her children to be front and center in neighborhood battles, as in this one against the roadway through Washington Square Park. Here her daughter, Mary, left, led a "ribbon-tying" ceremony in front of the park's arch in June 1958, celebrating an early victory in keeping traffic out of the cherished greensward. New York Daily Mirror/*Courtesy of Jim Jacobs*

In 1961, Jacobs published *The Death and Life of Great American Cities*, an attack on the planning tactics embodied by Moses. The book, like *Silent Spring* and *Unsafe at Any Speed*, exposed the destructive outcomes of an established orthodoxy: in this case, modernist city-building. As the book exploded into the cultural discourse of the time, it dramatically altered the way that people viewed cities. *Courtesy of Random House*

THE CITY PLANNERS ARE RAVAGING OUR CITIES!

☞ **They've put up gleaming stone and glass file cabinet housing which breeds delinquency and crime.**

☞ **They've built spacious green park areas that are avoided by everyone but bums and hoodlums.**

☞ **They've condemned and destroyed entire city blocks that are not slums, but attractive places to live.**

☞ **They've zoned our cities into intolerable patterns of dullness.**

Jane Jacobs says this and much more in her explosive new book, THE DEATH AND LIFE OF GREAT AMERICAN CITIES. Mrs. Jacobs shows that the city

planners have failed because they have overlooked the realities of urban life, and stripped our cities of the vitality and diversity which make them exciting places to live. She offers concrete, practical alternatives that can save our cities from the blunders of orthodox planners.

Harrison Salisbury of the *New York Times* hails this book as "the most refreshing, stimulating and exciting study of this greatest of our problems of living which I've seen. It fairly crackles with bright honesty and good sense."

William H. Whyte, author of *The Organization Man*, calls it "magnificent. One of the most remarkable books ever written about the city."

The Death and Life of Great American Cities

By JANE JACOBS

$5.95, now at your bookstore

RANDOM HOUSE

26

Jacobs spent long days and nights at her typewriter composing *Death and Life* and gazed out the window at 555 Hudson Street for inspiration from the "sidewalk ballet" of her Greenwich Village neighborhood. *Anthony Flint*

Battling Moses, Jacobs befriended up-and-coming city politicians such as Ed Koch and Carol Greitzer (pictured here with Jacobs and Greitzer's daughter Elizabeth). These politicians would play an important role in fighting Moses, city planners, and business interests keen on reaping the benefits of redevelopment. *Courtesy of Carol Greitzer*

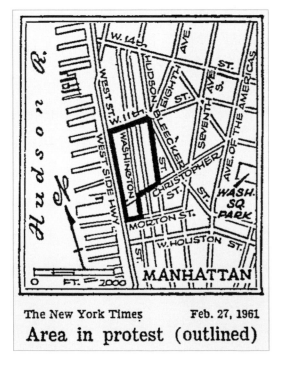

The New York Times   Feb. 27, 1961
Area in protest (outlined)

Jacobs read about the proposal to bulldoze her neighborhood in the *New York Times*: fourteen blocks, including hers on Hudson Street, would be designated a slum and redeveloped, wiping out the city life Jacobs had just celebrated in *Death and Life*. New York Times

Trained as a journalist, Jacobs understood the need to court the press. She made herself available for interviews throughout her battles against Moses and New York City planning officials, and cultivated relationships with reporters from publications ranging from the *New York Times* to the *Village Voice,* a start-up alternative tabloid. *John J. Burns Library, Boston College*

In the fight against the plan to raze fourteen blocks in the West Village for urban renewal, Jacobs marshaled the residents and businesspeople of the neighborhood and employed children as spies surveying city officials and developers. The neighborhood held book and bake sales to raise money, including this penny sale at St. Luke's Church. *John J. Burns Library, Boston College*

Moses sought expressways to run across New York, similar to his successful Cross Bronx Expressway, to relieve congestion and speed goods and services for the struggling New York economy. He used models, such as this one of the proposed Mid-Manhattan Expressway, as well as glossy pamphlets, and he even produced a film to argue for these multimillion-dollar infrastructure projects. *Black Star/MTA Bridges and Tunnels Special Archive*

Moses proposed the ten-lane, elevated Lower Manhattan Expressway, which would have run down Broome Street, obliterating hundreds of homes and businesses and the cast-iron architecture of the area. He characterized the area as dilapidated and worthless and suggested that the superhighway would signal progress and bring economic revitalization. *MTA Bridges and Tunnels Special Archive*

Father Gerard La Mountain, pastor of the Church of the Most Holy Crucifix on Broome Street, turned to Jacobs for help as his flock, including immigrants and small businessmen, was set to be uprooted by the massive Lower Manhattan Expressway, counting on her to draw media attention and galvanize political support. *Jack Manning*/New York Times/*Redux*

Jacobs saw Greenwich Village and SoHo as under siege by highway and urban renewal planners, who condemned buildings with the "hex" sign of the X; her son Ned, on stilts, stands defiantly before one example. Designating neighborhoods as blighted slums to her was a self-fulfilling prophecy, hobbling efforts for grassroots revitalization. *Ruth Orkin*

Moses had a flair for the theatrical and befriended Walt Disney (right, beside the musician Guy Lombardo), who shared a belief that sleek highways were the key element of modern life, and who contributed to exhibitions at the World's Fair. *MTA Bridges and Tunnels Special Archive*

Jones Beach was an early triumph for Moses, and he was a frequent guest at the Jones Beach Theater, where Guy Lombardo appeared with showgirls from a performance of the musical *Hit the Deck.* The Jones Beach complex epitomized Moses's vision of a great public country club. An avid swimmer, he regularly plunged into the ocean off the coast of Long Island for long solo workouts. *MTA Bridges and Tunnels Special Archive*

By 1967, Jacobs had grown more disenchanted with government and policy makers and joined a protest rally against the Vietnam War with her daughter, Mary, and husband, Bob. She would step up her radicalism in response to city planners and the proposed Lower Manhattan Expressway as well. *Fred McDarrah/Getty Images*

Jacobs with Susan Sontag and others in a New York jail, where they'd been taken after a Vietnam War protest. This was not the only time her activism landed her in jail. *John J. Burns Library, Boston College*

After the battle of the Lower Manhattan Expressway, Moses retreated from the spotlight, serving as a consultant and issuing memos to reporters, but spending more time at his Long Island home and bungalows on the beach; here he is shown with Mary, the secretary he married after his first wife died in 1966. *MTA Bridges and Tunnels Special Archive*

Worried that her sons would be drafted and discouraged by U.S. policies regarding cities, Jacobs settled in Toronto, battled a proposed freeway there, and eventually became a celebrated Canadian citizen. *Maggie Steber*

The cast-iron buildings of SoHo on Broome Street—the spot where the Lower Manhattan Expressway would have run—today are the sites of art galleries, designer boutiques, bistros, and the lofts of celebrities. *Jonathan Stephens*

Washington Square Park, with its signature arch and storied history dating to Henry James and beyond, is today one of New York City's most celebrated public spaces— as difficult to imagine bisected by a highway as SoHo with a ten-lane elevated expressway, and the quaint Greenwich Village replaced by drab housing towers. *Daniel Avila/New York City Department of Parks and Recreation*

When Jacobs lived on Hudson Street in the 1960s, Greenwich Village was a bustling place. Today the neighborhood has become one of the most desirable—and pricey—areas in any city in the United States. *Anthony Flint*

he changed the name of the community group to the Joint Emergency Committee to Close Washington Square to Traffic.

"We weren't trying to embrace all kinds of points of view about the Village, all kinds of political groups, all kinds of anything. We were trying to collect and concentrate on this issue, the people who felt as we did on that issue," Jacobs recalled later. "In order to dramatize this and clarify this, a name like that was necessary—not something like 'The Such-and-Such Association' . . . that's the reason Greenwich Village developed these strange and wonderful names, like 'The Committee to Get the Clock Started on the Jefferson Market Courthouse.' People knew what they were getting into. They weren't getting into ideology. They were getting into a particular thing . . . [We joined] people who believed in a particular thing and might disagree enormously on other things."

Though Hayes had attracted a wide range of activists to the cause, Rubinow and Jacobs sought to bring in even more firepower. They persuaded Eleanor Roosevelt to join the emergency committee, as well as the anthropologist Margaret Mead, who also lived in the Village. Jacobs asked her new friend the *Fortune* editor William "Holly" Whyte, author of the recently published book *The Organization Man,* to join, along with a respected local pastor, a prominent New York University law professor, and the publisher of the new alternative newspaper the *Village Voice.*

In the emergency committee's early strategy sessions, Jacobs stressed the importance of breaking down the effort into specific and manageable tasks. She realized that Moses was in a stronger position; he had been implementing his vision for urban renewal citywide for several years and was backed by powerful developers who hoped to get rich while reversing the city's economic decline. Construction of Washington Square Village, south of the park, was under way, and Moses would use this as a further argument for the highway. The developers there, he proclaimed, "were formally, officially, and reliably promised under the Slum Clearance Act a Fifth Avenue address, and access for the large new population in multiple dwellings replacing warehouses."

Jacobs advocated changing the terms of the debate away from the broader picture that Moses was painting. The emergency committee's best argument was that Washington Square was a park, and a park was no place for highways. Building on Hayes's strategy of accepting no compromise, Jacobs took the position that whatever adjacent development was under way, the park should remain a park, and no vehicles should be allowed. There should be no negotiation, she argued, and no acceptance of a slightly less harmful roadway, like Hulan Jack's proposal to reduce the number of lanes from four to two. If the roadway was built, and it connected to the Lower Manhattan Expressway, it would no doubt eventually be widened. Only killing the Washington Square roadway outright would put a stop to Moses's grander plans.

It would take discipline, Jacobs said. The neighbors must resist the temptation to negotiate or compromise, to accept trade-offs and scraps of concessions. It would also take a stepped-up public-relations campaign, and for that Jacobs helped recruit Lewis Mumford, the architectural critic at the *New Yorker,* whom Jacobs had befriended after her speech criticizing modern planning techniques at Harvard.

Years earlier, Mumford had critiqued Moses's plan for redesigning Washington Square as "absurd" and "a process of mere sausage grinding." In 1958, he furnished a statement to the emergency committee that was turned into a press release. "The attack on Washington Square by the Park Department is a piece of unqualified vandalism," Mumford said. "The real reason for putting through this callow traffic plan has been admitted by Mr. Moses himself: it is to give the commercial benefit of the name 'Fifth Avenue' to the group of property owners who are rehabilitating the area south of Washington Square, largely at public expense. The cause itself is unworthy and the method used by Mr. Moses is extravagant. To satisfy a group of realtors and investors, he is as ready to change the character of Fifth Avenue as he is to further deface and degrade Washington Square." He went on to condemn Moses's "insolent contempt" for common sense and good civic judgment. "Washington Square . . . has a claim to our historic respect: a respect that Mr. Moses seems chronically unable to accord any human handiwork except his own. [It] was originally used as a potter's field for paupers; it might now prove to be a good place to bury Mr. Moses' poverty-stricken and moribund ideas on city planning."

Mumford's suggestion that the Washington Square roadway was primarily to serve real estate developers had resonance. The foundation of urban renewal was to bring in the private sector—and in the case of the project south of Washington Square, a nonprofit, New York University, as well—to revitalize cities. Moses got no direct financial benefit from his relationship with the developers, but Mumford put him on the defensive by adding to the contention that the whole project was an insider deal. Moses hit back with a press release of his own.

"The public was told that this area was not substandard, that we were ruthlessly evicting small business firms which could not go elsewhere, that we were illegally substituting high-rental for low-rental residence, that our project was a 'steal,' 'giveaway,' [and the] 'sacrifice of perfectly good buildings,' " Moses said. "The critics failed to understand that Title I [the urban renewal program] aimed solely at the elimination of the slums and substandard areas. It did not prescribe the pattern of redevelopment, leaving this to local initiative."

Without private developers and New York University, the old warehouses would continue to be a fire hazard, Moses argued. "Who will clear out the rest of this junk?"

But Mumford's challenge prompted others who argued that urban renewal was no justification for destroying the park with a roadway. Within days, other prominent New Yorkers weighed in. Eleanor Roosevelt, an early skeptic of Moses's plans, devoted her "My Day" column in the *New York Post* to the controversy: "I consider it would be far better to close the square to traffic and make people drive around it . . . than to accept the reasons given by Robert Moses . . . to ruin the atmosphere of the square." Norman Vincent Peale, pastor of the Marble Collegiate Church, argued that "little parks and squares, especially those possessing a holdover of the flavor and charm of the past, are good for the nerves, and perhaps for the soul. Let us give sober thought to the preservation of Washington Square Park as an island of quietness in this hectic city."

And then there was Charles Abrams, a Columbia University professor and Greenwich Village resident who bore some resemblance to Moses, in terms of both his strong intellect and his patrician upbringing. Nothing less than the power of the people to maintain healthy city neighborhoods was at stake, Abrams argued. "Rebellion is brewing in America," he said at a crowded neighborhood meeting in July 1958. "The American city is the battleground for the preservation of [economic and cultural] diversity, and Greenwich Village should be its Bunker Hill . . . In the battle of Washington Square, even Moses is yielding, and when Moses yields, God must be near at hand." Abrams turned the speech into an essay for the *Village Voice* titled "Washington Square and the Revolt of the Urbs."

The high-profile support was encouraging. This was beginning to look like a fight that could be won. But Jacobs knew not to be overconfident. Employing her journalistic skills, she learned as much as she could about Moses, to better understand her foe. He seemed to control every function of city government from his lair on Randall's Island. He had years of practice battling neighborhoods and opponents, from Long Island to Spuyten Duyvil. To prevail, the neighbors would need a sophisticated strategy. In the evening strategy sessions of the emergency committee, Jacobs assumed the role of a war-room impresario in a modern-day political campaign and urged a three-pronged effort: continued grassroots organizing designed to draw in more allies, more pressure on local politicians, and a stepped-up campaign to gain attention in the media.

Greenwich Village in the late 1950s was fertile ground for bringing politicians into the cause—those in danger of being voted out, and newcomers trying to break in. Jacobs surveyed the political landscape with this in mind. A number of Greenwich Village residents were plunging into politics hoping to give the neighborhoods more of a voice at City Hall, and to change a government that did not seem to be listening. An ambitious young woman, Carol Greitzer, had befriended Jacobs and parlayed community frustrations into a job as a city councillor. "We were doing our own planning, and that really hadn't ever been done before," Greitzer said. "It was an exciting time."

Edward Koch, who later served as mayor of New York, began his career as well in those days, as a member of the Village Independent Democrats—an organization founded during Adlai Stevenson's 1956 presidential campaign to bolster liberal and progressive causes, and to support candidates against leaders still in power from the Tammany Hall political machine. Koch sought to shift politics away from patronage and political favors to true representation of ordinary citizens. Jacobs saw that men like Koch were seeking to make a name for themselves, beholden to no one in power, and eager to join a neighborhood cause that could give them publicity.

The politicians already in power required different treatment. Hulan Jack, the Manhattan borough president, seemed to be hearing the voices of opposition in the neighborhood, but was still clinging to the idea of some kind of new roadway through the park. A new champion was needed. One night as Jacobs drifted off to sleep, her husband woke her with the idea to tie closing the park to traffic to the upcoming election. The state assemblyman Bill Passannante was in a tight race against a Republican challenger, who opposed the roadway through the park. Passannante, Bob Jacobs said, could be encouraged to go a step further, by calling for stanchions at the park's perimeter blocking everything but bus and emergency vehicles. If he agreed, he would get the support of the emergency committee's sizable voting bloc; if he didn't, those votes would go to his opponent. Passannante very quickly became the first elected official to back the idea of closing off the park to car traffic. Jacobs also encouraged the neighborhood activists to appeal to a handsome young Republican running for Congress: John V. Lindsay, whose Democratic opponent quickly joined him in opposing the park roadway plan.

Jacobs and the other committee leaders continued to meet privately with the politicians, persuading them that the roadway battle was a central issue among voters. But Jacobs became even more convinced that one tool was more important than anything else to keep the public pressure turned up high on the Board of Estimate, the City Planning Commission, the mayor's office, and all the officials either elected or running for office: the media. A journalist herself, Jane Jacobs knew a few things about getting attention.

The 1950s was a time of change for newspapers in New York City. The number of newspapers had decreased from earlier in the century, but there was still the *New York Times,* the *Herald Tribune,* the *World-Telegram and Sun,* the *Journal American,* the *Daily News,* and the *New York Post,* and competition for stories was fierce. Jacobs knew that reporters feared getting scooped, and would be less likely to ignore a well-timed press release—especially one issued over the weekend, traditionally slow news days—if the neighborhood group could establish itself as credible and newsworthy. Using competition as leverage was the only way to counter the reporters' dependence on officialdom for information, a dependence that made them wary of printing critical comments about planners and commissioners. Nowhere was this more true than with Moses, who continued to have friends in high places at the biggest media outlets and froze out writers who strayed.

Not content with publicity in newspapers like the *New York Times,* which covered the battle thoroughly but always quoted Moses at length, Jacobs sought out different venues that would give greater voice to the neighborhood's sense of outrage. For this there was the *Village Voice,* which had been established in 1955 by Dan Wolf, Ed Fancher, and the novelist Norman Mailer as an alternative city newspaper that emphasized arts and culture—but also took on local and political issues with more of an edge and an opinion. The *Voice* dedicated itself to hard-charging reporting and criticism, ultimately winning three Pulitzer prizes, but it also covered neighborhood issues, paying special attention to the point of view of ordinary citizens.

The *Voice* journalist and Greenwich Village resident Mary Perot Nichols covered every hearing and rally on Washington Square Park—and later urban renewal in the West Village and the Lower Manhattan Expressway as well. Jacobs and Nichols became close friends over the course of the Washington Square Park battle, and Jacobs made sure the budding journalist had access to inside information. A good relationship with someone in the newspaper business was critical, Jacobs knew. Nichols's news stories and a *Voice* editorial made for a stirring defense of both community activism and the value of public space. "It is our view that any serious tampering with Washington Square Park will mark the beginning of the end of Greenwich Village as a community. Greenwich Village will become another characterless place," Wolf wrote on the editorial page. "Washington Square Park is a symbol of unity in diversity. Within a block of the arch are luxury apartments, cold-water flats, nineteenth-century mansions, a university, and a nest of small businesses. It brings together Villagers of enormously varied tastes and backgrounds. At best, it helps people appreciate the wonderful complexity of New York. At worst, it reminds them of the distance they have to cover in their relations with other people." When a Moses aide grumbled that the "awful bunch of artists" in Greenwich Village were a nuisance and couldn't agree to get anything done, Wolf proudly proclaimed that he hoped "there are thousands of nuisances like that within a stone's throw of this office."

While the *Voice* dedicated its pages to the fight, other media had to be drawn in. What the newspapers needed were good pictures, and Jacobs launched what would become a signature tactic: putting children front and center. They were the ones who used the playgrounds and ran around the park, after all. Jacobs deployed kids—dozens of "little elves," as she called them—to put up posters and ask for signatures on petitions. Young people, she soon realized, were irresistible to newspaper photographers; they were the perfect photo opportunity. There was precedent for a child becoming a symbol in a park battle. In 1956, residents near Central Park battled Moses over his plan to expand a parking lot for Tavern on the Green at Sixty-seventh Street. Mothers rolled strollers to the site and defiantly blocked the parks commissioner's bulldozers, and the image of a "little soldier"—a toddler refusing to cede her ground for construction work—became an enduring icon. Moses ultimately backed down, and Jacobs recognized a winning tactic when she saw one.

"She would bring the three children to the square on weekends to collect petitions demanding that the highway plan be canceled and the park permanently closed to traffic," recalled Ned Jacobs, Jane's son, who was seven years old in the spring of 1958. "This was during the beatnik era, and my brother and I were outfitted with little sandwich boards that proclaimed 'Save the Square!' That always got a laugh because people knew that 'squares' would never be an endangered species—even in the Village. These were also the dying days of McCarthyism. People were afraid—even in the Village—to sign petitions for fear they'd get on some list that would cost them their careers. But I would go up to them and ask, 'Will you help save our park?' Their hearts would melt, and they would sign. Years later, Jane recalled that we children always collected the most signatures."

Getting officials and the media to see battles through the eyes of children would continue throughout Jacobs's career. One day when she was shopping for long underwear at Macy's for her sons, Ned and Jim, the clerk asked whether it was for hunting or for fishing. "It's for picketing," she replied.

The tactics began to work. On June 25, 1958, responding to the residents' opposition, the city agreed to close Washington Square Park to traffic on a temporary basis while the roadway matter was put to further study. The next day, the *New York Daily Mirror* published a photograph of Mary Jacobs, three and a half, and Bonnie Redlich, four, holding up a ribbon that had been symbolically tied as a "reverse ribbon cutting." The caption read: "Fit to Be Tied."

~~~~~

The success of the neighborhood's media campaign did not go unnoticed by Moses. His riposte was to suggest that perhaps the emergency committee should be allowed to win—and be responsible when the area was hopelessly knotted by traffic jams. "There is something to be said . . . for letting unreasonable opposition have its way; find out by experience that it doesn't work. How can you choke off all traffic in Washington Square? It is preposterous."

The City Planning Commission continued to deliberate on what to do with the park while the vehicles were temporarily blocked and in July 1958 voted in favor of Hulan Jack's narrower road. Moses stepped up the rhetoric, vowing that his scheme would ultimately triumph "when drummed-up local hysteria subsides, mudslinging ends and common sense and goodwill prevail."

But by the fall of that year, with local campaigns in full swing, the emergency committee made a critical move: appealing to Carmine De Sapio, New York's secretary of state, Democratic leader, and de facto head of the Tammany machine. He was exactly the kind of old-school pol that Rubinow, Koch, and Greitzer and the rest of the Village Independent Democrats were determined to drive out of New York City government. But he was also a Greenwich Village resident. If he could be convinced to stand up against the roadway plan, it would have real influence. The New York University law professor on the emergency committee, Norman Redlich, was chosen as the envoy, and found a receptive audience in the Democratic party boss. De Sapio let it be known that the Board of Estimate should schedule a hearing, and that he planned to furnish some rare public testimony. Before he addressed the board, he was presented with a scroll listing some thirty thousand people who had signed in opposition to the roadway plan. Dozens of residents appeared outside City Hall wearing green "Save the Square" buttons and twirling parasols with "Parks Are for People" printed on them; among the crowd were Jane Jacobs, Shirley Hayes, and Eleanor Roosevelt.

Wearing his trademark dark glasses, which reflected the flashes of newspaper cameras, De Sapio asserted that Greenwich Village, as well as Washington Square Park, represented "one of the city's most priceless possessions and as such it belongs to every one of our 8,000,000 fellow New Yorkers . . . To change the character of this beloved central symbol of the Village would be, ultimately, to eradicate the essential character of this unique community."

Having worked with the influential De Sapio over the years, Moses knew that he had been checkmated. A month after the hearing, Hulan Jack, taking his cue from De Sapio, gave up on his two-lane roadway plan. The Board of Estimate directed the traffic commissioner to close the park to all but buses and emergency vehicles.

After so many fits and starts, this was the end of Moses's roadway plan—no Fifth Avenue address for his housing towers south of the park, no free flow of traffic. That fall, Moses addressed the Board of Estimate, in a desperate move for reconsideration. It was galling, the way he had let this get away from him. "There is nobody against this," he said. "Nobody, nobody, nobody but a bunch of, a bunch of mothers." Jacobs watched, both amazed and satisfied, as he turned and walked to a waiting car.

~~~~

The party to celebrate the victory took place on Saturday, November 1, 1958, at the base of the Washington Square arch. The carnival atmosphere brewed in the late morning with placards, children, "Square Warriors," balloons, and throngs of people. The event had an official name—the "grand closing" of the park to traffic. The members of the emergency committee set up a ribbon tying—as opposed to a ribbon cutting—as the big photo opportunity for the press. De Sapio, Hulan Jack, Bill Passannante, and Ray Rubinow all proudly held the green strip of fabric and smiled for the cameras. Jacobs stayed in the background.

Pink parasols bearing the slogan "Parks Are for People" and green buttons that proclaimed "Save the Square" were out again in force. Jacobs watched as reporters scribbled notes and photographers snapped away. Speakers read messages of congratulations that had been sent from New York's governor, Averell Harriman, Mayor Wagner, and Lewis Mumford. "I will do my utmost to see that this road is never opened again," said Passannante. "Look up the avenue. Any traffic jam? Any cars begging to come through the park? I see only people."

Just after noon, Stanley Tankel, a resident of West Eleventh Street, drove a battered old minibus festooned with a banner that read "Last Car Through the Park" under the arch and out toward Fifth Avenue.

About seven months later, the neighbors held another celebration, a masquerade ball attended by a thousand people, with more politicians and newspaper publishers and local artists. At midnight, someone held a lighter to a life-size cardboard car that had been assembled by a theater group, and the vehicle burned to mark the triumph over Robert Moses. Jacobs and all of Greenwich Village, it seemed, partied into the night.

The celebrations may have been premature, as the ban on car traffic was still intended to be temporary; the city considered it an experiment. But the weeks and months following the closing went better than anyone in the neighborhood could have hoped. As Passannante had observed on the day of the ribbon tying, the knotted traffic that Moses predicted never materialized. Because the New York City street grid in the area was so extensive, drivers had lots of options. The network absorbed the traffic flow. The experiment at Washington Square Park would become a principle of modern-day traffic engineering—that speeds are seemingly slower as drivers make their way through a traditional street grid, but they often get to destinations faster compared with a crowded, single express route. Some rethink the need to traverse the area by car, and find alternative transportation, like mass transit.

Moses did not accept defeat gracefully. In 1959, he refused to agree to close the park to vehicular traffic unless all the streets around the park were widened to eighty feet and all the corners of the greensward rounded off so, as Moses argued, traffic could navigate through the area better. But he had lost his influence on the matter of the park, and the city was in no mood to continue the battle with new proposals. The buses from the Fifth Avenue Coach Company continued to make their turnaround just past the arch.

Within two years, the buses would also be gone. Jacobs, by that time, had returned to her writing and played a less active role in this stage of the fight. But Shirley Hayes and Ed Koch, representing the increasingly powerful Village Independent Democrats, continued to press for the elimination of all motorized vehicles in Washington Square Park. A new parks commissioner, Newbold Morris, submitted to the pressure and urged the head of the transit authority to reroute the bus turnaround. With Mayor Wagner's blessing, Washington Square Park was permanently sealed off from all traffic, including buses, a few weeks before the assassination of John F. Kennedy in November 1963. One and a half acres of park were reclaimed, once the paved roadway areas were no longer necessary. This time, Koch and Hayes symbolically escorted a last bus out of the park.

The victory for the bunch of mothers was complete. Moses had been trying to fix Washington Square Park since 1935, and a quarter century later he was forced to give up. The achievement was infectious as neighborhoods across the city found a new voice in development, public works projects, and especially parks. Central Park became an important battleground. A year after the ribbon-tying ceremony at the Washington Square arch, Joseph Papp, head of the New York Shakespeare Festival, took on Moses over permitting for free performances there. New Yorkers assumed a new sense of ownership over public space.

For Washington Square Park, the aftermath of the road closing was mixed. The cozy brownstones remained on the north side, but the towers and parks of Washington Square Village—absent the grand gateway of an extended Fifth Avenue through the park—forever changed the character of the park's southern border. The street Moses wanted to become Fifth Avenue South was renamed La Guardia Place; a statue of the mayor, walking mid-stride, was erected in 1994, in front of shops in a low-slung building between two housing towers. New York University moved ahead with an aggressive plan for new campus buildings south of the park, most notably Bobst Library, situated at the spot where the Moses roadway would have emerged from the park. Built despite intense neighborhood opposition, the rust-colored modernist box by Philip Johnson casts shadows over the southern portion of Washington Square.

The park itself flourished and would become the outdoor headquarters for folksinging and the emerging 1960s counterculture, a staging ground for anti–Vietnam War protests, and a place to catch Bob Dylan on a Saturday afternoon playing his guitar at the fountain. For Jacobs, it was a perfect example of an unplanned and organic public space. The fountain basin with its outer stone rim, she wrote in 1961, is "a circular arena, a theater in the round . . . with complete confusion as to who are spectators and who are the show. Everybody is both, although some are more so: guitar players, singers, crowds of darting children, impromptu dancers, sunbathers, conversers, show-offs, photographers, tourists, and mixed in with them all a bewildering sprinkling of absorbed readers—not there for lack of choice, because quiet benches to the east are half-deserted."

The residents around the park continued to see themselves as stewards of the space; a new generation of mothers lobbied for better playground equipment and demanded action against the drug sellers and junkies that began to take over in the 1970s. Today, Washington Square Park is run by a privately funded conservancy, like Central Park's. Parents with strollers navigate through musicians, jugglers, and chess players. The town houses rival those on Fifth Avenue as desirable real estate, and nearby are hot spots in the city's restaurant scene, like Mario Batali's Babbo.

Contention over the space has not ended. In 2005, the city proposed yet another redesign—including plans for a uniform iron fence to line the entire park, and the relocation of the fountain so it lines up with the arch. Area residents are against the $16 million overhaul, claiming it would make the park too formal. They cite Jane Jacobs at every opportunity. The place has become indelibly associated with her; the memorial for her after she died was held in front of the arch.

~~~~

For Moses, the battle of Washington Square Park served as a worrying portent of things to come. He was particularly concerned that it would embolden the neighborhood forces to oppose all forms of progress for New York. It was also an embarrassing personal defeat, coming around the same time as the Manhattantown scandal—which involved private developers on the Upper West Side who were supposed to clear old tenement buildings but continued to operate them and collect high rents. Moses had handed off responsibility for the redevelopment as he had done in all his Title I projects, and only a handful of underlings were implicated in the profiteering. But the first negative editorials about Moses and urban renewal appeared in the major New York papers. The coverage of Washington Square Park had further chipped away at the Moses mystique, and in many ways more powerfully. Moses was the man in charge of parks and of designing the optimal layouts for the city's streets and buildings; for the first time, the notion was planted in the public consciousness that his plans might not always be best for the city.

After the Washington Square Park battle, Moses resigned as parks commissioner. During his tenure, he had more than doubled the green space of New York City, to nearly 35,000 acres, and added 658 playgrounds, 17 miles of beach, zoos, recreation centers, and ball fields. Washington Square Park was one of the very few projects left unfinished when he left the job.

Jacobs, meanwhile, grew more confident. Moses had come into her neighborhood and been turned back. And there was something larger at stake: ordinary citizens could see that they could challenge the top-down planning that Moses represented, not just in New York but in cities across the country. The Washington Square Park battle informed her emerging critique of contemporary planning. Her articles on Harlem and Philadelphia for *Architectural Forum,* and her speech in 1956 at Harvard, were leading to the same conclusion: the very things that made cities great were being systematically destroyed by people who didn't understand how cities functioned and who didn't know them intimately.

Throughout 1958, as the Washington Square Park battle was building to its crescendo, Jacobs began to put the essence of this argument into print. Her work at *Architectural Forum* and her involvement with the emergency committee had begun to attract notice. William H. "Holly" Whyte, the *Fortune* editor, commissioned her to write the essay "Downtown Is for People," which appeared in the April 1958 issue of the magazine. Shortly thereafter, the article was published as part of a compilation called *The Exploding Metropolis,* published by Anchor Books, a new softcover enterprise co-edited by Nathan Glazer and Jason Epstein, respectively the famous Harvard sociologist and the man who would go on to found the *New York Review of Books.*

Then the moment came that would be the turning point in her life and career. Recognized as an emerging writer about urban planning, she was invited to a conference on urban design criticism put on by the University of Pennsylvania in Philadelphia, sponsored by the Rockefeller Foundation. At a break for a reception outside the ivy-covered conference hall, Jacobs—a lone woman in the group, except for the male experts' spouses, in a calf-length dress and black heels and carrying a handbag—mingled with the leading theorists and practitioners of the day: Lewis Mumford, Ian McHarg, Louis Kahn, I. M. Pei, and Kevin Lynch. She also chatted with Chadbourne Gilpatric of the Rockefeller Foundation. Gilpatric followed up on the conversation by asking Jacobs if she had a larger project in mind, perhaps based on "Downtown Is for People." Yes, she said, she did.

"What I would like to do is to create for the reader another image of the city, not drawn from mine or anyone else's imagination or wishes but, so far as this is possible, from real life," she wrote to him in the summer of 1958. Gilpatric arranged for a $2,000 grant to get her started on a longer treatise on cities. Jason Epstein, who had gone from Anchor Books to Random House as an editor at large, successfully argued that a manuscript from Jane Jacobs about cities and city planning would make a great book. The publishing house agreed to a deal, and Jacobs received a $1,500 advance. The check arrived not long after the ribbon-tying ceremony at Washington Square Park, in November.

The men who believed in Jacobs had no doubt she would deliver on her promises. "You sort of fell in love with Jane when you met her," Epstein would later say. "She was exuberant, original, strong-minded—and a very kind woman."

And so as the 1950s came to a close, the strategy sessions for the emergency committee gave way to mornings and nights pecking away at a new typewriter—a Remington—on the second floor of 555 Hudson Street. The Washington Square Park experience was fresh in her mind, and it had been invigorating. Community organizing could make a difference. Yet she was about to discover that her words, in tandem with activism, could be more powerful still. She had defeated Moses in the trenches of New York City neighborhood politics. Now she was on the verge of publishing a book that would revolutionize urban planning, and turn the tide on Moses and all the other modernist master builders, as an act of intellectual radicalism.

FOUR

Urban Renewal in Greenwich Village

Sitting at her typewriter at 555 Hudson Street, Jane Jacobs rolled in another page of what would become *The Death and Life of Great American Cities.* The writing was going slowly. Nearly a year earlier, she had told the Rockefeller Foundation she needed more money and more time. When she was writing for *Vogue* and the *Herald Tribune,* the words had flowed a little more easily—in magazine articles, which were only a thousand words or so, Jane was adept at sizing up a subject. She quoted from her interviews at length and ticked off her observations with clarity and ease. But Jacobs found writing a book to be a much tougher enterprise, at times lonely and torturous.

The book was to be part report on the terrible things being done to cities and part explanation of what made them thrive. She had spent the previous four years traveling all over the country, studying what she considered the "sacrificial victims" of urban planning—in Philadelphia, where Ed Bacon was playing the role of Robert Moses, and in Boston, where the cluttered West End was being razed to make way for the towers of Charles River Park. She'd also gone to St. Louis, where she toured the Pruitt-Igoe public housing complex, designed in 1951 by the architects George Hellmuth and Minoru Yamasaki, a disciple of Le Corbusier's who would later build the twin towers of the World Trade Center in New York. Pruitt-Igoe was recognized as a disaster not long after its completion. The tall towers, touted as streamlined and efficient, instead were inhospitable places, from the parks at their base to the lobbies and elevators and stairwells, which bred muggings and other crime. St. Louis helped seal Jacobs's conviction that urban renewal, informed by the modernist architectural movement, was badly flawed. The planners and builders set on saving the American city were actually killing it, replacing slums and tenement housing with monolithic and dysfunctional buildings like Pruitt-Igoe or the Robert Taylor housing project in Chicago, another set of towers in barren open space where residents also quickly felt unsafe.

She had her examples of what didn't work. What she needed now was a way to articulate how cities really worked—an archetype of a vibrant city neighborhood. She had identified the basic elements of such a city: short blocks and a mix of buildings of different sizes, new buildings and old buildings, and, critically, a mix of uses—homes marbled in with stores, offices, restaurants, and cafés. The cities she toured all had older neighborhoods like that. But she needed to show that a mix of uses truly produced vitality, community, safety, and spontaneity, in ways that the isolated residential towers never could.

And then she heard the bagpipes.

Rising from her desk, she walked over to the second-floor window and parted the blinds. A man in a brown trench coat sashayed along the sidewalk, squeezing out a Highlands melody on the bagpipes. A crowd began to gather, some skipping and twirling and dancing as they followed. When he stopped, his followers applauded, along with many others who had appeared in the doorways of galleries and cafés along Hudson Street.

Jacobs smiled and let the blinds fall back in place, wondering who this little man was. But as she paused and peered out again, she began to think about the crowd that had gathered. Only on a block where there were so many different people could such a spontaneous and natural display of joy unfold. It was the block that was ready-made to indulge in the ephemeral: neighbors and strangers, safe and comfortable because they were never alone.

Throughout the writing of *Death and Life,* Jane often returned to that window to watch the life of Greenwich Village unfold: the longshoremen piling into taverns at the end of their shifts; the children getting out of the local schools; the morning choreography of trash cans being emptied and store owners sweeping the sidewalk in front of their businesses, the tailor, the barber, the butcher. There was Mr. Slube at the cigar store and Mr. Lacey, the locksmith, and Bernie at the candy store who loaned umbrellas and lectured youngsters when they asked for cigarettes. Mothers pushed toddlers in strollers, teenagers checked their reflections in storefront windows, and office workers picked up bundles from the grocer or the drugstore on their way home in the evening. It had a glorious functionality all its own, and Jacobs settled on a description that would endure for years to come: it was like a ballet. From morning into night, her neighbors and the shopkeepers and the workers all seemed to be part of an improvised dance, she observed, "in which the individual dancers and ensembles all have distinctive parts which miraculously reinforce each other and compose an orderly whole. The ballet of the good city sidewalk never repeats itself from place to place, and in any one place is always replete with new improvisations."

On one evening, a stranger emerged from a tavern to apply a tourniquet to the arm of a boy who had fallen through a plate-glass window, and a woman sitting on a stoop borrowed a dime to call the hospital. There were eyes on the street. It seemed to Jane that the physical arrangement of the neighborhood was itself enabling humanity's best instincts. She'd found the best example of a functioning and diverse city neighborhood right in front of her, right outside her second-floor window. Her block on Hudson Street would earn a starring role in a book that would change the world.

~~~~~

Jacobs continued to observe her little corner of Greenwich Village, which at the time was in the midst of a pivotal moment of change. Previously, the West Village had been a working-class neighborhood, attractive to immigrants and low-income families because of low rents, and was rundown in many ways. A short walk west from Washington Square Park, it had little of the park's storied history and Gilded Age charm. Though it was not unsafe, it had always been a space at the fringe, a place where railroad tracks fanned out across rough streets or soared overhead, delivery and tractor-trailer trucks unloaded and picked up their wares from the labyrinth below Fourteenth Street, meat packers and ball-bearing joint

warehouses and fabric way stations for hats and coats. The manufacturing plants stood around the corner from the simple rows of four- and
five-story walk-ups. The housing was affordable and plain, occupied by
dockworkers and municipal employees, many of them Irish Catholic and
blue-collar, raising families close to work. When Jane and Robert moved
into 555 Hudson Street in 1947, they were the equivalent of yuppies moving into a rough part of town, the same urban pioneering that goes on in
parts of Brooklyn or Newark today.

By the time Jacobs was writing *Death and Life,* more Puerto Ricans
and African Americans had begun to move in, along with white professionals like Jacobs and the gay men and women who would later give the
place its defining character. The mix of working-class and well-to-do led
to some tensions. The blue-collar workers felt threatened not only by the
low-income and racially diverse families moving in but also by the more
affluent people like Jacobs who were discovering the area, and the ensuing real estate speculation. Some buildings were being converted to luxury apartments seemingly overnight. Jacobs herself acknowledged that
too much "discovery" would knock the neighborhood out of balance.
"These real estate grabbers . . . you'd think there was oil under the ground
here," she said. The developers renovating big apartment buildings were
the culprit for rapidly increasing property values, she believed—not the
individual families, like hers, moving into fixer-uppers. Those newcomers, indeed, could keep assessed values from rising too fast. "Be patient
and fix up a house gradually, and keep the expense down by not ordering
a whole new bathroom," she advised in a newspaper article in 1963. "Buy
the odd fixtures you need second-hand in the neighborhood, and do as
much of the work as you can yourself." Still, as the West Village became
a place that was both rough around the edges and poised to be a ritzy
neighborhood, many of the Irish Catholics didn't stick around to see
which direction would prevail. The urban life was something many of
them were ready to surrender, anyway, and they traded their apartments
for small single-family homes in suburban settings like Staten Island.

Jacobs understood the complexity of what was going on, and knew
that the West Village somehow had to improve while also maintaining diversity and affordability. The neighborhood had to work for everybody.
The term "gentrification" was not much in use in those days, but the diversity she prized was obviously at risk if all those different people with
different skin colors, religions, and bank accounts couldn't live in proxim-

ity to one another. It wouldn't be easy, but Jacobs was sure that with the proper stewardship, the West Village could achieve that equilibrium. If any place had the ability to pull it off, she believed, it was blocks like hers. The West Village could both maintain its working-class character and benefit from the improvements the newcomers would bring.

Jacobs believed in the power of the people to improve their neighborhoods, in a grassroots, organic process she called "unslumming"—using both private and public funding to rehabilitate buildings and maintain economic diversity. Her idea emerged clearly in the manuscript of *The Death and Life of Great American Cities,* which she submitted to Random House in late January 1961.

The men who ran cities in Robert Moses's time saw things differently. Neighborhood improvement could not happen by incremental measures, and the federal government wasn't interested in trying to improve cluttered and outdated city neighborhoods. In the Moses worldview, reflected in the administration of Mayor Robert Wagner and a new team of planners Wagner appointed to carry out urban renewal, there was virtually nothing worth preserving in the patchwork of four-story buildings, manufacturing plants, and freight rail lines of the West Village. Parts of the neighborhood were teetering into decline, and parts were being subject to overheated real estate speculation: it was a perfect candidate for the government program that called for clearance and carefully planned "middle-income" housing—a program that sprang from the Moses vision to bring social and economic balance to New York City. It was a place to start over, from scratch.

~~~~~

Jacobs was paging through the *New York Times* on February 21, 1961—a month after she submitted her manuscript—when she saw the headline "Two Blighted Downtown Areas Are Chosen for Urban Renewal." The two "blighted" areas in the article were the neighborhood around Tompkins Square Park on the Lower East Side and fourteen blocks identified as the western section of Greenwich Village. The accompanying map clearly showed the targeted area, between the Hudson River and Washington Square Park, with the Jacobs home at 555 Hudson Street right in the crosshairs. The West Village was described by the city as a threadbare industrial zone with decrepit tenement buildings housing only about six hundred families who could be readily relocated. The government investment in rehabilitation and new construction to provide middle-income housing would be nearly $7 million, of which the city would pay a third, the article read. Before anything got under way, the city would conduct a study, initially to cost $300,000, to determine if the neighborhood could officially be designated as blighted.

Jacobs put down the newspaper, reeling. Her home and her neighborhood, the very neighborhood she had identified as a model of city living in the book she had just written, were now targeted by the urban renewal machine that Robert Moses had set in motion.

Reading about it in the newspaper was especially galling. Not long after he was elected mayor in 1954, Wagner had been promising a kinder, gentler form of urban renewal, with more citizen participation and a more open approach. Jacobs was disappointed that the new mayor's promises were apparently not so genuine.

Though his own father, as a U.S. senator, had sponsored the original federal legislation for urban renewal, Wagner acknowledged that Moses's implementation of the policy had been heavy-handed, and he ordered revised procedures for slum clearance in 1959. The new procedures were to include a better relocation process and more sensitivity to appeals for historic preservation, accompanied by changes in city zoning and a new master plan to show the big picture of where development in New York was heading. Neighborhoods and City Hall were set to work together in a united front for improvement, or so it seemed.

The political motivations behind this were clear. Despite his successes, Moses had given urban renewal a bad reputation during his tenure as head of the Committee on Slum Clearance, construction coordinator, and housing czar. Under him, officials and developers handed families in the redevelopment zones eviction notices that gave them only ninety days to move out before the bulldozers arrived while providing little actual help in relocating. There was a growing sense—fueled by the Manhattantown scandal, the Upper West Side project rife with financial improprieties—that too much power was being handed over to private developers, for whom community needs were not a high priority. During the construction of Lincoln Center, residents begged to stay in their brownstones. A local businessman set up camp in front of City Hall, protesting the loss of his livelihood. Their pleas were ignored. New Yorkers were beginning to see the human cost of ambitious redevelopment projects;

urban renewal had a public-relations problem, and it was one that Wagner intended to solve with the 1959 legislation.

Moses himself had grown frustrated with the difficulty of the challenge. He had pioneered urban renewal in New York City and established thousands of housing units, but it was an especially thankless task. Residents complained about conditions; there was never enough money to meet the staggering need for housing in New York City. Building a bridge or renovating a park was in contrast simpler—though after the defeat at Washington Square Park, Moses was also ready to end his tenure as parks commissioner. In 1960, he was named chief executive of the 1964 World's Fair, and as part of the deal worked out with the mayor and the governor, he agreed to relinquish his posts as parks commissioner, construction coordinator, and chairman of slum clearance while keeping his powerful position at the Triborough Bridge and Tunnel Authority. His focus returned to highways and bridges. It was now up to Wagner to take the Moses legacy of housing and urban renewal to the next level, while at the same time making the efforts more palatable to the neighborhoods; for this, the city needed a new team.

To lead the way, Wagner chose James Felt, the new chairman of the City Planning Commission. A scion of a New York City real estate family, Felt grew up on the Lower East Side in the second decade of the twentieth century, worked at his father's real estate business, and then struck out on his own with a company that specialized in assembling large parcels and relocating evicted residents. Felt was a diminutive, baldish man who favored bow ties, and while a major player in New York City real estate, he had considered becoming a rabbi and frequently quoted the Talmud. "He is a strong man who can control his passions, and who is able to convert his enemy into a friend" was among his favorite lessons. He marveled at the city's ability to reinvent itself and led an overhaul of New York City's zoning in 1961, which paved the way for streamlined modernist towers to replace the ornate wedding-cake-style skyscrapers of the early twentieth century. Felt also sought to relieve traffic congestion, reduce density in the city, and eliminate districts that didn't have a strictly defined, single function. Everything had its place, Felt said, pointing to charts he used in presentations to explain the new approach to zoning.

The other key figure tapped by Wagner was J. Clarence Davies Jr., another veteran of the New York City real estate business, whose father was responsible for the development of large swaths of the Bronx in the late nineteenth century. A dashing man who was also a decorated fighter pilot in World War II, Davies was a prominent leader in charities and the city's civic life. Utterly dedicated to the concept of urban renewal, he had been instrumental in the development of Lincoln Center and Cadman Plaza, another urban renewal project, in Brooklyn. Though he was president of the Citizens Housing and Planning Council and served on the Landmarks Preservation Commission, he had little patience for community activism, which he felt stood in the way of meeting the housing needs of all city residents. "When those needs are in conflict with the desires of neighborhood groups, the larger need will obviously prevail," he once said. Wagner made Davies chairman of the city's new Department of Real Estate and director of the Housing and Redevelopment Board, the agency that replaced the Committee on Slum Clearance that Moses had led.

The Felt-Davies combination was greeted by favorable editorials and press coverage, and Wagner proclaimed a new era for urban renewal, a more professional approach to planning, and a fairer process. The program even got a new name—"community renewal"—and the plan for the West Village was set as the debut.

Reading the *New York Times* article on the plan to raze her neighborhood, Jacobs surmised that the names had changed, but little else. A plan had been hatched without any true citizen participation—residents were being forced to react to a proposal. Urban renewal was dressed up in new language, but the basic Moses template remained—draw up plans in private, and push implementation before any opponents could effectively organize to object. And while Moses had stepped down from his leadership positions in housing and redevelopment, he made sure he remained in the mix, insisting for example, that Wagner keep him on as a member of the City Planning Commission. (When Moses saw that he had not been reappointed one year, and Wagner made up the excuse that it was an oversight in paperwork, Moses went out and grabbed an appointment form for city boards from a secretary, put his name on it, and pushed it across the desk to Wagner. The mayor, cowed by Moses's power and influence, signed it and wordlessly slid the form back.)

In addition, both Felt and Davies were very much in the Moses mold. They came from the world of New York real estate development and seemed to share Moses's distaste for citizen participation. Felt in particular had close ties with Moses and could be reasonably described as a protégé of the master builder's. In the 1940s, Felt had been in charge of relocation for evicted residents at Stuyvesant Town and Peter Cooper Village, the housing projects Moses developed along the eastern edge of Manhattan, essentially working at Moses's side. An aide to Wagner later conceded that Felt seemed to be a Moses apprentice: "I thought he would be ours. Instead he was Moses'."

Worse still, the blight study for the West Village had the whiff of revenge. When Moses had handed over the urban renewal portfolio to Wagner, Felt, and Davies, it had contained both projects under way and new areas of the city to be targeted. The Village had delivered the first major defeat for Moses, at Washington Square Park. It was entirely plausible—and, to Jacobs, seemed likely—that on the way out, Moses suggested where the bulldozers should go next and steered his successors right to Hudson Street.

Sometimes it seemed to Jacobs that unseen hands were behind all kinds of assaults on the neighborhood. Just one year before, in 1960, Jacobs's son Ned had seen surveyors laying down marks on the sidewalk on Hudson Street. He asked what they were doing and learned of city plans, unannounced to the neighborhood, for widening the street and shortening the sidewalk. As Jacobs tucked him into bed at night, Ned told his mother that it looked like they would lose the tree they had planted out front.

"No we're not, why do you say that? It's growing pretty well," Jacobs said.

He then told her what the surveyors had said. The next morning, Jacobs wrote up a petition and asked a local printer to make copies. Ned and his sister, Mary, set up a table outside 555 Hudson Street to gather signatures and taped a poster to the door: "Save the Sidewalks on Hudson Street." Jacobs formed the Save the Sidewalks Committee that year, sent the petition to the Manhattan borough president, and got the widening plan shelved. Also in 1960, she brought her children to picket in front of the governor's city offices to protest inaction on something that warranted government vigilance: the rampant luxury apartment conversions in the neighborhood.

After finishing her book, Jacobs had wanted to focus on her roles as writer and editor, but the urban renewal plans that Moses had set in motion could not go unanswered. That same morning after reading the article about the city's plans, Jacobs got on the telephone and went out onto the sidewalks and into the parks of the West Village, warning everyone she could that their beloved neighborhood was about to be razed.

Within days, more than two dozen residents banded together to form the Committee to Save the West Village, and Jacobs and a dentist who lived in the neighborhood, Donald Dodelson, became co-chairs. They hit the streets to enlist residents in the effort and to gather signatures for a petition demanding a one-month delay in the blight determination for the West Village. This would give them a window in which to disprove the city's claim. Jane went to the White Horse Tavern to spread the word, and her husband went to a bar frequented by Irish Catholic longshoremen to do the same, hoping that the topic might be raised at Sunday Mass.

Jacobs then moved into the next phase of combating the city—mobilizing West Villagers to show up at the city's public meetings, particularly those of the City Planning Commission and the Board of Estimate. Both panels were unaccustomed to receiving any large crowds on what were ostensibly routine agenda items, and the Villagers had a chance of making a big impact, Jane knew.

Two days after the *Times* story ran, a diverse group of more than thirty residents filed into a Board of Estimate hearing to demand an explanation of the blight study proposal. A Davies deputy on the Housing and Redevelopment Board assured the crowd that no plans had been made. The city was merely initiating a routine request for a survey under the terms of Title I, the urban renewal program, he said.

The residents protested. If that was true, then why, they asked, did the *New York Times* run an article about a "project" being teed up for the West Village? Prior to the meeting, Jacobs had secured a telegram from Representative John V. Lindsay to Mayor Wagner, asserting that the residents had not been given adequate notice of the city's intentions. It wasn't just the residents of the neighborhood who believed the process was flawed, she said, waving the telegram in the air.

Three days later, some three hundred people filed into the auditorium of St. Luke's School for the maiden meeting of the Committee to Save the West Village. Jacobs calmly read from the *Times* article on the study proposal and then gave her interpretation: the "study" would be perfunctory, and the project a foregone conclusion. The fourteen blocks would be deemed blighted. Once the neighborhood was officially so designated, people would not invest in the area, because they knew the bulldozers and wrecking balls would soon be upon them; buildings would be left to deteriorate, making the government's plans seem all the more justified, as the neighborhood morphed into the slum the officials had indicated it was. She had seen this many times before, Jacobs said. She had just documented the process, in New York and across the country, for her book.

"It always began with a study to see if a neighborhood is a slum," she said. "Then they could bulldoze it and it would fall into the hands of developers who could make a lot of money."

Reading the government boilerplate on the West Village plan, Jacobs told her neighbors that the process was only nominally about affordable housing. The study, she said, was the opening fraud of a government racket to clear the neighborhood of buildings and tenants to be replaced "by expensive versions of both, who paid higher taxes," recalled Village resident Erik Wensberg, an editor and a friend of Jacobs's. "If we liked our busy, friendly, frowzy neighborhood, urban renewal had to be fought."

But, Jacobs said, there was no reason to accept the inevitability of the city's plans. They would stand their ground and defeat the project outright. Indeed, she said, there should be no negotiations for a better deal. If they worked with Felt and Davies, they would come away with only scraps of concessions.

"The aim of the committee is to kill this project entirely because if it goes through it can mean only the destruction of the community," Jacobs said. When the blight study plan was defeated completely, "we will look for an alternative. We want enforced conservation of the buildings, not their destruction." This was a lesson she had clearly learned in the fight for Washington Square Park, where she had fought not for a narrower or less harmful roadway, but for no roadway of any kind.

Neighborhood and civic groups had tangled with Moses throughout his career as chief of urban renewal, but because of their willingness to compromise, their only victories were slight modifications in the plans, or better relocation for selected families. From 1951 to 1954, the Women's City Club issued reports detailing the great human cost of relocation in urban renewal, arguing not against urban renewal itself but for a more efficient and humane relocation process. At the urban renewal district around Bellevue Hospital, residents there did not try to stop the overall plan, but were satisfied to modify portions of the clearance plan by arguing for the rehabilitation of specific buildings. Those who tried to put a halt to urban renewal proceedings completely, like some of the twenty-one hundred households and hundreds of businesses in the way of the fifty-three-acre Lincoln Center redevelopment, had not been successful.

"The scythe of progress must move northward," Moses said, referring to the targeted seventeen-block area of Lincoln Square on the Upper West Side, a short distance from his recently completed New York Coliseum at Columbus Circle. The big institutional players, including Lincoln Center for the Performing Arts, the Metropolitan Opera, and Fordham University, sought to dilute at least some of the pain by providing better relocation services. Lifelong residents were being kicked out of their homes, after all, with no assurance that they would be given new housing that was comparable, or otherwise fairly compensated for their uprooting.

But the city's approach at the time was that residents like Augusta Hoening, who wrote to the governor protesting her eviction from the home she was born in on West Sixty-third Street, had to do their part for the greater good. At the ribbon cutting for Lincoln Center, Moses callously remarked that it was no more possible to rebuild a city without dislocation than it is to make an omelet without breaking eggs.

"We cannot rebuild a city without moving people," he said. "We do indeed sympathize with tenants and do everything we can to help them. [But] we cannot give everybody and their lawyer what they want." His message was clear: if the city lingered over every family that was moved out of a brownstone, no economic development project would ever move forward on time and on budget.

~~~

The Greenwich Village residents—the "Villagers," as the newspapers called them—had seen what happened at Lincoln Center, and wondered how they could argue against what Moses had convincingly characterized as progress for New York as a whole without being cast as villains themselves and, ultimately, defeated. Yet Jacobs rallied them like a football coach before a big game. Washington Square Park had been closed to traffic, she reminded them. The widening of Hudson Street had been stopped. They could fight, and had fought, City Hall.

Though she was tirelessly positive and supportive while around her fellow volunteers, Jacobs knew that gumption wouldn't be enough. Stopping urban renewal in its tracks would require a shrewd effort with multiple fronts—just like the fight over Washington Square Park, but with more additions to the strategic playbook, which she was making up as she went along.

Once again she turned to political leaders like Ed Koch, prominent in the increasingly active Village Independent Democrats; John Lindsay, then a congressman; and Assemblyman Louis DeSalvio, who were all looking to endear themselves to new constituencies. Once again she harnessed the power of the media, making sure reporters turned up to see the strength in numbers at the series of city meetings that would be held on the blight study plan; if the public wasn't allowed to speak, she knew that the residents would likely get quoted if they spoke out of turn and made a scene.

As the battle got under way, Jacobs also settled on a new strategy: to zero in on process and legal technicalities in order to discredit Felt and Davies. The new team, after all, had talked about citizen involvement, but they hadn't brought the West Village study proposal before the residents of the neighborhood, as Wagner's new procedures required. "The bulldozer approach is out," Wagner stated in the summer of 1961. "Any contemplated new improvements shall be in keeping physically and aesthetically with Village traditions."

Jacobs dismissed such promises as "pious platitudes" and pointed out that the Wagner team was, in reality, still operating under Moses's rules. The city had "gotten all their ducks in a row," wooing a carefully selected group—someone from the Greenwich Village Association, someone from a neighborhood political organization, and the monsignor of one church, St. Veronica's, who had been handpicked by a cardinal who was friendly with Moses. Jacobs pounced on this issue and filed a lawsuit charging that there was insufficient neighborhood-wide public notice of the renewal plans. For the first time, she turned to the courts to chasten the officials who had not followed the process that Wagner had instituted. Previously safe in the impenetrable labyrinth of government bureaucracy, Felt and Davies now cut corners at their peril.

Tipped off by friends in city government, Jacobs and the Villagers gathered intelligence about the officials' next steps and took every opportunity to confront them, hoping to catch them in a contradiction or expose intentions. Bob Jacobs weighed in with an important strategic insight: always ask the officials to be clear about their ultimate plans, he said, and if they deny the existence of a project or plan, get it on the record. That way they couldn't push ahead without being caught in a denial. Spending long hours on process was a dreary business, but it carried a big payoff. If Felt and Davies could be shown to be maneuvering behind the scenes, they could be publicly shamed, weakening their positions under the mayor. The tactic was also helpful in blunting neighborhood groups that the city had co-opted. The Committee to Save the West Village would announce that a group was about to endorse urban renewal; the group would deny it, and "once they denied it, they couldn't do it," Jacobs said.

A decade before Watergate, Jacobs was employing the techniques of modern-day investigative journalism, another tactic of which was following financial trails. She was on the lookout for any evidence of an insider deal—any consultant or developer who could benefit from redevelopment and was helping to make the case for urban renewal on the front end.

On many nights, committee leaders would meet at the Jacobs home, sitting around the dining room table drinking martinis and smoking cigarettes. As more and more people stopped by, Jacobs disconnected the doorbell and began leaving the door unlocked. But the place where one could really feel the pulse of the West Village fight was the Lion's Head, a coffee bar later to become an infamous watering hole for editors, columnists, and reporters.

The interior of the Lion's Head was essentially a big living room filled with tables and chairs where patrons could sit and drink coffee while reading the *Village Voice* and the *Villager*, as well as newspapers from England and France. With his business now threatened, Leon Seidel, the proprietor, plunged into the West Village fight with as much verve as Jacobs. Reporters made a habit of stopping in to pick up on the neighborhood's tactics, and Seidel was always available for quotations. Leaflets could be dropped off at 1:00 a.m. to be copied, and would be ready the next morning thanks to a printer friend of Seidel's. Seidel, who later ran unsuccessfully for the New York City Council, "got information almost sooner than anyone else and then spread it almost sooner than anyone else. You just dropped in at Leon's to get the news even if you weren't getting a coffee or dinner or anything," Jacobs said.

At the Lion's Head, the Villagers mapped out their plan of attack. They had filed the lawsuit and petitioned City Hall for a delay in the official study proposal. Now they needed to prove to the city that their neighborhood was not a slum—that the conditions of buildings were not unhealthy or deteriorating so badly they could not be rehabilitated. It would be difficult and expensive to hire outside experts to perform this work, so the residents volunteered to conduct a study themselves—surveying building owners, residents, and shopkeepers about the conditions of the West Village block by block.

The survey takers relied on the expertise of Lester Eisner, regional administrator for the Federal Housing and Home Finance Agency, who told them what they needed to look for to blunt the official rationale for slum clearance: the condition of buildings as documented by square footage, number of occupants, kitchen and bathroom facilities, and rent paid. Eisner had become an impromptu adviser to the committee after one of its members persuaded him to take a walking tour of the neighborhood. Impressed by the diversity, the range of incomes, and the general health of the area, Eisner didn't see the West Village as a strong candidate for urban renewal.

He told Jacobs that if they engaged with the city at all, or made any specific requests for amenities and improvements, they would then be considered complicit in the plans; the city could then claim that there was community support for the urban renewal plan.

"We understood we should be extremely careful not to say, 'Wouldn't it be nice if the area had such-and-such,' " Jacobs recalled. Eisner confirmed Jacobs's conviction that their only chance of success was to kill the city's plans outright.

The Villagers fanned out, knocking on doors, collecting the information for the study to be presented before the Board of Estimate at the end of March. "The city wants our houses and businesses torn down," the volunteers' leaflet read, in both English and Spanish. "To save them we urgently need detailed information on the area. Please cooperate when our representative calls." When all of the necessary information had been gathered, a Villager who was a senior research analyst for an advertising agency supervised the compilation. The results showed about 1.3 rooms to a person, no consistent evidence of deterioration, and adequate bathroom and kitchen facilities, among other evidence that the area wasn't a slum.

Though Jacobs and others were pleased at the outcome of the survey, the committee stayed on task, continuing with its multipronged effort. It circulated a petition urging the new Manhattan borough president, Edward R. Dudley, to derail the renewal plan. "I urge you to vote in the

Board of Estimate against the proposed urban renewal project for the West Village," the petition read, over a stack of hundreds of signatures. "It would destroy a healthy neighborhood. It is unwarranted and unwanted."

As the survey takers jotted information down on clipboards and young children gathered signatures, Seidel held court at the Lion's Head.

"They brought this proposal out of a clear blue sky and left us less than a month to present an alternative plan, but they have not produced any evidence that the neighborhood needed renovation," he told reporters, brandishing reams of assessment documents that showed an increase in property values. "Does this look as if the neighborhood was decaying? It takes years to establish yourself and pay off your initial cost, and it is all wiped out if you are forced out by redevelopment. You don't just move it somewhere else. You have to start again."

Sensing a David and Goliath story, the newspapers began to send reporters to investigate the brewing Greenwich Village rebellion. Jacobs took the journalists on tours to show them the neighborhood wasn't blighted.

"We couldn't go two steps without children appearing with handfuls of signed petitions," a *Herald Tribune* reporter wrote after taking a tour with Jacobs, whom she described as a "down-to-earth . . . mother who's bringing up three children" as well as a leading urban critic. The campaign to save the neighborhood had momentum, Jacobs told the reporter, precisely because of what was valuable about the neighborhood—a printer willing to run off leaflets for free, a shopkeeper devoting his time, the neighbors out on the street watching out for one another, all reflecting a tight fabric of community.

A *New York Times* reporter did his own analysis, cataloging the "old but sound" one- and two-family homes, with high ceilings, large fireplaces, and wooden beams. He found that only one rooming house and three hotels lacked private bathrooms. The report was accompanied by a photo spread showing West Village residents tending to a tree on the sidewalk in front of their home, an imported-goods warehouse, neighbors talking with Jane Jacobs on Hudson Street, and the cozy living room of an apartment at 661 Washington Street.

~~~~~

But the battle was just beginning. City officials stayed on course with their blight study plan, shelving the survey so carefully put together

WRESTLING WITH MOSES { 111

by the West Villagers. It was standard practice for cities to portray targeted neighborhoods in the worst possible terms—even employing photographers to hunt for the slightest deterioration in wooden beams and the darkest, most cramped crawl spaces as evidence—and the survey the committee had presented didn't square with those objectives.

Davies, head of the Housing and Redevelopment Board, said the West Village had been targeted as a blighted area based on the fact that there was a mix of uses in the neighborhood, considered a "deficiency" under the guidelines of Title I. Rooming houses, obsolete building types, and excessive density—all of which existed in the West Village, and all of which Moses had cited in previous urban renewal projects—were other indicators of blight. In other words, it didn't matter what the Villagers had found in their house-to-house survey. Under the urban renewal guidelines, the neighborhood by definition was a candidate for redevelopment.

For the city's first big counterpunch, Felt and Davies took a page out of the Moses playbook: divide and conquer. Moses had employed this tactic on Long Island and in the Washington Square Park battle, cultivating support among some residents by promising improvements, thereby dividing the opposition. At a meeting of the Greenwich Village Association, another neighborhood group opposed to the West Village plan, Davies's deputy Walter S. Fried let it slip that he expected one thousand people to show up at the next Board of Estimate meeting to support the city's plans. When pressed on that prediction, Fried replied that the supporters were from the Middle Income Cooperators of the Village, known as Micove, which had just spawned a subsidiary group, the West Village Site Tenants' Committee. This committee, he said, had been formed for the specific purpose of lobbying for urban renewal in the neighborhood and all the affordable housing it would bring.

Micove had been founded in anticipation of a vast housing redevelopment plan in SoHo; when that proposal fell through, Micove became a citizens' group without a housing project. Charlotte Schwab, the group's leader and a recent transplant from Maine, said she'd become interested in the West Village proposal when she read about it in the newspaper. When the SoHo housing project had been proposed, she said, "we had hundreds of applicants . . . from the West Village who desperately needed moderate-priced housing." When the city proposed new housing as part of the West Village urban renewal plan, "we decided to support it. Micove would like to become a sponsor of low-cost housing."

Jacobs acted quickly to counter Micove's involvement, describing it as a "puppet," "invented and nurtured by the Housing and Redevelopment Board or its handpicked site sponsor." The city needed to find a citizens' group to indicate they had "participation," Jacobs knew, and Micove served the purpose. She told reporters that Schwab had been promised an apartment in any new housing that was built, which Schwab denied; when pressed, the housing board said that the one thousand citizens had simply come forward on their own, clamoring for the affordable housing that the West Village redevelopment would bring.

Micove was not the only group that supported the West Village plan. In March 1961, the Citizens Housing and Planning Council, a powerful civic group headed by Roger Starr, leaked its position to the newspapers, saying the city did not "intend to level the area, to destroy its notably good housing, to tamper with that neighborhood character of which the residents are justifiably proud," and should be allowed to proceed.

Jacobs and four other civic groups issued an immediate rebuttal, saying there was no assurance whatsoever that the city planned to clean up only old factories and warehouses in the neighborhood. Jacobs's sources inside City Hall left no doubt that there were no specific plans for preservation, only clearance and redevelopment.

The Citizens Housing and Planning Council had drawn attention by planting the story over a weekend when news was slow; Jacobs countered by banding together citizen representatives from across the city where urban renewal had been proposed, and also by recruiting new intellectual firepower—similar to Lewis Mumford and Charles Abrams in the battle of Washington Square Park—to criticize the West Village urban renewal plans as a flawed policy. The commentators included the sociologists Nathan Glazer and Staughton Lynd and the art historian and urban design critic Martin James. Jacobs would later suggest that, like Schwab at Micove, real-estate-connected board members of the Citizens Housing and Planning Council stood to benefit from redevelopment in the West Village.

But the strategists behind the West Village urban renewal effort—Wagner, Felt, Davies, and David Rockefeller, who publicly supported urban renewal in New York City, even though the family foundation had funded Jacobs's critique of it in *Death and Life*—were on to something. The mission of urban renewal, as they saw it, was to create more affordable housing, in a city that never seemed to have enough. The West Village urban renewal plan, in this perspective, could potentially be a savior against gentrification.

"I think it should be so obvious . . . that, if the Village area is left alone and if no middle-income housing is projected by the board, which is the only way it can be, eventually the Village will consist solely of luxury housing, which we, of course, will be powerless to prevent," Davies wrote to a colleague. "This trend is already quite obvious and would itself destroy any semblance of the present Village that [Jacobs and her allies] seem so anxious to preserve."

Fortunately for Jacobs, the lawsuit she had filed, *Jacobs v. the City of New York,* paid dividends just when they were most needed. On April 27, 1961, a New York Supreme Court judge issued an order demanding that the mayor, the Board of Estimate, the City Planning Commission, and the Housing and Redevelopment Board all justify the proposal for determining whether the West Village was blighted. The city had failed to comply with the requirement to hold a hearing on the plans, which Wagner himself had put in place.

With Jacobs leading the way, neighborhood activists and the attorney for the Committee to Save the West Village marched into City Hall to present the court order to Mayor Wagner himself at a meeting of the Board of Estimate. They wore slogans on their lapels and cheap sunglasses adorned with a masking-tape X on each lens, intended to symbolize the mark of a condemned house. An Associated Press photographer snapped away, and the image of the protesting residents was published around the country and around the world, much to the delight of Jacobs and the Villagers, who were beginning to attract attention for identifying what was wrong with urban renewal. Jacobs saw the X as an important visual symbol of the looming threat that plans for urban renewal posed to neighborhoods.

"People who get marked with the planners' hex signs are pushed about, expropriated, and uprooted much as if they were the subjects of a conquering power," she wrote in *Death and Life*. "Thousands upon thousands of small businesses are destroyed, and their proprietors ruined, with hardly a gesture at compensation."

Jacobs sought to use the judge's admonitions to drive Felt and Davies from office.

"We are prepared," she said, "to prove that the Housing and Redevelopment Board has practiced vast deception in its procedures." Years before the body counts and secret invasions of the Vietnam War and the cover-up of the Watergate break-in, Jacobs was portraying a government that, far from being there to help, could not be trusted.

Wagner laughed and said he could not comment on the court order because he had just received it. But the eight hundred Villagers who turned out for the meeting sensed that with the judge's decision, there was a shift in momentum.

After the hearing, Felt pushed ahead with an aggressive public-relations campaign, promising to hold a citywide hearing on the "new" and more nuanced urban renewal program to rebuild New York. Some areas, like Tompkins Square in the East Village, needed a complete over-haul, but others could be more surgically redeveloped. Citizens would have their say, he claimed. In a *New York Times* article, Felt said that re-newal meant conserving and improving existing structures and relating any new development to the established neighborhood, implying that the Villagers' criticism of the program had been misguided.

At a hearing in May 1961, several New Yorkers lauded the city's re-newed commitment to citizen involvement. "We particularly commend the announced procedure of frequent public hearings as the program de-velops," said Miss Juliet Bartlett of the Women's City Club of New York. "For the first time, planning is to precede the choice of sites," said George Hallett from the Citizens Union. Roger Starr from the Citizens Housing and Planning Council announced that the era of Robert Moses was over, replaced by better planning and more affordable housing. Jacobs dis-agreed, saying that the commission was more interested in expanding the city's tax base than in providing better living conditions for low- and moderate-income families. Hers was the solitary voice of dissent.

In June 1961, Jacobs and the Villagers made their next move. At City Hall, while the planning commission deliberated on the West Village urban renewal plan, they handed a petition to the mayor's secretary de-manding the resignation of both Felt and Davies, who had "discredited their offices" by pushing so aggressively on redevelopment and failing to respect the wishes of the neighborhood. The petition demanded that an impartial official consider the ouster. The state assemblyman Louis De-Salvio said the Villagers had been pushed to drastic action because they felt railroaded. "They don't want or need bureaucratic interference with their way of life," he said.

At first, Wagner was defensive. It was preposterous, he said, that his appointees would be accused of unproven unethical conduct. Reacting to the petition, some rival neighborhood groups also rose to Felt's defense. But in August, with a primary election coming up, Wagner signaled that he was softening on the idea of urban renewal in the West Village.

"I want to say for the record that I shall vigorously oppose any study which would contemplate a change in the basic character of Greenwich Village," he said, hailing the area's small-town character, local color, and rich heritage.

Still, the mayor's statement wasn't enough for Jacobs, who said that if Wagner was really concerned about the well-being of Greenwich Village, he would order the entire plan shelved.

~~~

Over the next few weeks in that fall of 1961, the political pressure to shelve the plan mounted. The state comptroller, Arthur Levitt, running against Wagner for the Democratic nomination in the primary, promised that he would scrap the plan if elected. Carmine De Sapio, in a fight for the leadership of the local district of the Democratic Party, demanded that the mayor take a clear stand one way or the other, before the primary.

On the eve of the vote, Wagner succumbed, saying he was "deeply concerned and sympathetic with the people of the West Village neighborhood in their desire to conserve and to build constructively upon a neighborhood life which is an example of city community life at its healthiest." He asked the City Planning Commission to shelve its proposal and start over, urging a more "constructive approach to community-wide planning [that] will have the sincere cooperation and will engage the enthusiasm and talents of the citizens of the Greenwich Village community as a whole." Jacobs and the Villagers had successfully kept the spotlight on the mayor, until he concluded that if he pushed the West Village plan any further, he would be accused of operating just as Moses did.

Felt promised to give Wagner's request "earnest consideration," but he had already decided to plow ahead, despite losing the boss's support. As a planner schooled by Moses, Felt believed he could persevere with the project despite the opposition, even from a superior. Felt wrote in a report that the mayor had a right to request a withdrawal of the project, but "such a request does not destroy the independence of the commission," and that even in the face of substantial opposition the commission would be "derelict in its duty" if it yielded. "The argument that community opinion, as expressed at the public hearing, must dictate the commission's decision, misconstrues the function and responsibility of the commission and the nature of the public hearing," the report said.

In a meeting that Wagner requested with Jacobs and the Committee to Save the West Village, the mayor suggested the Villagers could defuse the whole controversy by publicly accepting a map describing the area—"to save Mr. Felt's face," Jacobs said. They would not have to worry about any action beyond the map, Wagner promised; he would make sure there were no bulldozers and no follow-through on urban renewal there. The committee rejected the deal and said they would go to court if necessary to continue the fight.

Unable to convince Jacobs to make the face-saving gesture, Wagner issued a statement reiterating his opposition to the plan and promising to vote against it should it come before the Board of Estimate.

Then Felt and the City Planning Commission made a shocking announcement. On October 18, 1961, at a packed City Hall meeting, the commission stated that behind closed doors, it had already designated the West Village as a blighted area suitable for urban renewal. The commission released the report that Felt had written defending its independence.

"Down with Felt! Down with Felt!" Jacobs and the Villagers chanted, immediately rising from their seats and rushing forward. The crowd accused Felt of making a secret deal with a builder, David Rose Associates, to push ahead with urban renewal in the West Village, so yet another private developer could make a profit redeveloping New York City. The planning commission's action was illegal, and the mayor had been "double-crossed."

Felt pounded the gavel and called for order. He nodded to the police officers he had summoned to contain the unruly crowd. The Villagers were aghast. The commission had acknowledged public opposition—and then, almost proudly, announced that the voice of the people would be ignored.

Trying to maintain control, Felt spoke into the microphone, reminding the crowd that it was not a public hearing and citizens were not allowed to make statements. But he granted time to Assemblyman Louis De-Salvio, and the crowd quieted to hear their ally speak.

"By this reprehensible and strange decision," DeSalvio declared, "you have sent the urban renewal program of this city, state and federal government back to the dark ages of Robert Moses, and his arbitrary and inhuman procedures."

Felt suggested that DeSalvio and other elected officials meet with him privately, to work things out behind closed doors. The Villagers around Jacobs went wild.

"You are not an elected official!" said Stephen Zoll, a resident of Christopher Street and an editor at the Macmillan book publishing company. "You have made a deal with David Rose!" Felt ordered the police to remove him. "Your name will be remembered in horror!" Zoll cried, as several officers escorted him away.

"You belong with Khrushchev!" shouted a woman. "How dare you assume such authority? Who the hell do you think you are making decisions in the interest of builders?"

A shaken Felt pounded the gavel and called a recess. During the break, he put in a call for ten more police officers. The citizens' feistiness, which would be commonplace later in the 1960s and right up to today, was unheard of in 1961, let alone at a meeting of the New York City Planning Commission.

"This is the most disgraceful demonstration I have ever seen. We cannot operate on the basis of disorderly conduct," Felt told reporters.

An hour later, Felt called the meeting back to order, with men in blue surrounding the hearing room. The remaining Villagers demanded a new hearing and continued their chants about Felt making a deal and doublecrossing the mayor.

"You will be obliged to arrest anyone who interrupts the meeting," Felt said to the police. When James Cuevas, an actor who lived on West Street, refused to be silent, two officers picked him up and carried him out feetfirst. They escorted a few other Villagers out, though they made no arrests and at times chatted affably with their charges.

There would be no more hearings, Felt said, trying to remain calm. The project would go to the Board of Estimate. He pounded the gavel again as the Villagers stood and protested. The meeting is adjourned, he said, and he slipped out a side door.

~~~~~

Where Moses had remained in the background, rarely showing up at hearings and avoiding confrontations as much as possible, Felt never had that luxury. His mandate was, supposedly, a better public process. This made him the perfect foil for Jacobs; she knew that the bow-tied commission chairman would eventually be forced to explain himself when confronted by the finger-pointing Villagers.

Felt tried to avoid confrontation as best he could, employing Moses's tactic of scheduling meetings at the last minute, but Jacobs had a "mole" in City Hall who filled her in on their times and locations. In evening meetings just about every week for months, Felt looked out across the meeting room only to see Jacobs in the front row. His Talmudic patience soon turned to dread, and he wasn't the only one. Some commissioners felt physically threatened; and two pro-urban-renewal citizens' groups, the Citizens Housing and Planning Council and the Citizens Union, said that the Villagers' conduct endangered future hearings and warned against their "dangerous attack on democratic institutions." The United Neighborhood Houses of New York and the Citizens' Committee for Children of New York also condemned the residents' behavior, and the city housing authority commissioner called it "ignorant, neurotic, dishonest, slanderous, disorderly and disgusting."

But it was the beginning of the 1960s, and a change was already washing over Greenwich Village and all of New York. Faith in authority had steadily eroded in the 1950s, and questioning political leaders and calling out injustice were becoming socially acceptable. The folksingers gathered by the fountain at Washington Square Park, and Bob Dylan came into town with his harmonica and announced that the times were changing. In this new era, it was not the protesters that were the outrage, but the City Planning Commission itself, with its arrogant dismissal of the voice of the people and its secrecy. Felt not only met behind closed doors but ordered official seals to be removed from city vehicles prowling the neighborhood. The distrust was palpable, and Jacobs made plain the necessity of civil disobedience.

"We had been ladies and gentlemen and only got pushed around," she said. "We were not violent. We were terribly alarmed at what is happening in our neighborhood and our city . . . so yesterday we protested loudly."

The confrontation at the City Planning Commission prompted Jacobs to dig deeper into the private developers who stood to benefit from slum designation and clearance, and to see if they were behind some of the resident groups backing urban renewal. She had enlisted neighborhood children to be on the lookout for developers' agents—she called them "creepers"—who fanned out through the blocks of the West Village and asked questions about living conditions. With the help of the young spotters, Jacobs was able to trace some creepers back to David Rose Associates, the firm slated by the city to rebuild the area once the demolition plans were approved.

Then she took the detective work a step further. Flipping through her saved correspondence, Jacobs discovered that one of the firm's associates, a man named Barry Benepe, had written her a letter asking about a travel fellowship. Then she noticed that the press releases from neighborhood groups supporting the city's plans looked remarkably similar—whenever the letter r appeared in both documents, it was dropped slightly. Jacobs hired a forensic expert, who confirmed that the developer's correspondence and that of the supposedly citizen-based groups backing urban renewal, including Micove, originated from the same typewriter. The typewriter was traced to a clerical office near Columbia, and Erik Wensberg, Jacobs's friend who worked at the university, stopped by to investigate. He saw a telegram from Rose Associates on a desk in the office.

The revelation was explosive. From the beginning, Jacobs was suspicious about the pro-urban-renewal citizens' groups, which had conducted a door-to-door campaign to convince hundreds of Villagers to sign a petition supporting redevelopment. Jacobs interviewed the residents who had signed the petition herself, and learned that the petitioners were describing the plans inaccurately, promising benefits far exceeding what was proposed. She documented the deception by obtaining more than a hundred notarized statements from the Villagers—who she now knew had been duped not just by opposing neighborhood groups but by the very company that stood to reap the financial benefits of redevelopment in the West Village.

Her moment to go public with her findings came at a neighborhood strategy session at the Lion's Head the day after the raucous City Planning Commission meeting. Surrounded by angry residents and members of the press, Jacobs presented a manila folder containing documents she said proved this collusion—including the résumé of a consultant who boasted he had sketched out plans for the West Village urban renewal project. Under Title I, the urban renewal legislation, the city was supposed to first identify slums and only then bring in the private sector to revitalize them; Jacobs was asserting that developers had taken over the entire process, in a moneymaking real estate scheme.

"It's the same old story," Jacobs said. "First the builder picks the property, then he gets the Planning Commission to designate it, and then the people get bulldozed out of their homes."

Rose and the consultants Jacobs had named denied that plans had secretly been drawn up, or that they had any such influence over the decisions of the city. James Kirk, the head of the Neighbors Committee, former president of the Greenwich Village Association, and a resident of the neighborhood for some sixty years, also denied a connection to the builders, and claimed it was Jacobs who was the bully.

"For the past ten years, dock workers, truckmen, longshoremen and people like that who lived in the Village near their pier work have had to move away because of evictions," he told reporters in October 1961. "Their buildings were torn down to make way for new luxury apartment buildings, or they were converted into smaller apartments which are too expensive and not large enough for their families." Urban renewal, he said, would give those hardworking people the affordable housing they needed.

Kirk genuinely viewed urban renewal as a solution for a rapidly gentrifying neighborhood, but his pleadings were too little too late. Jacobs had planted the notion that corruption was afoot, in addition to the bureaucratic arrogance and secret maneuverings. As the November election approached, Mayor Wagner was in good shape to be reelected, but he was still getting hammered by independent rival candidates for bungling the West Village situation. He needed the fourteen-block slum designation, and the proposal for urban renewal there, to go away for good.

Felt and Davies, battered by the negative press coverage of meetings where New Yorkers were being carted off by police, and then the revelations about Rose Associates, were at last ready to back down.

Davies was the first to capitulate, reluctantly concluding that there was little chance of overcoming the tarnishes on the West Village plan. On October 23, 1961, the Housing and Redevelopment Board issued a statement saying it would no longer pursue the West Village blight study plan—notably citing not the public's but rather the mayor's vigorous opposition to it.

Jacobs didn't allow herself to get too excited, because there was still work to do—the planning commission still needed to remove her neighborhood from its targeted list of slums—but she knew she'd triumphed. She had proven that the "new" urban renewal program put forth by Wagner reflected little genuine reform: there was minimal public participation, just as in the days of Robert Moses, and the wide latitude granted to private builders fostered the perception that power and greed were driving the process. She had proven that urban renewal plans issued from City Hall were not inevitable. And she had shown that ordinary citizens could successfully challenge authority—a pioneering act that would resonate throughout the 1960s.

Within a year, Davies resigned, and Felt stepped down as chairman of the City Planning Commission a year after that.

~~~~

With that battle won, Jacobs returned to the domestic tranquillity she so loved. She baked cookies and made plans for Thanksgiving dinner while collecting press clippings that described her as Joan of Arc and Madame Defarge leading the people to the barricades, a conquering citizen-hero who left politicians quivering in her wake. In November 1961, the *New York Times* ran its first full profile of Jacobs, under the headline "Critic at Large," describing her as a "vigorous, bespectacled, gray-thatched woman" who "does not believe in supervised play." But her celebrity was just beginning.

Having proved herself a tenacious and street-savvy neighborhood tactician, starting in September 1961 she was also an author, whose book would change the course of urban planning across the country and around the world. Indeed, just as the city began to back down on the West Village urban renewal plan, Random House released *The Death and Life of Great American Cities*.

The book was billed as a shocking and revolutionary work that took on a singular establishment: the government bureaucrats, planners, architects, traffic engineers, developers, and construction consultants who were shaping the nation's cities. "The City Planners Are Ravaging Our Cities!" was the banner headline on a Random House advertisement for the book, and it captured Jacobs's basic charge: that the men who were supposed to be improving American cities were, incredibly, laying waste to them. Indeed, the book's opening lines nullified the work they'd been doing for years. "This book is an attack on current city planning and rebuilding . . . To approach a city or even a city neighborhood as if it were capable of being given order by converting it into a disciplined work of art is to make the mistake of substituting art for life."

Before *Death and Life,* urban planning wasn't a subject much talked about beyond architecture schools and public works commissions—but Jacobs had opened it up and made it accessible, even exciting. Hers was a folksy, commonsense analysis, free from jargon. At first, only a few thousand copies were released, but the paperback would eventually be snapped up by tens of thousands in the first few years of publication, and hundreds of thousands thereafter. Writing about what was going wrong in American cities, what was right about them, and how ordinary citizens could restore dignity to urban life, Jacobs asked her readers to get involved. Proud to be a mother with no college degree and no formal training in urban planning, she told them to go out and observe how cities work, just as she had done. The planners at their drafting tables, and Robert Moses with his determination to get things done, had forgotten the power of simple, thoughtful observation, she charged. They were building cities without understanding how they best functioned, blinded by the arrogance of believing they could be planned in the first place. To them, cities were problems to be solved, and solutions were isolated housing towers and stores crammed into strip malls, on straightened and lengthened street blocks and amid windswept plazas—none of which worked for the people for whose use they were intended. The barren open space and the wide roadways built to accommodate traffic drained the life out of cities. What the planners could not or would not see, Jacobs wrote, was that the successful model of thriving urban life was right before them—in the very neighborhoods being bulldozed.

The book was the first of several public challenges to established institutions made during the 1960s. Rachel Carson's treatise on pesticides, *Silent Spring,* which appeared in 1962, essentially started the modern environmental movement; in 1963, Betty Friedan confronted male domination in business and culture and the unnecessary tedium of the housewife in *The Feminine Mystique;* Michael Harrington's *The Other America* inspired the war on poverty; and by showing how corporate bureaucracies refused to adopt basic safety measures like seat belts, Ralph Nader and his *Unsafe at Any Speed* blazed the trail for consumer advocacy. The authors of all these books employed the tactics of investigative journalism to identify flaws in American politics, policy, and culture in the postwar period through the 1950s, and called into question the confident course that the country was taking.

Because her principles are so widely embraced in planning, design, and government practices today, it is difficult to appreciate just how radical *Death and Life* was at the time. Urban renewal and highway building were the accepted policies of urban planning. The principles of modernism and modern city planning were being taught at all the nation's architecture schools. Academia, the entire planning establishment, all the leading thinkers on cities, and all the most swaggering practitioners of urban renewal had it wrong, Jacobs said. "The economic rationale of current city rebuilding is a hoax," she wrote. "The means to planned city rebuilding are as deplorable as the ends." Planners were reducing city and countryside alike to a "monotonous, unnourishing gruel," all coming from the "same intellectual dish of mush." Her statements were audacious, made all the more bold by the fact that she was a woman with virtually no credentials criticizing the work of an almost entirely male group of professional planners, academics, and government officials.

In *Death and Life,* Jacobs took on Moses's planning dogma piece by piece. Where Moses and his followers took a dim view of the density of older neighborhoods, believing it led to overcrowding and unhealthy conditions, Jacobs said density was a great thing, and density with diversity was ideal. Most older neighborhoods were valuable because they had both, in all their chaotic and organic forms. Across America by 1960, planning had also called for the strict separation of "uses," or the basic functions of life—living, working, manufacturing, entertainment, and culture—based on the principles of 1920s zoning, itself the product of the times when slaughterhouses and tanneries were cheek by jowl with tenement houses. But for the modern city, Jacobs was saying just the opposite: that successful neighborhoods mixed these uses, with stores and workplaces and residences and cultural entertainment all jumbled up together in close proximity. "Intricate minglings of different uses in cities are not a form of chaos," she said. "On the contrary, they represent a complex and highly developed form of order."

Moses's line of thinking also held that traffic congestion was a bad thing in the city, and that the city could compete with the suburbs only if cars and trucks could get around easily on superhighways. But Jacobs was saying just the opposite: that congestion in cities deterred car use and encouraged people to walk, or bike, or take the subway. Besides, she said, the big new highways always seemed to fill up with vehicles in short order. The places without them, like Washington Square, got along remarkably well. Traffic found its way through the urban street grid just fine; if one street had a traffic jam, drivers could just head over to the next street that was parallel.

Jacobs made four basic recommendations for successful neighborhoods: a street or district must serve several primary functions; blocks should be short to make the pedestrian feel comfortable; buildings must vary in age, condition, and use; and population must be dense. Hudson Street—unplanned in contrast to the grand housing developments of urban renewal—was a perfect example of diversity and strength in numbers, what Jacobs referred to as "eyes on the street." Whether neighbors or strangers, people are safer in dense areas because they are almost never alone.

In her analysis of what made a successful park—landscaping and amenities that adults and kids could actually use, smaller rather than bigger, and framed by "edges" of urban vitality rather than sweeping, windswept plazas—Jacobs was like a child telling a manufacturer the ingredients for a successful toy. Her homespun expertise exposed just how much the planners and the modernist firms had gotten away from the needs of the human beings who actually inhabited the city.

Perhaps the most radical aspect of *Death and Life* was the notion that planning a successful downtown redevelopment, or housing and parks and a successful neighborhood, wasn't really possible at all—that cities and city neighborhoods had an organic structure of their own that couldn't be produced at a drafting table. Jacobs was suggesting not only that planners were doing their work badly but that it was pointless for them to be doing their work at all.

Called "a brashly impressive tour de force" by the *New York Times,* *Death and Life* was regarded as a breath of fresh air by most critics. But the establishment that Jacobs was challenging saw things very differently. In government, planning, and academia the book was considered a collection of outrageous, flawed, preposterous, and dangerous ideas.

Unsurprisingly, Robert Moses was one of the first to try to dismiss it. In the book, Jacobs chastised Moses's plan to blast the roadway through Washington Square Park and ridiculed his thinking that plazas and empty open space could make up for the housing slabs that Moses himself admitted could be "ugly, regimented, institutional, identical, conformed, faceless." She criticized the Moses plan for the Lower Manhattan Expressway, which the master builder was just beginning to push in earnest

WRESTLING WITH MOSES } 125

as Jacobs was writing the book, as a typical example of ramming freeways through urban environments and destroying them in the process.

"Robert Moses . . . has made an art of using control of public money to get his way with those whom the voters elect and depend on to represent their frequently opposing interests," she wrote. "This is, of course, in other guises, an old, sad story of democratic government. The art of negating the power of votes with the power of money can be practiced just as effectively by honest public administrators as by dishonest representatives of purely private interests. Either way, seduction or subversion of the elected is easiest when the electorate is fragmented into ineffectual units of power." The statement was not just an expression of the rationale for campaign finance reform decades later but a manual for advocacy. Jacobs was warning city residents not to let themselves become disempowered.

Sitting in his New York apartment at One Gracie Terrace, Moses justifiably viewed *The Death and Life of Great American Cities* as an indictment of both his tactics and his fundamental philosophy of urban planning. Moses did not issue a public comment. That he would leave to others. But he did type out a one-page letter to Bennett Cerf, Random House's co-founder, who had sent him a copy of the book:

Dear Bennett:

I am returning the book you sent me. Aside from the fact that it is intemperate and inaccurate, it is also libelous. I call your attention, for example, to page 131.

Sell this junk to someone else.

Cordially,
Robert Moses

The rebuttals came quickly, from legions of government officials, urban planners, and virtually all of the leading thinkers in academia. The Moses protégé Edward Logue, head of the redevelopment agency in Boston, called it "a plea for the status quo." Edmund Bacon and Holmes Perkins, leading planners of the time, also inveighed against the book. Dennis O'Harrow, director of the American Society of Planning Officials—the precursor to today's American Planning Association—captured the planning profession's feeling about the book: "Mrs. Jacobs has presented the world with a document that will be grabbed by screwballs and reactionaries and used to fight civic improvement and urban renewal projects for years to come . . . The Jane Jacobs book is going to do a lot of harm. So batten down the hatches, boys, we are in for a big blow!"

Many of the book's critics focused their attacks on Jacobs's lack of formal training in urban planning. When Jacobs's friend Erik Wensberg asked Lewis Mumford what he thought of the book, Mumford, who was stung by Jacobs's criticism of his writing in the pages of *Death and Life*, responded with derision. "In asking for comment," he said, "you are in effect suggesting that an old surgeon give public judgment on the work of a confident but sloppy novice, operating to remove an imaginary tumor to which the youngster has erroneously attributed the patient's afflictions, whilst overlooking major impairments in the actual organs. Surgery has no useful contribution to make in such a situation, except to sew up the patient and dismiss the bungler."

In a scathing review for the *New Yorker*, Mumford again called Jacobs a "sloppy novice," making note of "schoolgirl howlers" in the book, what he considered egregious misreadings of planning history and urban design theory.

It was as if "Mrs. Jacobs had visited Pompeii and concluded that nothing makes a city so beautiful as covering it with ashes," wrote Roger Starr, the head of the Citizens Housing and Planning Council, who had been defeated by Jacobs in the West Village fight—and whom she considered "a professional stooge for project builders."

"She describes her folksy urban place on Hudson Street with such spirit and womanly verve that she has made a considerable number of readers believe it really exists," Starr wrote. "No mere socio-analyst, but a reformer, too, Mrs. Jacobs tells us how we can cast off the wicked spell" of such urban theorists as Ebenezer Howard with his garden cities and "find our way back" to city neighborhoods characterized by diversity, noise, and crowding. "The rest is easy, chum. You takes $20,000 out of your savings . . . and you buys a house in a part of the city that's known as a slum . . . and you and your like-minded (and like-financed) neighbors 'unslum' it. This means, Mrs. Jacobs admits, reducing the neighborhood population, i.e., throwing out the people who were living there, and remodeling for expensive apartments or single family occupancy."

Starr had hit on the most stinging critique of Jacobs's theories: if no low-income housing was planned or built, her vision of organic city growth would do little to curb gentrification. And after all, the underlying motivation that drove many urban renewal projects and public housing plans was to help the poor. A growing underclass required a helping hand from government, and liberals of the time believed that affirmative action on their behalf was necessary. Greenwich Village could not be replicated on the scale that was needed, these critics argued, to accommodate the hundreds of thousands of low-income and, increasingly, minority families in such desperate need.

While under fire from the left, Jacobs was embraced by the right. Like many radicals, she leaned toward the libertarian end of the political spectrum, and many conservatives responded positively to the book's message. Her critique of centralized government planning was music to the ears of William F. Buckley and the *Wall Street Journal* editorial page writers. The free economy, the *Journal* said, has all the virtues of the "messy" city neighborhoods Jacobs was defending: chaotic interactions and individual drive that cannot possibly be planned or controlled. Martin Anderson, a professor at Columbia who would later work in the Nixon administration and push the "devolution" of responsibility from the federal to state and local governments, within three years published *The Federal Bulldozer,* his own detailed indictment of urban renewal. Conservative groups fighting the use of eminent domain—government's constitutionally protected ability to "take" private property for roads or new development that is considered to be for "public use"—cite Jacobs to this day.

Drawing praise from surprising quarters, and controversy from everywhere in between, this middle-aged mother from Scranton had become a sensation. She was photographed by Diane Arbus for *Esquire.* Feature stories about her and her book appeared in *Newsweek* and the *Saturday Evening Post. Vogue* magazine would eventually call her "Queen Jane." She was invited to a luncheon at the White House by Lady Bird Johnson; she accepted on the condition that she could talk about urban amenities rather than beautification and tulips. Mary, her preteen daughter, screened her calls, including those from the mayor, who was calmly informed that Mrs. Jacobs was unavailable until after 4:00 p.m. She inscribed a copy of *Death and Life* to Eleanor Roosevelt, writing, "In appreciation, and with admiration, from the author who has personal reason to be grateful to you not only as a General Citizen but as a supporter of the people on Washington Square and the Lower Manhattan Expressway fights."

With the book in stores and getting attention, Jacobs went national— not so much on a book tour as on a whistle-stop campaign, sweeping into cities struggling to revitalize. In many cases she was only a few steps behind Moses, who was being hired as a consultant for downtown renewal plans from Pittsburgh to Portland, Oregon. Invited by civic groups seeking a fresh perspective on revitalization efforts, she grew more strident each time she was taken on a tour of redevelopment. Forget the big parking garages, she said in West Palm Beach. Just keep the stores and cafés open at night.

Flying into Pittsburgh, a city that had turned to Robert Moses for advice beginning in 1939, Jacobs toured the Northview Heights public housing project, a set of ten-story towers, walk-ups, and row houses isolated from the established residential areas, built by the local housing authority on the Moses–Le Corbusier towers-in-the-park model. She pronounced the project "bleak, miserable, and mean." Another Pittsburgh neighborhood plan, Jacobs said, was "homogenized, dull, unimaginative, doing nothing for the community but leading it astray . . . Pittsburgh is being rebuilt by city haters." Could the city get help from new consultants? No, the visiting author proclaimed. "There isn't a good planner in the nation. Every one of them has had the same bad training."

Naturally, local officials did not appreciate the remarks she made to local newspapers.

"You must have heard the old adage that a half-truth is similar to a half-brick, because it can be hurled further," wrote the Pittsburgh housing administrator Alfred L. Tronzo the day after the visit. "By comparison with the crowded, narrow, dangerous, dirty, rodent- and bar-infested streets in downtown New York—and the Greenwich Village area, which you call more ideal—Northview Heights to many thoughtful citizens, would seem a veritable paradise." Useful urban criticism, he said, "cannot be achieved by star-gazing from the second floor window of a Greenwich Village flat—while anxiously awaiting the 3 a.m. closing of the neighborhood pubs as an omen that all is well in the land."

On a tour of Philadelphia, Jacobs told an interviewer: "Planners always want to make a big deal of everything they do . . . In urban renewal you need new buildings—I have no quarrel with that—but there are plenty of good buildings here. Why tear them all down?" She liked

Philadelphia as it was, she insisted. But recent development was dreary, insufferably monotonous, isolated, and barren.

~~~~~

Back in New York, Jacobs was heralded as a new kind of public intellectual, blending urban theory and streetwise activism. She was the "Madonna misericordia to the West Village . . . who has probably bludgeoned more old songs, rallied more support, fought harder, caused more trouble, and made more enemies than any American woman since Margaret Sanger," said the *Village Voice*.

As *The Death and Life of Great American Cities* gained in prominence, it became an inspiration, guidebook, and bible for not only a new generation of planners and architects but ordinary citizens as well. "We don't live in no slum," an African American woman declared at a City Hall protest of plans to raze her block and replace it with housing towers in the early 1960s. A copy of *Death and Life* was tucked under her arm. "We don't want to live in no project. We want to stay where we is, but we want it fixed up the way she says."

The book placed Jacobs alongside the jazz musicians and abstract painters of Greenwich Village, who were challenging established ideas and systems, albeit in very different ways. Emerging from 555 Hudson Street, or enjoying a cigarette and a beer at the White Horse Tavern, she was often approached by fans asking her to sign the book and self-styled community activists seeking her counsel. But she never considered herself a member of the avant-garde, and disliked the limelight. "I like attention paid to my books and not me. I don't know who this celebrity called Jane Jacobs is—it's not me," she said. "My ideal is to be a hermit . . . and do my work. I just detest when I'm around somewhere and strangers say, 'Are you Jane Jacobs?' and engage me in conversation in this obsequious way. That has nothing to do with me. You either do your work or you're a celebrity; I'd rather do my work." She did, however, clip just about every newspaper and magazine article ever written about her. She sent copies to her mother and kept a comprehensive scrapbook.

If she enjoyed being the go-to person for quotations about urban renewal—New York City reporters covering the metropolis kept her number handy—it was only because it afforded her greater influence in neighborhoods and urban planning. She took every opportunity to urge other New Yorkers to organize and rebel and demand their voices be heard, just as the Villagers had done. When, in February 1962, the City Planning Commission finally dropped the West Village's slum designation for good, Jacobs didn't stop to relish the victory for a moment. Instead, she tried to transfer the good fortune to neighborhood struggles elsewhere in the city. "Our sympathy goes out to other areas that are now being victimized by the Planning Commission," she said.

As a published and, increasingly, quite prominent author, Jacobs found herself invited to everything from demonstrations to congressional hearings. In October 1962, she was invited to testify before a Senate subcommittee on banks and insurance companies withholding loans in deteriorating neighborhoods targeted by urban renewal or freeway construction. "I'm talking about banks and insurance companies that withhold loans because they consider them bad risks," she said. The blacklisted areas were selected "often because Negroes have moved in," and the neighborhoods "deteriorate because it is impossible to get money for improvements."

She also became active in the fledgling historic preservation movement in New York City. In the years following the West Village victory over urban renewal plans, neighborhoods had begun to clamor for blanket protection against demolition and development by being designated as special districts of heritage, character, and historic significance. Greenwich Village was early in line for this protection, which would later become commonplace in cities across the country—tellingly, in the districts most heavily visited by tourists seeking to experience the genuine urbanism of places similar to London or Paris.

Jacobs was leery of the idea of trying to freeze a neighborhood in time and put it under a kind of museum glass, but she did object to the wanton demolition of historic buildings. When word leaked out that the city planned to demolish Pennsylvania Station, the 1910 Beaux Arts masterpiece, and replace it with the bland redevelopment of Madison Square Garden, Jacobs picketed alongside the architect Philip Johnson and others, showing up in a felt skirt and top, her trademark costume-jewelry necklace of oversize beads, and white gloves.

Jacobs joined the Action Group for Better Architecture in New York, which pledged to fight "every step of the way" the "would-be vandals" who sought to destroy historic buildings. The group pleaded with the City Planning Commission to consider the architectural and historic attributes of Penn Station, holding demonstrations and writing letters to the editor. But business and political leaders saw the Madison Square Garden redevelopment as a way to revitalize that section of midtown Manhattan, and the planning commission swiftly granted the permits for demolition. In spite of the group's efforts, the big columns of the train station were toppled, and the stone eagles adorning its cornices were hauled off to be dumped in a swamp in the Meadowlands. But the demolition was a turning point, as it forced many New Yorkers to recognize what Jacobs was saying: that new was not necessarily better, and that there was value—human and cultural capital—in the built environment that already existed around them.

~~~~

Though Jacobs cared deeply about historic preservation, it was housing that worried her the most in the aftermath of the publication of *Death and Life*. She had fought off urban renewal in the West Village—and in the process killed off plans for hundreds of below-market-rate homes. As the planners had predicted, real estate speculation had intensified throughout Greenwich Village, and many residents were finding themselves priced out. Jacobs understood that she needed to change tactics if she wanted to make a useful contribution to the housing crisis. Determined not to work with city officials, she set out to show the entire planning system—from government officials to academics to planners and builders—a proper example of city building, with a construction project the neighborhood would lead itself.

The West Village Houses was a radical idea from the start: 475 apartments in forty-two five-story redbrick walk-ups, arrayed on vacant parcels—designed by the community, for the community, with no demolition or relocation required. Jacobs and the West Village residents came up with the idea for the project shortly after the defeat of the blight designation plan for their neighborhood. The Committee to Save the West Village had actually promised Mayor Wagner to lay out its own, community-based vision of neighborhood improvements, once, in Jacobs's words, "the threat of dictatorial redevelopment was lifted." Now that the bulldozers had been thwarted, the neighborhood residents, organized under the renamed West Village Committee, met to discuss how this vision would take shape.

Instead of tall, massive, barracks-like projects, the West Village Houses would be a harmonious addition to the existing neighborhood. The buildings would provide housing for families, with three-bedroom apartments and no studios or efficiency apartments. Elevators had become infamous for fear and crime in the Moses-era public housing towers, so the apartments would be built as walk-ups, even those on the fifth floor. There would be stoops, front gardens, and small backyards similar to Jacobs's own at 555 Hudson Street on the ground floor. There would be a public park for all residents to use, commercial space for local shops, and no big parking lots.

"The West Village Houses was a preventive measure, to make sure it was there in case the neighborhood ever got fingered again," recalled Erik Wensberg, a member of the Village committee. "The reason Greenwich Village was targeted was the low density. The effort was to increase the density gracefully."

The tenants had to be ethnically diverse—white, black, Puerto Rican. As the plan came together, the residents established two basic ground rules: there must be consensus on all actions; and not one person or family would be involuntarily moved. On the last page of the brochure for the project was a drawing of a fragile bird and, underneath, the West Village Houses' motto, a Jacobs creation: "Not a single person—not a single sparrow—shall be displaced."

The audacious idea that a neighborhood could take charge and build its own housing was front-page news. "It appears certain that the program will be highly controversial, pitting its advocates against the nation's city planners," the *New York Times* reported.

Remembering the grassroots tactics that Saul Alinsky employed to organize ordinary citizens in shaping the downtrodden districts of Chicago, Jacobs brought the West Village neighborhood together again, this time not to show up at planning commission meetings with Xs on their glasses but to pore over blueprints and learn principles of urban design. Her comrade in arms was again Leon Seidel, owner of the Lion's Head, who had become chairman of the Committee to Save the West Village. The citizens of Greenwich Village raised the $3,500 needed to pay an architect to draw up plans. Rachelle Wall, an off-Broadway producer who lived in the neighborhood, donated *Renoir, My Father* and two dozen other books for a two-thousand-volume book sale. Others donated expertise. The architectural historian Henry Hope Reed gave a free lecture on the neighborhood; Len Lye, a sculptor and moviemaker, held benefit screenings, and his wife extracted tips on real estate development and financing from the real estate office where she worked. The Lion's Head charged admission of $1.60 for cookies and coffee and a copy of the brochure. "We are really not against renewal," said Rachelle Wall. "This will show that we have a constructive side."

The West Village Committee issued a statement that Jacobs helped write in May 1963, explaining the new approach: "It is widely believed that new housing on high-priced city land must consist of tall or massive buildings if it is to come within middle-income rentals. It is also widely believed that land costing a developer in excess of $8 a square foot cannot be used for middle-income housing. Both beliefs are entirely erroneous, as is shown by the West Village plan cost figures."

The financing for the $8 million project would come from a combination of public funds and money from the International Longshoremen's Association; the state would provide low-cost mortgages and tax incentives to the developers, under New York's recently passed Mitchell-Lama housing act.

Jacobs knew the importance of getting a good architect to design the scheme. But she quickly found that no New York firm would agree to do the work, because they were fearful of alienating New York City officialdom and losing out on lucrative projects. After much research and cajoling on Jacobs's part, the Chicago firm of Perkins & Will was hired instead. Housing officials from New York state government, who had grown critical of the city's housing and renewal plans in general, agreed to do economic feasibility studies.

At City Hall, official reaction was curt. Fearing a ripple effect that would wrest control of redevelopment, the housing bureaucracy had little interest in seeing a citizen-led redevelopment project succeed. The financing would never work, the critics said, and in any case who would want to walk up five flights of stairs?

But the project needed the city's cooperation. For one thing, the area was zoned commercial. The elevated freight rail line, the High Line—the remaining portion is today a stunning linear park above street level—had run through the parcels and been partially dismantled. The site of the proposed West Village Houses had the feel of a deteriorating manufacturing district.

Developers eyeing the area, meanwhile, were irritated by a citizen-led effort to build on what they considered their territory. One in particular, William Zeckendorf, who sought to build luxury high-rise towers adjacent to the West Village Houses, dismissed the project as "a triumph for eggheadedness that is economically impossible to build." Jacobs immediately challenged him. "If you tried to evict us, there would be blood in the streets," she said, to which Zeckendorf replied: "I'm just relaxing and waiting for the Villagers to fall flat on their faces."

In the years following the defeat of the blight designation plan, Jacobs and the Villagers persevered, though the project took much longer than anyone had envisioned. The city bureaucracy made getting permits diffi-cult at every turn, and construction was delayed year after year, leading to cost increases from $8 million to $25 million. It was only in 1969 that a new city housing and development administrator gave his backing to the plan, and construction got under way. The West Village Houses were completed in 1974, and a family moved into the last three-bedroom unit in 1976.

While hard at work on the project in the planning stages, Jacobs helped circulate handsome renderings and documents she hoped would prove that the financing would work out. But she did not anticipate the problems that would eventually arise.

As costs increased, many features had to be eliminated, such as mansard roofs and the number of windows. As so often happens with de-sign, the whole package suffered when these details were stripped away, leading Paul Goldberger, then the architecture critic for the *New York Times,* to scorn the "unrelieved plainness" and "basic dreariness" of what turned out to be nondescript, big red boxes.

Originally envisioned as a home-ownership opportunity, the West Vil-lage Houses became primarily subsidized rental apartments—and some Greenwich Village residents complained that the rents, at about $420, ap-proximately $100 to $200 lower than the monthly market-rate rent at the time, didn't really constitute affordable housing but were more for the middle-class and other privileged denizens of the Village. Some even sug-gested the houses were tailored for the burgeoning gay population.

Yet the promise of the West Village Houses never died in Jacobs's mind. Even if the price of the new homes was not as low as she would have liked, the project still served as a "windbreak" against market forces and gentrification, she believed. They remain so to this day, amid brown-stones renovated by celebrities such as Sarah Jessica Parker and Matthew Broderick, and in the shadow of gleaming towers by the architect Richard Meier, where condos go for $3 million and up.

And for Jacobs, the real triumph was that the neighborhood had taken charge, laying out an alternative to the housing towers that Moses and his successors had built in the age of urban renewal. The West Village Houses project presaged today's common practice of projects financed by neighborhood-based, nonprofit community development corporations, guided by the principles of "community design," where residents identify the features they want. And Jacobs was recognized for being an exceptionally effective leader of the pioneering effort. On the day the West Village Houses plan was announced, the *New York Times* ran another profile of the "contentious" and "iconoclastic" community organizer and author, under the headline "Crusader on Housing." The writer noted that while "she has been denounced by officials who have tangled with her . . . those who know her find Mrs. Jacobs a warm and witty friend."

Years before, Robert Moses had been lauded in the newspapers for reinventing New York City. As the plan for the West Village Houses was unveiled, it was Jane Jacobs who was crowned as a new expert of city planning—as someone not just fighting proposals but putting her ideas from *Death and Life* into action.

In those years of the early 1960s, following the publication of her book and the tours of other cities, Jacobs lived her life in Greenwich Village as an author, an activist, and a mother of three children. The first engagements with Robert Moses and his protégés had turned out well. Washington Square Park was closed to traffic. The urban renewal bulldozers had been turned away from the West Village, her own plan for housing was under way, and her activism in historic preservation would soon lead to a special designation for all of Greenwich Village, requiring approval from the Landmarks Preservation Commission before any building could be altered. She had published a book that repudiated everything Moses stood for.

But her battle with the master builder was not over yet.

CROSS MANHATTAN ARTERIALS

LOWER MANHATTAN EXPRESSWAY
MID MANHATTAN EXPRESSWAY

AND RELATED

IMPROVEMENTS

DOWNTOWN REDEVELOPMENT
THE CENTRAL CITY
POST OFFICE
THE NEW EAST SIDE

Looking east along route
of Lower Manhattan
Expressway from Hudson
River to East River

FIVE

The Lower Manhattan Expressway

While Jane Jacobs fought off the bulldozers in the West Village, Robert Moses was preparing to take his highway building to the next level. By 1961 he was well on the way to building nearly six hundred miles of roadways: parkways in Westchester and Long Island, bridges such as the Triborough—the "hanging highway in the sky"—and towering elevated roadways like the Gowanus Parkway, crisscrossing the outer boroughs of the city at the expense of the hapless neighborhoods through which they slashed. "It has long been a cherished ambition of mine to weave together the loose strands and frayed edges of New York's metropolitan arterial tapestry," he said. "The Triborough Bridge Authority has provided a warp on the metropolitan loom, the heavier threads across which the lighter ones are woven." Now he hoped to complete the network: to connect the major bridges with high-speed roads, thereby making the entire metropolis easily navigable by car.

Fortuitously, Moses's aspirations had aligned perfectly with the vision of President Dwight D. Eisenhower, who in 1956 had signed the National Interstate and Defense Highways Act, calling for a vast network of superhighways in and around the country's major metropolitan areas, and deep

OPPOSITE: The Lower Manhattan Expressway, proposed to run through modern-day SoHo. *MTA Bridges and Tunnels Special Archive*

into suburban and rural areas as well. It was the thick of the cold war, and the military needed a speedy way to transport nuclear missiles, troops, and vehicles in the event of a confrontation with the Soviet Union. It was also the era when the American automobile grew bigger and more powerful, outfitted with plush interiors for comfort on longer journeys and adorned with chrome and tail fins. The car had become the ultimate expression of personal mobility, not just for special weekend trips but for daily life, commuting to work, taking kids to school, and running errands; gasoline was cheap and supplies seemingly boundless. The project before America was to build the basic infrastructure to support this mode of transportation—a road network unprecedented in scope.

In 1953, Moses, overseeing new highway construction in New York in his position as chairman of the Triborough Bridge and Tunnel Authority, entered and won an essay contest sponsored by General Motors called Better Highways, which asked for reflections on the need for more highways. He was awarded $25 for his commonsense plan for a first-class highway network for the entire country, to be financed by a penny increase in the federal gas tax. Moses was one of the earliest and most prominent supporters of the National Interstate and Defense Highways Act, which ultimately produced the forty-seven thousand miles of superhighways that Americans know and use today. "Greater convenience, greater happiness and greater standards of living" would flow from this massive public works project, said Eisenhower, who thought of the idea after a slow trip across the country by car. The establishment of an interstate system came with a tantalizing promise for state and local governments: Washington would pay 90 percent of the cost of any expansion or completion of the network.

Suburban and rural areas jumped at the free money, extending fresh asphalt into cornfields and ranch lands and remote valleys occupied by Christmas tree farms and summer camps. Developers capitalized on the new access to land for subdivisions, shopping malls, and office parks. In the 1950s the periphery of urban centers was the new frontier, as predominantly white and middle-class families, as well as corporations, headed for what were then wide-open spaces. But cities sought a piece of the action, too. Though they were crowded with buildings and boasted miles of sidewalks and extensive public transit systems, the nation's older, big cities figured that a superhighway retrofit would be a force for transformation, allowing them to keep pace with the booming suburbs and rural frontiers. Highways through cities would allow them to make crucial connections with the increasingly dispersed region all around and, city governments and planners believed, would reduce traffic congestion on knotted surface streets as well.

Moses's broad experience attracting government funds, and his diligent study of the interstate highway bill, allowed him to ensure that New York was first among major cities to receive funding. In 1955, he teamed up with the New York City Port Authority and published the *Joint Study of Arterial Facilities,* calling for a second deck on the Henry Hudson, four new bridges in the New York City area, and, if federal funding could be secured, two major crosstown expressways, one through midtown and one across lower Manhattan.

The crosstown routes weren't a centerpiece of the arterials report, but they were a priority for Moses. And they were no ordinary, ground-level highways. New York's congested urban terrain meant that they would have to soar and sweep and dive through the city; they would be highways that poked straight through skyscrapers, highways with housing on top, highways that dipped belowground and rose a hundred feet in the air. Though this futuristic marriage of superhighways and urban redevelopment was first imagined by Le Corbusier, Moses also drew inspiration for the task from an unlikely source: Walt Disney.

Moses had long admired Mickey Mouse's creator, an urban planner in his own right who would carefully lay out transportation systems for his theme parks. Moses was particularly intrigued by Disney's prognostications on cars, technology, and transportation systems. In 1958, the Walt Disney Studios produced an eight-minute animated film called *Magic Highway U.S.A.* for an episode of its television program *Disneyland.* Narrated in the authoritative bass of a newsreel, the film showed gleaming white highways and cloverleaf interchanges, overpasses and bridges and tunnels. In the future, the voice-over said, these roads would glow, disperse fog, and melt snow, and cars equipped with radar would ultimately drive themselves—something the U.S. Department of Transportation would ultimately work on in the years ahead.

"Prefabricated bridges and overpasses move quickly into place," the narrator says in the film, predicting an automated frenzy of construction, with trestles and cantilevers molding to mountainous topography. As the population spreads across vast areas, the roadways will become wider and faster, and "the commuter radius will be extended many miles." Tomorrow's living will be closely integrated with the highway system, the narrator goes on, as the film shows a couple with a child heading out in the morning from a motor port. After conducting some business in the car by videoconferencing, the mother and the son break off for the shopping center, and the father heads to work. "Office buildings will combine unique parking and elevator services. From his private parking space," the narrator concludes, tongue in cheek, "Father will probably have to walk to his desk."

The Disney film took as a given that the highway would play a vital role in civilization in the years ahead: "It will be our magic carpet to new hopes, new dreams, and a better way of life for the future."

The vision was for a technologically advanced environment for suburban commuters, but Moses believed the magic carpet could both connect the city to the suburbs and make the city itself function better. Moses would go on to befriend Disney, and in planning the World's Fair of 1964, he asked Disney to put on four exhibitions, including the Magic Skyway, sponsored by Ford Motor Company, and General Electric's Progressland. The glimpses of a gleaming future and the animated robotics Disney tested out at the fair—including a moving figure of Abraham Lincoln— proved so popular that Disney briefly considered creating a permanent theme park at the World's Fair's Flushing Meadows site; instead, he opted for better weather and twenty-seven thousand acres of flatlands and cattle pastures in Orlando, Florida.

In Disney, Moses saw a flair for drama and theatrics, and the power of dreaming big. With the federal government opening its wallet, Moses pressed his engineers to be unrestrained in their sketches—to draw on-ramps that swept in wide circles leading to tunnel portals, and skyways that blasted through the heart of the city, even if it required massive demolition and clearance and the relocation of people and businesses. Federal money could make these big plans not only possible but inevitable, Moses believed. If New York didn't grab the funding, it would go somewhere else—forsaking thousands of construction jobs and consulting and engineering contracts.

And it was a popular idea, too. For years, many New Yorkers had been clamoring for the kind of complete highway network Moses was proposing. Truckers and CEOs whose businesses depended on the movement of goods had complained about congestion in Manhattan and lack of access to the island since the end of World War I. Four bridges had been built across the East River at the turn of the twentieth century, and in 1921 a new Port Authority was formed to make similar connections across the Hudson on the West Side—the Holland Tunnel, the Lincoln Tunnel, and the George Washington Bridge. In 1929, the Regional Plan Association, or RPA, published a master plan to complete the network, which it claimed would reduce the cost of doing business, increase economic activity, and accommodate the growth of the tristate (or New York, New Jersey, and Connecticut) area. The RPA was founded in 1922 by a prominent group of civic and business leaders; its goal was to create a regional plan for a broader New York metropolitan area, with an infrastructure that extended well beyond city limits. The 1929 blueprint laid out seven major new east-west routes—one across Brooklyn, one across the Bronx, and the rest across Manhattan.

The five new routes in Manhattan included one at the very top of the island, linking the George Washington Bridge and the Bronx; another across Harlem at 125th Street, from the Triborough Bridge to a planned additional span across the Hudson River; another in the area of Fifty-seventh Street, also providing access to another new bridge vaulting the Hudson; a midtown corridor at Thirty-fourth Street, stretching from the portal of the Lincoln Tunnel all the way over to the portal of the Queens Midtown Tunnel; and finally, the crosstown route from the Holland Tunnel to the Manhattan and Williamsburg bridges, providing express access straight across the southern portion of Manhattan Island: the Lower Manhattan Expressway.

Officials in city and state government embraced the RPA plan, but it was Moses who, ten years later, took the blueprint and began to push ahead to make it reality. The crosshatch of highways—Jane Jacobs later called them "laces" across a long boot—would connect Manhattan with the region all around, allowing smooth travel in, out, and around the metropolitan area. The concept fostered by the RPA was that highways would be like arteries that kept the blood pumping; under Moses, the roadways were called "arterials" in official city documents in the decades that followed the publication of the RPA's master plan.

The New York Port Authority, which built the George Washington Bridge, started the first crosstown route, a twelve-lane, half-mile roadway dubbed the Trans-Manhattan Expressway, which would usher traffic coming off the George Washington Bridge across the tip of Manhattan Island to the Harlem River. This extended off-ramp replaced the existing condition of bridge traffic being dumped into the neighborhood of Washington Heights at 178th Street.

Moses would build on this section of road to construct what would become one of his most infamous projects, and the first crosstown highway—the Cross Bronx Expressway. The vision was for an uninterrupted ride across the Hudson River on the George Washington Bridge, across the northern section of Manhattan, across the Harlem River, and through the borough of the Bronx. His proposed superhighway, nearly seven miles long in all, required blasting tons of rock in submerged sections, crossing a hundred streets, seven other highways or parkways, and nine subway or rail lines, an elaborate elevated interchange with the New York and New England thruways—and would slash through one mile of densely populated neighborhoods in the Bronx. Over fifteen hundred families would be forced to relocate. Begun in 1948 and completed in 1963 at a cost of $128 million, the Cross Bronx Expressway represented Moses's dominance over neighborhood objections in that period, and the project is remembered to this day as a case study in brutally overriding citizen participation in roadway planning. As Robert Caro later wrote in *The Power Broker*, the Cross Bronx Expressway broke up thriving and diverse immigrant enclaves and jump-started the economic and social decline of the Bronx.

Moses knew it would be difficult to plow through the Bronx neighborhoods of East Tremont and West Farms, home to middle- and working-class Jewish and Italian families, but he was also particularly inflexible on the route of the Cross Bronx Expressway. Moving it just two blocks south, to the northern section of Crotona Park, would have spared hundreds of families from having their homes destroyed. Tenants' groups and a handful of elected officials pleaded for the change, but Moses would not budge. The homes were bulldozed, and many residents, especially renters, complained they got very little assistance to relocate.

Moses didn't dwell on such human costs. For him, the Cross Bronx Expressway was a perfect example of how a New York City highway could qualify for federal funding. It had created a seamless highway running from New Jersey, across Manhattan and the Bronx, and on to the thruways leading to upstate New York and New England, to Connecticut, Boston, and Maine. Motorists and trucks could also use the route to head back down into Queens and into Long Island. Before it became reliably clogged decades later, the Cross Bronx shaved substantial time off the trip across the top of New York City for cars and trucks, and completed a missing link in Interstate 95, the mighty East Coast highway that would ultimately run from Maine to Florida. Eisenhower and the 1956 National Interstate and Defense Highways Act called for completing connections in a national network; Moses delivered by filling in a major gap.

The promise of federal funding was an important factor as Moses tried to build the other crosstown expressways, which posed even tougher challenges than the Cross Bronx.

Though Moses liked the RPA's suggestions for two crosstown express-ways at 125th Street and at Fifty-seventh Street, he ultimately chose not to pursue those routes, in part because they made sense only if two new Hudson River crossings were built, and those spans never made it past the conceptual planning stages. Instead, he focused on two major east-west routes outlined in the RPA plan—the Mid-Manhattan Expressway and the Lower Manhattan Expressway. Moses began to campaign for these highways in the 1940s, persuading the public-works-obsessed mayor Fiorello La Guardia to allow him to move ahead with engineering plans. Both the Mid-Manhattan and the Lower Manhattan crosstown routes were included in the City Planning Commission master plan for a new arterial network in 1941, and blessed by the New York state legisla-ture in 1944. By 1949, the job of building these cross-Manhattan express-ways was fully under the control of Moses's Triborough Bridge and Tunnel Authority. Funding for these costly roadways remained uncer-tain—until the interstate highway act passed in 1956, providing 90 per-cent of the $350 million ultimately needed for both expressways. Moses was set to turn the blueprints into reality.

The Mid-Manhattan Expressway would connect the Lincoln Tunnel, which ran under the Hudson River from New Jersey to Manhattan's West Side, with the Queens Midtown Tunnel, which ran under the East River and emerged in Queens. A new highway connecting these two tunnels would provide a seamless route from New Jersey, across Manhattan, and into Long Island. It was slated to run along Thirtieth Street, a narrow cross street lined with hotels, cafés, schools, and stores. All the buildings on the south side of Thirtieth Street would have to be demolished to make way for the elevated six-lane roadway that Moses envisioned. New development would rise along the route, however, and the sleek, modern new buildings would actually become part of the highway. In the render-ings that Moses circulated showing the Mid-Manhattan Expressway, the elevated highway runs right through proposed new office buildings, at about the third floor. Pedestrians and delivery trucks are depicted in the sketches occupying the conventional surface streets below.

The cost of the project was estimated at $77 million, but it was eligible for 90 percent federal funding, because in stretching from northern New Jersey through the Queens Midtown Tunnel and out onto booming suburban Long Island, it would become an interstate. Despite the relative availability of funds, however, opposition was fierce from the start. Several organizations, including the Thirtieth Street Association, the fur industry, the Murray Hill Home Owners Association, and the Midtown Realty Owners Association, came out against the plan. The Associated Fur Manufacturers, representing six hundred members and twenty thousand workers, said the forced relocation of the city's top outlets in the fur industry—located largely along Thirtieth Street—"may well be severe enough to destroy it." These were largely affluent and politically influential forces, based in part in a busy and thriving district that was now threatened by Moses's vision.

Mayor La Guardia's successor, William O'Dwyer, was mesmerized by the idea of the Mid-Manhattan Expressway. But outside of Moses and his team, the skyway struck many as too brutally disruptive. Acknowledging this difficulty, the Regional Plan Association suggested a tunnel instead, which would have cost roughly twice as much. Moses dismissed the idea, arguing that a tunnel would be too difficult from an engineering perspective, too expensive to pass muster with federal funders, and inadequate for moving a large volume of traffic because only four lanes could be accommodated underground. Fiddling with the scheme, he said, would only lead to delays.

He continued to lobby for the Mid-Manhattan Expressway as Vincent Impellitteri succeeded O'Dwyer, followed by Wagner and then finally John Lindsay in 1966. Moses sought to convince each new chief executive of the project's viability, and maneuvered to give the superhighway an aura of inevitability. He agreed to build a third tube for the Queens Midtown Tunnel on the condition that the Mid-Manhattan Expressway be built. Congestion was bad at the time and would only intensify, he argued, with the anticipated influx of cars and trucks through the 1950s and 1960s. Midtown was going to suffer from "the worst problem of traffic strangulation in history." He even started land acquisition for the highway, buying a parcel near the Queens Midtown Tunnel in anticipation of the first stage of the futuristic skyway. But the day after that purchase, the powerful interests aligned against the project revealed their influence. Mayor Lindsay declared his final decision against the Mid-Manhattan Expressway, characterizing the project as a boondoggle. The parcel Moses had acquired for the highway was turned into a playground.

Shortly thereafter, Moses concluded it was pointless to invest any more energy in the doomed project. As his parting shot, he predicted that midtown traffic would continue to worsen and would have to be dealt with eventually. But he was set to move on, to the final and greatest hope of realizing a crosstown superhighway through the heart of New York City—the Lower Manhattan Expressway.

The basic rationale for Lomex, the project's nickname, was as compelling as connecting the midtown tunnels on either side of Manhattan, if not more so. Lomex would connect a Hudson River tunnel and two East River bridges that currently dumped traffic into the congested streets of Manhattan. On a map, a favorite form of persuasion for Moses, a connection looked like an achievable and obvious solution to the mile of chaos and gridlock between the portal of the Holland Tunnel and the on-ramps of the Manhattan and Williamsburg bridges. And the payoff was huge: the extension of Interstate 78 from New Jersey to Long Island would be another major contribution to the interstate network, and thus would be eligible for 90 percent federal funding. But that was not all. Perhaps more than any other roadway project he pursued, Moses saw Lomex as a way to spark economic development. The highway would move traffic, reduce congestion, and retrofit the entire area—now beset by low property values and diminishing tax revenue—with a modern amenity with a half-dozen local off-ramps that would symbolize a neighborhood on the move. The rationale made sense to business leaders in the downtown chamber of commerce, who were working on other revitalization plans, including the emerging vision of soaring twin towers at the southern tip of the island.

"The route of the proposed expressway passes through a deteriorating area with low property values due in considerable part to heavy traffic that now clogs the surface streets," Moses wrote in the *Joint Study of Arterial Facilities* in 1955.

> Construction of the expressway will relieve traffic on these streets and allow this locality to develop in a normal manner that will en-

courage improved housing, increased business activity, higher property values, a general rise in the prosperity of the area, and an increase in real estate tax revenues. This has been the experience again and again in localities in the city where modern parkways and expressways have been built. The Grand Central Parkway and the Belt Parkway have produced these results, and it is now happening along the Long Island Expressway. There is every reason to expect that it will also happen in the case of the Lower Manhattan Expressway.

The Lomex model in Moses's Randall's Island office—the one with the Lucite handles to lift out the blocks of old buildings and replace them with a highway—made it look easy, but reality was more complicated. Moses chose a narrow east-west lane called Broome Street, named for New York's first alderman after the Revolutionary War, as the best route for the highway. The elevated, ten-lane roadway required a 350-foot-wide corridor, superimposed on Broome Street and all the buildings on the north side of the street. The entire route was thickly settled, from the neighborhood that would later be known as SoHo to Little Italy, Chinatown, the Bowery, and the Lower East Side; the grand total for proposed demolition was 416 buildings that housed 2,200 families, 365 retail stores, and 480 other commercial establishments.

Moses promised that all the businesses and residents would be properly relocated, but the project required a massive rearranging of humanity and commerce before the furious assembly of concrete and steel could even begin. And it came at a substantial price. When Moses first got approval to draw up plans in 1940 from Mayor La Guardia, the project had a price tag of $22 million; over the following thirty years it would jump to $72 million, then $88 million, $100 million, and finally $150 million.

But Moses had seen cost increases before. The projects were always worth it in the end. He wanted this highway built.

~~~~~

On a summer day in 1962, Father Gerard La Mountain emerged from the Church of the Most Holy Crucifix, turned right, and started to walk down Broome Street toward the Hudson River, his monk's robes sweeping along the sidewalk. The street was pocked with crumbling pavement and cobblestones, cluttered with cars and delivery trucks, and lined with ornate cast-iron five- and six-story buildings on either side. A filmy grime seemed to cover everything, and black fire escapes zigzagged down the facades. But it was home. And soon it would all be gone.

As the neighborhood's residents passed him on the sidewalk, La Mountain, who had arrived as the church's pastor in 1960, tried to imagine the destruction that was coming: a superhighway fifty feet in the air, with traffic roaring above, obliterating the city blocks to his right—apartment buildings and businesses and not only his church but five others, all razed to clear the path. He shuddered at the thought. His parishioners, an eclectic flock of retirees and longshoremen, immigrants from Italy and Eastern Europe and increasingly Puerto Rico, had become resigned to the point of being depressed, convinced by the newspaper coverage that the Lower Manhattan Expressway would soon be built. The expressway had consumed his time as the new pastor of the Church of the Most Holy Crucifix, located on Broome Street between Mott and Mulberry streets in the thick of Little Italy—and right in the middle of the proposed highway. The neighborhood had been condemned, bringing a kind of paralysis to the area. Nobody could make plans. The congregation's homes would be destroyed, and the people would be scattered to parts unknown, evicted and subject to what most believed would be an inadequate relocation process. It was hard to go to Mass in their beloved church, three stories high with an inlaid bell tower and wood-carved front door, knowing it would soon be smashed by a wrecking ball.

La Mountain hadn't expected to arrive fresh out of seminary and plunge into a political fight. But he had done what was necessary, joining the Committee to Save Homes and Businesses in the Second Assembly District, strategizing with the local assemblyman in an office above a liquor store a few blocks down in the Lower East Side, organizing meetings, and even getting an audience with Mayor Wagner to plead against the looming destruction. The mayor had listened but made no promises.

The defense of the neighborhood was a full-time job, and La Mountain needed help. Having done all he could to convince city officials not to destroy his church, La Mountain embarked on a mission that would change everything, or at least he hoped it would. He was headed to Hudson Street to knock on the door of Jane Jacobs; he had heard about her successful fight against urban renewal in the West Village and thought she might be able to help.

When he arrived at her home and explained why he'd come, Jacobs welcomed him into the cluttered living room at 555 Hudson Street to hear him out. She, too, was aware of the plans for the Lower Manhattan Expressway; part of the rationale for Moses's plan to extend Fifth Avenue through Washington Square Park was to connect with Lomex, and she had warned against the folly in *The Death and Life of Great American Cities.* She listened as the pastor explained how Moses was hard at work again, pushing big plans, marshaling the New York City establishment, and coldly arranging for the eviction of thousands of people and businesses. He was moving fast. Following the *Joint Study of Arterial Facilities* and passage of the interstate highway act in 1956, he had successfully placed Lomex on the map of planned arterials, which had been submitted to the Board of Estimate and the New York City Planning Commission for approval. He laid plans for acquiring the land for the highway and had already commissioned some preliminary work, including a revamp of the Manhattan Bridge and its on-ramps to accept the new highway connection and an eighty-foot section of the highway's foundations at Broome and Chrystie streets.

Scattered merchants and small-business owners had spoken out against the plan at a City Hall hearing of the planning commission in late 1959. But in the months that followed, their voices were drowned out by bigger downtown business interests—including David Rockefeller, who had sparred with Jacobs on Greenwich Village redevelopment. Moses had expertly positioned Lomex as not just a roadway but economic salvation. "Not to be overlooked in examining the benefits of the Expressway is the tremendous stimulus it will provide to the program of the Downtown–Lower Manhattan Association," Moses wrote in one of the many glossy brochures he produced for the project. "This group of distinguished downtown leaders, headed by David Rockefeller, is assiduously tackling a giant task—the rehabilitation of Lower Manhattan. These citizens have undertaken a project of stunning scope. They deserve nothing less than the complete cooperation of our elected and appointed city officials."

La Mountain and the merchants had successfully drawn in the New York state assemblymen representing the area, the most vocal of whom was also familiar to Jacobs: Louis DeSalvio, the state legislator who had been so helpful in the West Village urban renewal fight. DeSalvio—a stout, balding man with heavy black-rimmed glasses and a passing resemblance to Truman Capote—was a Catholic and a member of the Elks and

Knights of Columbus, and had been serving in the New York state legislature since 1941. Donning a crisp suit every day, he made a career of taking up his constituents' causes, and Lomex was high on the agenda. Together with fellow Democratic state senator Joseph R. Marro, DeSalvio filed a bill in Albany to delete state authorization for the expressway, arguing that the city already had a backlog trying to relocate residents displaced by other projects, and that adding over two thousand more evictions would create "great hardship and suffering to the families involved." Instead of an elevated highway, the lawmakers suggested improving Canal Street, a wider surface boulevard just south of Broome Street.

The Manhattan borough president at the time, Louis A. Cioffi, also sought assurances from Moses that the residents and businessmen would be smoothly relocated before committing to the highway. In response, the City Planning Commission and the Board of Estimate ordered a new study of the needs of tenants in the right-of-way, though it would be performed by Relocation and Management Associates Inc., a Moses-friendly firm that had worked on the Lincoln Center redevelopment. That would buy some time, Jacobs thought as she listened to La Mountain, but she saw that the opposition had fallen into the trap of negotiating, thereby accepting the highway as a fait accompli. If the fight remained framed by the need for a better relocation process, the forces behind the expressway would prevail.

Jacobs appreciated the extent of La Mountain's challenge. Moses had been working the relocation issue masterfully. He encouraged the editorial writers at the *New York Times* to complain that delay-inducing studies were "tampering with the future of the city." In the summer of 1960, he warned the Board of Estimate, which he complained had already postponed action four times, that it must approve the route or the federal government would walk away from the project, along with tens of millions in funding. The city would be left to pay millions for design contracts that had already been commissioned, modifications to the Manhattan Bridge, and the foundation work at Broome and Chrystie streets. It would be pure folly to abandon a project that was effectively already under way, he argued. He had already put his stake in the ground. Besides, Moses said, only about a hundred families would need to be relocated in the early phases; there was plenty of time to make sure the process went smoothly.

Cioffi, the borough president, continued to be a voice for the residents. "There is no point in pushing these people out until we know where they are going," he cautioned. DeSalvio complained that Moses was "hitting us below the belt" by scaring the city into thinking the federal largesse would be lost. But in the early fall of 1960, the city government approved the route for Lomex, and prepared to authorize Moses to make condemnation and property purchases for the right-of-way. Mayor Wagner assured residents that those slated for eviction would have ample time to learn where they would be relocated. "No hasty action is in sight on the project as a whole," Wagner said, in a vague attempt to placate those in the highway's path, some of whom vowed to leave the city entirely if forced out.

The report by Relocation and Management Associates claimed there was "ready availability" of loft space nearby and throughout the city to absorb the evicted families and businesses. "Those businessmen who are interested in finding space and continuing their operations in New York City should be able to do so," the consultants said. Even as things were going well, Moses railed against any hint of questions or hesitation, decrying to a reporter "the folly and interminable delays, postponements and evasions which continue to bedevil the building of the Lower Manhattan" expressway.

In February 1962, La Mountain and the parishioners of the Church of the Most Holy Crucifix received yet worse news. The newspapers, thanks to a Moses leak, reported that Mayor Wagner had dropped any lingering misgivings and had thrown his full support behind Lomex. City Hall's unqualified backing appeared to make the roadway a foregone conclusion; construction on the first stage, from the West Side Highway to Sixth Avenue, would begin soon. The neighborhood reeled. "Where can I go?" asked Mike Squecciarine, sixty-five, a retired iceman living with his daughter in an apartment at 390 Broome Street. Four doors down, a barber across from the police headquarters building mourned the loss of the business he started in 1925.

La Mountain and DeSalvio helped organize two busloads of residents to picket City Hall at a subsequent hearing, but Moses's trusted ally Arthur Hodgkiss, the city traffic commissioner, the Downtown–Lower Manhattan Association, and the Automobile Club monopolized the proceedings with calm testimony in favor of Lomex. The deputy mayor even threatened to have DeSalvio removed by police for speaking out of turn. Approvals for property condemnation sped along. The City Planning Commission also brushed aside a detailed alternative submitted by the Committee to Save

Homes and Businesses in the Second Assembly District for a viaduct down Canal Street.

Moses maintained momentum for the project by portraying opponents as naysayers taking potshots at progress. On one occasion, after accepting a plaque from the Affiliated Young Democrats, as Lomex protesters picketed outside, he observed that New York "tolerates blackmailers and slanderers in the name of news and lets its virtues go unpublished and unsung."

A brighter moment came at a June hearing of the Board of Estimate, when protesters read a letter by Eleanor Roosevelt—who had similarly weighed in against the roadway through Washington Square Park—urging the city not to build Lomex. "Don't approve this road if you want to remain in office," Leon Seidel of the West Village Committee, who had joined the fight, told the Manhattan borough president, Edward R. Dudley. DeSalvio urged the board to kill the "mad visionary's dream" to "cut the city's throat with this stupid idea." The board members sat and listened passively.

That was where things stood, La Mountain told Jacobs. The opposition was starting to be heard. Now they needed to take the fight to the next level, and they needed Jacobs's help.

La Mountain's tale was as familiar as it was disturbing to Jacobs. But in the summer of 1962 she was preparing to leave *Architectural Forum* for good and devote herself full-time to writing books. She wasn't sure she wanted to spend the hours she knew would be required for another neighborhood fight. As she led La Mountain to the door, she agreed to come to his meeting as an observer.

A few days later, as she walked into the tiny auditorium of the Church of the Most Holy Crucifix, Jacobs was immediately reminded of the community meetings in the West Village urban renewal fight. Close to a hundred people were there, plotting the next moves in the fight with palpable energy. She surveyed the crowd and could see that La Mountain had recruited not only residents but politically active organizers; a few weeks before, he had noticed pamphlets on the radiator near the front door of the church from the Downtown Independent Democrats that said, "People of Broome Street: We're Here to Help You," and invited members of the reform group. One leader, Estelle Rome, made calls to boost attendance. Jacobs was also struck by the diversity of the group La Mountain had gathered: there were Republicans and Democrats, businessmen and professionals, piano teachers and artists, Catholics, Jews, and Protestants, socialists and conservatives alike. Rosemary McGrath had come from the Greenwich Village chapter of Young Americans for Freedom, and there was rumored to be representation from the Mafia in Little Italy. Nobody ever said anything outright, but it was widely known that La Cosa Nostra had joined the fight against the destruction of its power base.

Jacobs listened as La Mountain led the discussion and stressed the need for unity, suggesting that all in opposition to Lomex should consolidate under one Joint Committee to Stop the Lower Manhattan Expressway. This wasn't just Broome Street's fight, he said. Moses was promising that the highway would improve the neighborhood, but everybody knew that the city blocks anywhere near the roaring, elevated structure would quickly deteriorate. The people and businesses along Third Avenue in Brooklyn, in the shadow of the towering Gowanus overpass, built twenty years before, could attest to that.

When La Mountain introduced her, Jacobs addressed the group and quickly dropped her detached-observer status. She began to ask questions, trying to determine what chess moves Moses was likely to make, get a better sense of where the mayor stood, and learn what promises had been made for the relocation of businesses and residents. She listened to the answers for what seemed like hours.

When she emerged from the church, Jacobs followed La Mountain's steps back toward Hudson Street. On the journey, she did what she had done in New York City since she arrived from Scranton: she scrutinized the neighborhood, trying to learn how it functioned through careful observation.

In spite of having been dubbed Hell's Hundred Acres by city firefighters who were constantly responding to blazes that ignited from chemical-soaked floors, stored toxics, and other materials in the area's manufacturing buildings, this swath of Manhattan wasn't lacking in architectural splendor. The Church of San Salvatore, just down from the Church of the Most Holy Crucifix, bore cherubs and gargoyles in the Italian Renaissance style known as rococo. The fire station, home base for Engine Company 55, had the symmetrical arched stone windows of the Renaissance revival; the police headquarters at the corner of Broome and Centre, a classic Beaux Arts building by Hoppin, Koen & Huntington, was built in the monumental style of Edwardian Baroque, common in prominent public buildings in London.

Jacobs observed that many of the buildings in the area had facades made of cast iron, a construction method she recognized from her stint at the magazine the *Iron Age*. Iron was cheap, and the plates of the facades were prefabricated and assembled on-site. It was also, critically, a fireproof material. The cast-iron buildings of SoHo, built beginning in the mid–nineteenth century, were arguably the first step in the evolution of the sky-scraper, which would move steadily from masonry to glass and steel. The buildings Moses wanted to bulldoze represented an important moment in history—a vibrant new commercial district of stores, storage, and man-ufacturers, built by men dedicated to creating a uniform elegance. The cast-iron buildings of Broome Street, with their repetitive columns remi-niscent of Rome, had come to be known as the "Palaces of Trade." The E. V. Haughwout building at Broome and Broadway housed a department store that had been the Tiffany of its day when it opened in the late 1850s; it housed the city's first passenger elevator. The six-story Gunther Building at 469 Broome Street, a fur warehouse and fabric showroom by the archi-tect Griffith Thomas, had a corner-curving facade of rolled glass, Corin-thian columns, and lavishly decorated cornices and balustrades.

These buildings were beautiful, Jacobs thought, and—anticipating the artists' lofts and fancy restaurants that would mark the area in the decades to come—they could be renovated and reused. There was an el-egance to the area, and the scale of the place was comfortable. Down-town had its towers around Wall Street, but the skyline stepped down around Broome Street and throughout Greenwich Village, rising again to a forest of towers at midtown. The low-slung area was a Paris-like reprieve from height.

It was the people inhabiting the area that made it truly remarkable, however, as Jacobs would later learn through her own research. Hell's Hun-dred Acres—the proposed corridor for the Lower Manhattan Express-way—was home to companies that employed 12,000 people, primarily blacks, Puerto Ricans, and women, in roughly 650 small businesses and 50 larger industrial establishments. The majority of the businesses produced textiles, fashion accessories, and cheap daily necessities of life. Their em-ployees earned about $80 per week on average.

The working-class character of the area was evident all along the route where Lomex would run. Along Broome Street were lofts and one-room apartments, a live poultry market, mom-and-pop shops, and inexpensive places to eat. The pasta eateries of Little Italy were not far from the eclectic food stalls of Chinatown. At the corner of Broome and Chrystie streets—the spot where the work was scheduled to begin on the foundations for Lomex, adjacent to a subway tunnel—was a long vertical park named for FDR's mother, Sara Delano Roosevelt. Moses himself had built it, and the melting pot that was New York City could be witnessed on any weekend morning, on the benches and on the soccer fields. Beyond the park toward the East River, the neighborhood became a bit rougher and cluttered in appearance in the Lower East Side. The five-story walk-ups near the Manhattan and Williamsburg bridges were filled with immigrant families, Slavs, blue-collar workers, and many others. It wasn't the Upper East Side, but people had a roof over their heads, and factories nearby and affordable stores for the basics on just about every corner.

During the West Village fight, Jacobs recalled hearing about a city plan to raze part of the neighborhood. Before backing off the proposal, the Wagner administration had targeted twelve blocks in the area south of Houston Street, or SoHo, as it would come to be known, for urban renewal, to make way for low- and middle-income housing towers. As she headed back to the West Village, the parallels with her own neighborhood were clear. Here was a place that had all the elements that she had described as the model of city living in *The Death and Life of Great American Cities*. And here, again, the city planners thought they could tear it all down and create something better.

Urban renewal spared SoHo. Now Moses was proposing a highway that would destroy the neighborhood for good. Perhaps thinking he could steamroll the residents and small businesses along Broome Street much easier than in midtown, Moses was poised to do as much harm as any urban renewal scheme, or more. La Mountain's flock was being assaulted by a new enemy that Jacobs would dedicate the rest of her life to fighting: the urban freeway. Moses wanted to pave big swaths of the city, and someone needed to stand up and fight it. "It's all part of a huge interstate network . . . they're getting it approved a piece at a time so people won't be able to grasp the whole picture," Jacobs said later. She believed that if the highway building wasn't stopped immediately, they'd "be fighting the tentacles of this stupid octopus forever."

She had made her decision. She would join the fight. Within days, she and her old ally DeSalvio were named co-chairs of a re-branded community organization: the Joint Committee to Stop the Lower Manhattan Expressway.

~~~

M oving quickly to try to seize momentum, Jacobs obtained the known schedule for official hearings on anything relevant to the highway proposal. She helped organize the residents—most of whom had rarely ventured outside the cluster of city blocks of their neighborhood—to clamber onto buses and make the short trip to City Hall. Building on the success of the ribbon tying at Washington Square Park, she helped orchestrate photo opportunities to make the opposition more theatrical— outfitting residents at one hearing with gas masks, symbolizing the soot and exhaust they envisioned filling the air if Lomex was built, and then organizing a parade through the neighborhood modeled after a New Orleans funeral march. With the help of the local artist Harry Jackson, Jacobs sought to conjure the death and destruction of a neighborhood—a theme that would resurface again and again, with pickets in the form of tombstones, adorned with skulls and crossbones and the slogan "Little Italy—Killed by Progress," or, simply, "Death of a Neighborhood." In turn, because Lomex was an act of violence, it must itself be "killed," as the protest signs said. There was a steady rain on the evening of the funeral march down Broome Street, but still enough light for photographers to take pictures. About a hundred protesters met in the rain at the corner of Broome and Sullivan, and they all stopped near Mulberry Street in Little Italy, near the Church of the Most Holy Crucifix, for speeches. Jacobs addressed the crowd after DeSalvio, the state senator Joseph Marro, and the state representative Leonard Farbstein, decrying the uprooting of more than two thousand people. The marchers walked all the way to the Upper East Side to Gracie Mansion, the gated home that Moses himself convinced Fiorello La Guardia to buy to be the New York City mayor's residence, and delivered a letter to Mayor Wagner, urging him to cancel land acquisitions for Lomex.

In short order, fighting Lomex became a cause célèbre. Bob Dylan— not yet the celebrity he would soon become, somewhere between the albums containing the songs "Blowin' in the Wind" and "The Times They Are A-Changin' "—wrote a protest song about the Lower Manhattan Expressway, listing the melodic street names in the area—Delancey,

Broome, Mulberry—and provided it to the anti-highway campaigners to sing at future demonstrations.

Moses and his allies responded in typical fashion: a few zealous activists must not be permitted to stand in the way of the city's future. "Every delay gives added hope to those who indulge themselves in partisan politics and who make municipal progress a dirty word," said William J. Gottlieb, president of the Automobile Club of New York. Private developers deal with the relocation of tenants all the time, he said, and "these improvements would not have happened if the men behind the private projects had wavered each time a voice was raised in protest."

Wagner had promised a full report with a specific timetable for relocations, and put a young Hispanic politician, Herman Badillo, in charge of it. When Badillo failed to produce the report on time, Jacobs reminded reporters that Wagner himself had promised there would be no expressway if no "feasible relocation plan . . . [was] produced." City Hall showed some signs of nervousness. As about a hundred residents marched outside carrying pickets and paintings expressing their opposition to the Lower Manhattan Expressway, the mayor and the Board of Estimate again delayed a vote on condemnation proceedings, agreeing to wait until after the November elections of 1962. The residents were "outraged at this cat-and-mouse game of postponement," Jacobs proclaimed.

The city finally released Badillo's report in December, asserting that new housing would be found for all displaced residents. The Joint Committee to Stop the Lower Manhattan Expressway issued a statement that the report "cannot bail out this scandal-ridden expressway proposal that Robert Moses has been trying to bulldoze through this city since the 1940s." What the city should be releasing for public scrutiny is engineering and economic data that prove the highway is feasible and necessary, the committee said—especially since other east-west routes were newly available, such as the Cross Bronx Expressway and the Verrazano-Narrows Bridge.

At the same time, Jacobs recruited new allies, such as Lewis Mumford, the architecture critic for the *New Yorker,* to the ranks of those speaking out against the highway. Approaching Mumford had not been easy, since Jacobs had criticized him in *Death and Life* and Mumford had panned the book in the *New Yorker.* But Mumford had begun to sour on the idea of a vast highway network in and around New York, and the over-reliance on cars. In a *New York Times* story he was quoted saying that

Lomex "would be the first serious step in turning New York into Los Angeles . . . Since Los Angeles has already discovered the futility of sacrificing its living space to expressways and parking lots, why should New York
follow that backward example?"

Others rallied to the cause: the New York Society of Architects; Artists
Against the Expressway, founded by Jim Stratton, who has also been
credited with coining the term "SoHo"; and the Lower East Side Businessmen's Association, whose unofficial headquarters was Ratner's dairy,
a restaurant in the path of the highway on Delancey Street, owned by
Harold "Hy" Harmatz. Leon Seidel from the Lion's Head and Rachelle
Wall, veterans of the West Village fight, also joined the merry band of
highway fighters.

Jacobs also continued to cultivate the media. Ordinary citizens fighting City Hall made good copy, and she was expert at spotting reporters
she knew needed a quotation. Approaching the television reporter Gabe
Pressman at one rally, she provided the sound bite she knew would make
the evening news: "The expressway would Los Angelize New York." The
press was intrigued by what Jacobs was suggesting—that instead of accommodating the automobile, New York City should actually make it
harder to drive everywhere. The dense urban neighborhoods would function much better by relying on mass transit, walking, and bicycles.
Though today New York is following her advice, building new subway
lines and deterring traffic by keeping tolls high and parking costly, fifty
years ago working against the car was the ultimate contrarian notion. The
Moses view seemed to make much more sense. "We always have been
trying to catch up instead of keeping ahead of traffic congestion," he said.
His highway network "may be postponed at enormous ultimate cost, but
it cannot in the end be avoided, for you cannot just wish the automobile
away."

It was a precarious business to stand up to Robert Moses, as La
Mountain discovered just before Christmas in 1962. One evening, La
Mountain informed Jacobs that he would not be able to come to a critical Board of Estimate hearing on the project, saying he had to visit a sick
friend in Massachusetts. But in fact he had been summoned to a meeting at an archdiocese office behind St. Patrick's Cathedral in midtown,
where a church administrator informed La Mountain that he should
lower his profile in the fight against the Lower Manhattan Expressway.
He was ordered not to breathe a word of this instruction. No one could

ever prove how the silencing of the unruly pastor came about, but Moses did have close ties with the archbishop of the diocese, Francis Joseph Cardinal Spellman.

At the Board of Estimate hearing, with La Mountain absent, Jacobs was left to play the role of master of ceremonies, introducing speakers. DeSalvio took to the microphone and let loose against Moses. "Except for one old man, I have been unable to find anyone of technical competence who truly is for this so-called expressway," he said. This "cantankerous and stubborn old man" should "realize that too many of his technicians' dreams turn into a nightmare for the city." The proposed highway was a "monstrous and useless folly," said Jacobs, one of forty-four opponents to testify. The arguments for it, she said, amounted to "piffle."

The comments had their intended effect. The press began to portray the highway in overwhelmingly negative terms, and the mayor and the Board of Estimate had little stomach to stand up for it. On December 11, 1962, Wagner backed off just enough to allow the Board of Estimate to halt the condemnation proceedings for the corridor—and to begin the process for removing Lomex from the city map of planned arterials. Most New Yorkers didn't know about the victory, because the action came in the middle of a two-day citywide newspaper strike, leaving a tiny Italian-American paper, the *New York Daily Report,* with the scoop: "Downtown Expressway Plan Killed."

The merchants, artists, liberals, and conservatives of the Joint Committee to Stop the Lower Manhattan Expressway rejoiced. Jacobs's message was being heard: the city is for people, not cars. In solidarity, Jacobs planted a tree with La Mountain in front of the church on Broome Street.

"We won! Isn't it marvelous!" Jacobs scrawled to her mother on the side of the headline in the *New York Daily Report.*

"You can well imagine what went on behind the scenes!" she wrote in the margin of a December 12 *Village Voice* story headlined "Political Powerhouse Kills Broome Street Expressway." The note was to her brother and his wife. "A traffic man told me this was the first time in the whole United States a (federal) interstate highway had been killed. Love, Jane."

The only thing left to do was to convince City Hall and the New York state legislature that the Lower Manhattan Expressway should be "demapped"—removed from official city documents as a proposed arterial.

But as Jacobs would later say, bad projects have to be killed several times before they go away for good.

~~~~

Moses bided his time. He had waited out the opposition before. He let Jacobs relish the victory for the first few months of 1963—and then mounted an aggressive campaign to bring Lomex back from the dead. The highway was crucial for relieving congestion and hugely important for economic development, he believed, and had been unfairly pilloried. He promised a new, comprehensive report on the rationale for all the planned arterials, including the Lower Manhattan Expressway, and again warned that any talk of "demapping" the expressway was a "clear invitation to remove huge sums of federal and state metropolitan arterial funds to other more progressive communities." The Downtown–Lower Manhattan Association, joined by the Regional Plan Association and new allies, such as the Citizens Union and the Commerce and Industry Association, urged the city to reconsider.

"No matter where a construction project is planned, the people of the area object very strenuously," said Peter J. Brennan, president of the Building and Construction Trades Council of Greater New York. "If our city planners were to give in to all of these people, our city would still be a cow pasture with Indians running around."

Now Jacobs was being portrayed as obstructionist. "I have yet to hear of anything in New York that [her] group is for," said the city transportation commissioner, Henry Barnes. Jacobs was "a Jeanne d'Arc protesting [on behalf of] the people . . . [but] in the years to come she will be known as the one who has done the most to keep New Yorkers from progressing." Nevertheless, Jacobs and DeSalvio went back to work, tramping down to the City Hall hearing room for more testimony and chances to get quoted in the morning papers, trying to stir up more outrage that Moses was seeking to revive a plan that had been voted down by elected officials. "Just who does this high priest Moses think he is? Does he know more than Mayor Wagner or the people who know how to run this city?" De-Salvio frothed before the planning commission, which entertained a reconsideration of the project. "Moses is convinced he's a junior God."

In 1964, Moses was sworn in as chairman of the Triborough Bridge and Tunnel Authority—his sixth six-year term at the agency. After the cer-

emony, the wily seventy-five-year-old found himself surrounded by reporters. Despite the setback in 1962, the Lower Manhattan Expressway
would soon be built, he predicted. He hinted at a plan to build housing as
part of the project, to accommodate evicted residents. "It's before the
mayor for action. I wouldn't spend any time talking about it if I didn't
think it was going to be built."

The pro-highway forces began to loom larger—more and more business, real estate, and civic groups were urging construction, along with
the American Institute of Architects and the Municipal Art Society, both
of whom warmed to the project as a major redevelopment of a sagging
section of the city. The building trades grew more vociferous, too, arguing
that the project would provide jobs for two thousand construction workers. The Joint Committee to Stop the Lower Manhattan Expressway responded by trotting out a different group of union workers—waiters and
bartenders and deliverymen, who said that Lomex would obliterate ten
thousand jobs. The opposition flaunted its diversity, designating different
leaders for the SoHo section, the Italian community, and the Spanish-
speaking residents of the neighborhood. Anthony Dapolito, the unofficial
mayor of Greenwich Village, formed a citywide group against the expressway to bolster the committee's work. Members of the Joint Committee to
Stop the Lower Manhattan Expressway filed suit to prod the city to take
action one way or the other; small property owners complained about declining property values, and big banks like Manufacturers Hanover said
they put expansion plans on hold, amid the uncertainty. Lomex "would
turn downtown Manhattan into a construction camp for years," Jacobs
said, while also predicting that mid-Manhattan and upper Manhattan expressways would quickly follow if Lomex went through.

"The basic problem in New York is that the government long ago
ceased to be a government of and for the people it governs," Jacobs told
the editorial writers of the *New York Herald Tribune* in an interview. "The
people of the city are being utterly disregarded."

In the midst of the standoff, proposals for a newfangled Lomex began
to emerge. In a reprise of its proposal for the Mid-Manhattan Expressway,
the Regional Plan Association proposed putting the highway underground, presaging Boston's Big Dig by forty years. A "cut and cover" section toward the on-ramps to the Williamsburg Bridge would allow parks,
open space, housing, and other development over the sunken roadway.
The American Institute of Architects called for a completely fresh ap-

proach to designing a less disruptive roadway. One architect suggested going in the opposite direction—lifting the highway higher, in a Habitrail-like tube he called a "sky tunnel," a hundred feet above the streets and many buildings, reducing the need for demolition. By contrast, the City Club argued that the plan for demolition didn't go far enough: a wide swath on either side of the elevated highway should be razed so the city could start over with new parks and residential buildings, forever wiping away the hundred acres of "hopeless commercial slums."

As he did with the Mid-Manhattan Expressway, Moses dismissed the idea of a tunnel, citing the expense of digging under Broome Street, which would mean weaving over and under subway lines and thick bundles of utilities and water and sewer lines. He told the papers the idea of depressing the highway would save no money and few buildings—and was depressing in and of itself, as one *Daily News* headline put it. An elevated roadway had the added virtue, he said, of providing fourteen hundred new parking spaces under the structure. But Moses's most important work was behind the scenes, stirring the growing impatience and frustration at City Hall, questioning why a perfectly sound proposal couldn't proceed as is, and encouraging powerful allies like David Rockefeller and Harry Van Arsdale, president of the New York City Central Labor Council, to keep up the pressure on Wagner. "We better start planning for five or six expressways that will take us across Manhattan," Van Arsdale said.

Moses had reclaimed momentum in favor of the project. The members of the Board of Estimate, the equivalent of a city council, changed their views depending on who was most vociferous at the time—community opposition in 1962, and then business and civic groups three years later. The board reversed course, reopening the process for land acquisition. Mayor Wagner flip-flopped as well. In what would be his last term, he decided not to cave in to neighborhood pressure. He first hinted at his decision by vowing there would be no more postponements: "We're not going to stall this thing along." Convinced that the project was crucial for the city's economic development, he made the stunning announcement in May 1965: The $110 million Lower Manhattan Expressway, paid for with $90 million in federal funds, would proceed. Construction would begin as "quickly as possible," and the two-hundred-foot-wide, eight-lane elevated roadway, with the final dozen blocks submerged from the Bowery to the Williamsburg Bridge on-ramps—his concession to make at least part of the roadway submerged where it was most technically feasible—should be completed by 1971. As part of the project, the Triborough Bridge and Tunnel Authority would build a massive $10 million housing complex at the site of the Beaux Arts police headquarters building to accommodate 460 evicted residents from the Broome Street area.

"Most gratifying," Moses said when called for comment about the mayor's decision.

As residents gathered for special prayer services in the churches set to be bulldozed, the city prepared to take bids on the first construction contracts. "A world is being destroyed, a way of life," said a weary La Mountain, defying the orders from his superiors to keep quiet. "There are people here 80 years old who have never lived anywhere else. The neighborhood is everything to them."

It was once again a dark time for Broome Street. Members of the Joint Committee to Stop the Lower Manhattan Expressway lashed out at Wagner for turning on them. But his term was coming to an end, and he had announced he would not seek reelection; he would later become ambassador to Spain. Moses, it seemed, had won.

There was only one hope: a dashing young Republican congressman named John V. Lindsay was running for mayor of New York. The charismatic forty-three-year-old had first befriended Jacobs during the battle over Washington Square Park and then remained an ally in the urban renewal fight in the West Village. He wasted little time joining the citizens opposed to Lomex, staying in touch with Jacobs to get a sense of what the people of the neighborhoods were thinking. It soon became clear that he viewed opposition to the Lower Manhattan Expressway as a way to cultivate the support of a large constituency, and adopted it as a key part of his platform.

Lindsay began to speak out against the destruction the project would bring and proposed an alternative loop around the southern tip of Manhattan. In the summer of 1965 he stepped into a helicopter with the architect Philip Johnson to view the city from above and came away "depressed" by the physical landscape that Moses had wrought. The sight of the elevated Prospect Expressway in Brooklyn "made it imperative to re-examine expressways and what they do to cities," he said.

Lindsay called Wagner's lame-duck endorsement of the project "an outrage" and urged the administration to leave the decision on the Lower Manhattan Expressway to the next mayor. Moving ahead with the first construction contracts, he said, was "a basic contempt for the wishes and welfare of the people who make up the neighborhoods of New York City. We have learned—or should have learned—that elevated structures are outmoded."

Lindsay campaigned through the summer of 1965 and became Jacobs's biggest ally. He promised to use his position as a congressman to hold up federal funding and the approval process from Washington. His Democratic opponent, the city comptroller, Abraham Beame, also questioned the need for Lomex and sympathized with the people in its path. Beame, however, did not satisfy Jacobs with his commitment against it, and she echoed comments by a rival describing his "little accountant's mind." Lindsay narrowly defeated Beame and moved into City Hall promising a new era for New York, one that did not include a highway through lower Manhattan. Moses watched and waited as yet another mayoral transition—the fifth of his career—got under way.

~~~~

With this new obstacle in place, Moses redoubled his efforts to convince the press and the public that the area that would become known as SoHo was not worth saving. To build on the perception that the neighborhood was blighted, Moses hunted down damning statistics on building code violations, fires, vacant buildings and lots, and declining property assessments from every corner of the city bureaucracy. "We would appreciate photos or records of our department indicating the conditions of these buildings inside and out," he wrote to the building commissioner. He urged the city transportation chief to furnish "candid interior photographs" of buildings in the path of the expressway, juxtaposed with the promise of "sanitary substitute housing" that would be built as part of the project. And he made sure the record was made available to reporters: One of every five buildings partly or completely vacant. No new development since 1929. Most of the residents had lived there six years or less. Two-thirds of the residential buildings in the highway's path had pending Building Department violations, one-third of the commercial buildings had Fire Department violations, and hundreds lacked adequate fireproofing. The assessed property value along Broome Street was under $20 a square foot, compared with $660 around Wall Street.

The grim portrayal opened the way for downtown businessmen to argue that SoHo was dragging down all of lower Manhattan. "That area is our neighbor," said David Rockefeller. "Nobody likes to have an unfortunate neighbor next door. The expressway will be the occasion for a lot of clearing and opening up. It will bring in a lot of light and air," he said, echoing the modernist theories of urban renewal.

There was certainly a lack of investment and plenty of boarded-up buildings, countered Jacobs and others—particularly Hy Harmatz, the restaurant owner—but it was because the threat of the highway had been looming for more than twenty years. No sane business would locate in the corridor, and no banks would invest in alternative improvements. The same thing happened when neighborhoods were targeted for urban renewal, Jacobs said. It was a self-fulfilling prophecy: the neighborhood was blighted, and so a highway should go through it; but the neighborhood was blighted because the city planned to put a highway through it. And even with the death sentence on the area, some businesses continued to thrive there—and Moses was not including in his calculations the loss of tax revenue that would occur when they were displaced.

By the time Lindsay was elected, however, another potent defense of Broome Street had emerged: the nascent historic preservation movement. Starting in earnest in the early 1960s, a coalition of New Yorkers began to rise up against the demolition of historic buildings, including Penn Station. In response, the city formed the Landmarks Preservation Commission in 1965, amid increased awareness that New York's architectural and cultural heritage was being lost, despite the possibility in many cases for the historic buildings to be spruced up and reused. Not only individual buildings but entire districts—Greenwich Village was among the first in line for this honor—were becoming eligible for historic designation. No demolition or alteration could occur if the landmarks commission deemed that buildings had historic significance and character.

Proving that significance required hard work and research, and one young woman in particular came to the defense of the "Palaces of Trade" in the path of the Lower Manhattan Expressway: Margot McCoy Gayle. Born in Kansas City, Gayle had become politically active at a young age, campaigning to repeal the poll tax while living in Georgia. In 1932 she married and raised two daughters in New York, working as a radio writer and then running unsuccessfully for city council in 1957. Her first foray into local politics came when she led the fight to stop the razing of the Jefferson Market Courthouse, an 1877 Victorian Gothic building with turrets and a clock tower, in Greenwich Village. She went on to found the Friends of Cast Iron Architecture in 1970, led tours of cast-iron buildings, and distributed logo magnets that could be slapped on the buildings to test for iron. Author of the book *Cast-Iron Architecture in America,* Gayle would almost single-handedly ensure that SoHo was declared a landmark district. The 139 iron-front buildings in SoHo today, she proudly proclaimed, are more than any other place in the world.

Like Shirley Hayes, Margot Gayle would be an important ally for Jacobs, although the two never became close friends. Gayle and Jacobs had first met during the campaign to save the Jefferson Market building in Greenwich Village and repair its big clock. Gayle's practical approach, Jacobs later wrote, "not only culminated in saving and reusing the building, but taught me (and many others) the importance of starting with doable things and building upon those."

In the Lower Manhattan Expressway fight, historic preservation became quite literally a roadblock. In 1966, the city ratified a Landmarks Preservation Commission designation for the E. V. Haughwout building at 488–492 Broadway, at the corner of Broadway and Broome—directly in the path of the expressway. Moses lobbied hard to keep the classic cast-iron building from getting historic protection and interfering with his condemnation and demolition schedule. The building was of "dubious historical and artistic value," he wrote to the city's transportation administrator. "Certainly this is no way to dispose of the Lower Manhattan project." Moses also fought to keep the Beaux Arts police headquarters building from getting protection; he wanted to demolish it and build housing at the site for residents displaced by the highway.

Margot Gayle had successfully introduced historic preservation as a new issue in the Lomex fight. But Moses sought to change the subject. What was really at issue was not a few quaint old buildings but the way the area was being choked by congestion.

Traffic jams were something everybody could relate to. Despite the largest public transit system in the world, more and more commuters were using single-occupancy vehicles to get in and around the city, mixing uncomfortably with taxis and buses and delivery vans and freight trucks of all kinds. From the end of World War II to 1960, getting around by motorized transportation had become notoriously difficult. Congestion along Canal Street, the major east-west boulevard across lower Manhattan two blocks south of Broome Street, was a cause for concern for the economic health of lower Manhattan, Moses argued. It was often faster to walk. Congestion was bad for city neighborhoods, leading to deterioration and the worsening of slum conditions and declining property values. The highway would improve conditions within a several-block radius—a kind of salvation by expressway—and pave the way for economic growth in the area.

"One of the principal reasons for the undesirable character of the neighborhood is the ever-present heavy traffic with its accompaniments of congestion, noise and confusion," wrote M. J. Madigan, president of Madigan-Hyland Inc., one of Moses's favorite engineering consultants, which Moses had hired for the project. "Construction of the Lower Manhattan Expressway will remove this burden from the local streets and will allow the area to develop its own character with benefit both to residents, to local business and to the city of New York as a whole."

"What is now little more than a fume-filled traffic corridor will become a true neighborhood," a Moses deputy added.

For Moses, the Lower Manhattan Expressway had become an obsession; with the Mid-Manhattan Expressway defeated, it was the one chance to prove that crosstown routes would be the city's salvation. The moment had come to put a public-relations campaign into high gear. Moses ordered his consulting firm to publish a new, colorful brochure detailing the "inescapable logic" of the Lower Manhattan Expressway. But to make the case as powerfully as possible, he turned into a filmmaker. *This Urgent Need,* an eight-minute production in 16-millimeter black and white, depicted "the slow strangulation of a neighborhood, and of a city." Every day, more than 70,000 vehicles attempted to cross Manhattan in the area of Broome Street, taking thirty minutes for the trip at two to three miles per hour. Another 200,000 vehicles trying to move north and south faced this "blockade," while 100,000 more idled on the Manhattan and Williamsburg bridges, waiting to get in. Three-quarters of a million people were being delayed, "a tragic waste of man-hours and money, measured in tens of millions"; delivery trucks couldn't get to local businesses, speeding the decline of an area that already had the lowest growth rate, lowest property values, and lowest tax revenue. Images of "For Rent" and "No Loitering" signs flash across the screen.

"Now, look at the solution," the film's narrator continues, his tone becoming cheerful: "a Lower Manhattan Expressway," part of a national system of interstate and defense highways, paid for almost entirely by state and federal funds, providing an "express connection" between local Manhattan streets and New Jersey, Brooklyn, and Queens; it will serve 450,000 vehicles, remove 60 percent of through traffic from local streets, "cut accident and injury," save fifteen million man-hours and $25 million a year. "We must have a Lower Manhattan Expressway now."

Jacobs and the Lomex opponents, however, spotted some flaws in the argument. The highway would have two Manhattan exits. How much would that help local traffic and delivery trucks get around? They had indeed caught Moses in a conundrum: he'd told the city officials that most of the usage of the new road would be local, but had simultaneously assured federal officials that most vehicles would speed right through Manhattan. As Interstate 78, Lomex would essentially be a bypass. SoHo, Little Italy, Chinatown, and the Lower East Side would be decimated so Long Island and New Jersey could have a free transportation corridor.

Building new roads to accommodate this traffic was itself a fool's errand anyway, Jacobs argued, because the freshly built highways just fill up with the cars and trucks that flock to them. That view was endorsed by some dissidents within the Wagner administration, including Henry Stern, the future parks commissioner. "Traffic is usually self-generating," Stern said. The phenomenon had already been witnessed in some of the other roadways Moses had built in New York—free-flowing on opening day, but soon so popular, hopelessly clogged.

When John Lindsay was inaugurated as mayor in 1966, he faced a stark choice: preserve the neighborhood or build a highway to accommodate the swift flow of traffic, accepting the idea that it would jump-start economic development. Ultimately, the construction workers—the benefactors of federal largesse, along with consultants and engineers and others whose businesses existed because of such projects—would change his mind. Peter Brennan, president of the Building and Construction Trades Council, threatened a citywide work stoppage by 200,000 workers in protest of delays on major projects, including Lomex. "Stop blocking traffic—and jobs!" the labor pickets said.

As a candidate, Lindsay found it easy enough to criticize Wagner's stance on Lomex, but now that he was in office, he found himself faced with a desperate need for economic development and construction workers threatening to strike. He began to think the highway might figure in after all, as part of a transformation of all of lower Manhattan. But he knew he couldn't simply reverse course and support the same project he had castigated Wagner for endorsing. So he set out to design a better road.

~~~~

When Lindsay acknowledged that some kind of multilane highway was necessary to traverse lower Manhattan, Broome Street held out hope that if he really meant that, he would surely build a tunnel all the way across the island and leave the neighborhood on the surface un-scathed.

A tunnel was indeed one of three alternatives Lindsay was consider-ing, in addition to a new route around the southern tip of Manhattan and a proposal to merely widen an existing crosstown thoroughfare, either Canal Street or Houston Street. The spin by the administration was that the mayor was keeping true to his campaign pledge, which was to aban-don the Lower Manhattan Expressway as proposed. But as he sent his planners to their drafting tables, the fresh ideas kept reverting to the basic Moses plan.

In the spring of 1966, Lindsay hired a consulting firm that came up with a possible solution—a new version of the skyway that had been pro-posed years earlier, eighty feet high and soaring above the buildings of Broome Street, which could be left intact. The ramps of the roadway could run right through the upper floors of buildings. A "high expressway of suitable design would permit light and air to reach homes, stores and factories and would scarcely be noticed by local travelers down below," a draft report said. A Lindsay aide said it would solve the traffic problem "without knocking down half the town." A narrow, double-decked struc-ture, with eastbound traffic on one level and westbound traffic under-neath, was also considered.

The skyway scheme was ultimately rejected—and so was a deeply bored tunnel. Word of a "secret plan" to reconfigure Lomex with a combi-nation of elevated platforms and more shallow sunken sections leaked out in the spring of 1967. Ed Koch, Carol Greitzer, and Paul Douglas, who had been named as a new liaison between City Hall and the lower Man-hattan community, sent a telegram to Lindsay warning that any proposal that wasn't a deep tunnel from the Hudson to the East River, or that ran along the southern edge of Manhattan, was "a complete betrayal of the principles and concepts proclaimed by the . . . administration. It is in direct contradiction to the principle of routing traffic around or under Manhattan."

Finally, Lindsay swallowed hard and unveiled his new version of Lomex. The new plan was front-page news on March 28, 1967. The Lower Manhattan Expressway should be built, he announced, but as a truly modern superhighway, based on what engineers call "cut and cover" construction—an open trench running along the north side of Broome Street, requiring extensive demolition but also making possible new air-rights development over the sunken highway. Depressing the road opened up urban design possibilities—a center mall, park space, and housing. Broome Street and Kenmare Street, one block to the north, would be made into three-lane surface routes on either side. On-ramps connecting to the Holland Tunnel and the West Side Highway would be above grade, but otherwise the roadway would dive down in an "open cut" at about Sixth Avenue and remain submerged until it rose up again to join the entrances of the Manhattan and Williamsburg bridges. Where the Moses plan required the demolition of 2,000 homes and 800 commercial and industrial buildings, the Lindsay proposal called for razing only 650 homes and 400 commercial structures. Construction would begin in 1969, and the new price tag would be $150 million.

The reconstituted Lomex was "probably the most dramatic breakthrough the nation has yet seen in the planning of highways through congested urban areas," Lindsay said, but he knew the people of Broome Street would not share his perspective. Lindsay tried to differentiate himself from Moses, but Jacobs saw that the basic corridor was exactly the same. "The underground idea is better than the elevated highway proposal, but we don't want to see any highway at all," DeSalvio told a reporter for the *Times*.

Even Lindsay's attempts to create excitement by linking housing to the highway and promoting futuristic possibilities of air-rights development—one scheme by the architects Ulrich Franzen and Paul Rudolph called for a series of structures straddling the highway that looked variously like pyramids and towering bookshelves atop the sunken road—were reminiscent of Moses's Le Corbusier–inspired vision for the Mid-Manhattan Expressway. The "City Corridor" would marry the superhighway and modernist urban development, just as Moses dreamed. The solution to the displacement of people was to make housing part of the highway.

The simple highway Moses started working on back in 1940 had turned into a swerving, diving road with parks and the potential for *Jetsons*-like housing on top—but the public response remained muted. "The in-out, over-and-under proposal that has come out of this attempt to defang the monster makes no one very happy," the architecture critic Ada Louise Huxtable later wrote in the *New York Times*. "Ducking subways, utilities and the water table, it struggles above and below ground in a series of curious compromises of tortuous complexity, complete with enough entrances, exits and connections to turn Lower Manhattan into a concrete no-man's land. Displaced people will now number in the low thousands rather than the high thousands. It is a question of degree; do you kill a city or maim it?"

The residents of lower Manhattan were exasperated. The project was off under Wagner, then back on again; then off under Lindsay, then back on. "The citizenry never wins the battle on this project. When we beat them, they take the package back, dress it up a little and offer it again in the hope we'll wear out," said Koch, who had moved from congressman to the city council and remained a staunch anti-expressway ally. "It doesn't matter who the mayor is."

Jacobs couldn't agree more. It didn't matter who the mayor was, because the one constant since 1940 had been Moses, who kept the pressure on and made sure the bureaucratic machinery remained intact to move ahead with the construction project, regardless of a change in administrations. It didn't even matter that Lindsay had removed Moses from his official role as city arterials coordinator; he had just as much influence from his perch at the Triborough Bridge and Tunnel Authority. It was eerily reminiscent of Wagner's replacement of Moses with Felt and Davies to lead the housing and urban renewal agenda. Moses was still the man behind the curtain. It was critical, Jacobs said, to remember the origins of this "ridiculous" idea—"the product of stupid, incompetent minds."

~~~~

As the expressway fight moved into the tumultuous year of 1968, it was only one of many tensions tearing at New York. The assassination of Martin Luther King and the ensuing race riots, economic decline, and the Vietnam War revealed an established order increasingly frayed. The city pulsed with rebellion and challenge; citizen activists felt emboldened to question just about everything. In the tumult, both Moses and Jacobs moved into new phases of disenchantment, and were pushed to extremes.

From his power base at the Triborough Bridge and Tunnel Authority, Moses, seventy-nine years old, continued to roll out big ideas even as the Lomex project was delayed. One of them was a 6.5-mile bridge from Oyster Bay, Long Island, to Rye and Port Chester, New York, at the Connecticut state line. The monster span, just shy of the record-setting Chesapeake Bay Bridge Tunnel project in Virginia, would allow Long Islanders to get to New England without going through New York City.

But though Moses was still dreaming big, getting New York officials to go along with his plans was becoming more difficult. He found himself challenged publicly as never before. The New York State Senate subpoenaed him to explain his funding arrangements with the federal government; newspaper photographers captured the moment when he was handed the subpoena. Congressman William F. Ryan ordered an inquiry into Moses's purported amassing of millions in federal grants for projects that had not been fully approved. Even old allies on the Triborough Bridge and Tunnel Authority board challenged him, notably George V. McLaughlin, who objected to the publication of the new brochure justifying Lomex, when a new mayor had been elected and should have been allowed to make his own decision.

Moses was unaccustomed to affronts of this kind, and cut back on public appearances even more. He decamped from One Gracie Terrace to Long Island and Great South Bay. His first wife, Mary, had died in 1966, following a long illness. For most of the half century she was married to Moses, Mary was supportive, outfitting her husband when he wore suits, shirts, and shoes to the point they disintegrated. But she seemed disappointed that Moses remained distant and so focused on his career, and began drinking. The same year Mary died, Moses married his longtime secretary, Mary Grady, an employee of the Triborough Bridge and Tunnel Authority who had already spent time with Moses. It was a second marriage of singular but very private devotion, and Moses looked forward to evenings at home with "Mary II," as some aides secretly called her. Often he would plunge into the Atlantic Ocean for a long solo swim before dinner.

Jacobs, meanwhile, was feeling marginalized for her own reasons. She grew more discouraged at how her government kept pressing ahead with bad plans, despite all the pleas and counterarguments she and the citi-zenry had made. "I hate the government for making my life absurd," she told a magazine interviewer years after the Lomex fight. She had re-mained an outside agitator from the day she answered the State Depart-ment interrogatory on her communist leanings, but it seemed that an even more intense brand of radicalism was required for the government to even take note of those it was supposed to represent.

On a spring day in 1967, she locked arms with protesters against the Vietnam War, blocking the entrance to the Whitehall Street induction center. It was a three-day demonstration, and the police began to cart off the protesters one by one. Jacobs was arrested along with the writer Susan Sontag, the poet Allen Ginsberg, the writer and activist Grace Paley, the pediatrician Benjamin Spock, and 259 others. Jacobs was photographed in a crowded, fluorescent-lit jail cell, sitting patiently with Sontag, behind bars. The two women chatted about the dynamics of dissent.

When she first took up the neighborhood fight in the West Village, Ja-cobs was able to catch New York officialdom off guard, with her peppery quotations and photo-op stunts. Now she was a known commodity, and City Hall had grown inured to her tactics. They were not listening. As she now realized, it would take more dramatic gestures to get attention for the cause against the Lower Manhattan Expressway.

~~~~~

The hearing on the Lower Manhattan Expressway at Seward Park High School on April 10, 1968, was hastily scheduled, but Jacobs heard about it just in time to meet with the Lomex opponents beforehand. They agreed that the meeting was a sham. The New York State transportation agency wanted to collect public comments on the project to fulfill its obligations under new rules designed to gauge the impact of major proj-ects on the surrounding area. The officials would just be recording the comments and putting them in a report. It wasn't as if anything anybody said would change their minds about moving ahead with the project. This was a meeting that needed to be disrupted, Jacobs said. The opponents should take a stand with an act of civil disobedience.

Her prediction that the Seward Park High School gathering was no true public hearing was confirmed when she arrived at the auditorium after 9:00 p.m., after the meeting had started. The state had set up an in-formation table in the entryway with copies of a glossy pamphlet called "A

Better Lower Manhattan," which touted Lomex as a solution to crippling congestion, enabling the speedy delivery of goods in lower Manhattan and revitalizing the tawdry slums that had festered in the area. She took a pamphlet, wrote her name on the sign-up sheet for speakers, and took a seat at the front of the hall.

It was then she noticed that the microphone had been set up so the speakers addressed the crowd, and not the transportation agency officials seated at a table on the stage. The residents and small-business owners went up one by one, saying the highway would devastate their lives and their homes. As a stenotypist moved her hands rhythmically over the key tabs of her machine off to the side, the speakers were constantly reminded of a time limit. A man talking about the dangers of air pollution was told he was taking too long. The audience began shouting questions about the project, but the transportation men said they were there only to provide basic information and hear testimony. The local representative of the Liberal Party, which had broken from both Democrats and Republicans to back progressive, "good government" candidates, was at the microphone when the crowd began their chant of "We want Jane."

At the microphone, Jacobs made her comment that the citizens were oddly addressing themselves and not the officials. John Toth, the top official from the New York Department of Transportation who was chairing the hearing, came down from the stage to turn the microphone around, and Jacobs swiveled it back. "Thank you, sir, but I'd rather speak to my friends," she said. "We've been talking to ourselves all evening as it is."

Her speech was succinct. At a time when affordable housing was scarce, the government proposed destroying the homes of two thousand families. At a time when unemployment was high, the government wanted to wipe out small businesses and warehouses and factories representing thousands of jobs, many of them held by minorities. The government, she said, was acting like inmates of an insane asylum. The people didn't want this highway, but no one was listening. And she issued her warning: "If the expressway is put through, there will be anarchy."

It was time to give the "errand boys" who "had been sent by their betters from Albany" a message to take back to the capital, as Jacobs recalled later. She announced that she would walk up the steps to the stage behind her and march past the officials' table in a silent protest. Anyone who felt as outraged as she did was welcome to join her.

The residents who had met with Jacobs before the hearing sprang to their feet, taking her cue as they had planned. They were joined by several others—about fifty in total—who followed Jacobs up the steps and onto the stage. "You can't come up here," Toth said. "Get off the stage!" When Jacobs informed him that the citizens were going to march across the stage and down the other side, Toth summoned the New York City police officers assigned to the meeting. "Arrest this woman!" he shouted.

The terrified stenotypist, seated off to the side of the officials' table, picked up her equipment and batted at the protesters as they walked ominously close by. Patrolman Joseph McGovern asked Jacobs to move away from the marchers. Then the moment came to execute what had been discussed in the opposition's pre-meeting plan: make a mess of the stenotype paper, so the record of the hearing would be destroyed. One protester, Frances Goldman, grabbed a bunch and tossed it into the air. Others trampled the wads of paper that had tumbled out onto the stage as Toth and the transportation men tried to gather up the evidence of their hearing. What a grand melee, Jacobs thought. The stenotype tape of the hearing was all over the place, like confetti.

Jacobs climbed down from the stage, where the patrolman had told her to remain. "Listen to this! There is no record!" she announced into the microphone. "There is no hearing! We're through with this phony, fink hearing!"

Their work done, the protesters came down from the stage and gathered around Jacobs, who called for everyone to leave in an orderly fashion and go home. That was when she felt a hand on her arm—the plainclothes precinct captain who informed her she was under arrest. Toth was charging her with disrupting a public hearing, he informed her. She would have to come to the nearby station for booking.

The police made it clear to her that they did not agree with the order to arrest her but they had no choice. Ashen but calm, Jacobs walked out of the Seward Park High School auditorium and climbed into the back of the squad car.

"Well, here I have been arrested again!" she wrote to her mother the next day, after she had been released from the Seventh Precinct station house, with a promise to appear in court. "I'm afraid you will have a jailbird daughter, or anyway one whose conduct is disorderly." Getting arrested was a surprise, but it was "better than just lying down and taking all this crookedness . . . I hope you won't think too badly of me."

Jane Jacobs's arrest was the talk of the town. The newspapers first ran brief accounts and then followed up with longer stories. "Jane Jacobs Seized at Roadway Protest," said the headline in the *New York Post*. And the story just got better. When Jacobs reported to the Centre Street court-house on April 17, she was informed by the assistant district attorney Ed-ward Plaza that she was no longer being charged with disorderly conduct. Instead, the charges had changed, and she would be arraigned in crimi-nal court on charges of second-degree riot, inciting a riot, criminal mis-chief, and obstructing public administration. She was also prevented from participating in any further anti-expressway protests, though that in-junction was later dismissed. She was rebooked back at the precinct sta-tion, photographed, fingerprinted, and questioned, and informed she faced imprisonment on each charge anywhere from fifteen days to a year. A trial would not likely occur before summer.

The riot charge was more than Jacobs had bargained for. But the gov-ernment's move only strengthened her resolve. The events of the evening as recited by the prosecution "bear no relation to what happened," she said. She had been targeted as a rabble-rouser and a high-profile oppo-nent of the Lower Manhattan Expressway to make other citizens cower: she was being made an example.

"The inference seems to be," she told reporters after she learned of the riot charge, "that anybody who criticizes a state program is going to get it in the neck."

If Moses thought the arrest of Jacobs would finally silence his neme-sis and speed the construction of Lomex, he was quickly proven wrong. All of New York, it seemed, rushed to the defense of the nationally ac-claimed author of *The Death and Life of Great American Cities*. "If this is how they are going to treat distinguished citizens who protest projects which are against the good of the community, then God help our city," said Leon Seidel. Ed Koch described the Seward Park High School rebel-lion as "the first real public hearing we have been able to obtain on the ex-pressway." The architecture critic Peter Blake said Jacobs was laughingly being accused of "stenocide," and that the initial charge of disorderly con-duct was "pretty ridiculous . . . of course Jane Jacobs is disorderly. That's her job!"

Resolving a legal battle against a riot charge would have been stressful under any circumstances, but for Jacobs it was particularly troubling be-cause of the plans she had made for that summer. To the shock and dis-may of her friends, she had decided to leave New York.

Her husband, Robert, had landed a commission to design a hospital in Toronto. He loved the city, and the family agreed to pack up 555 Hudson Street and drive north across the border in a Volkswagen bus. Jacobs's growing disillusionment was part of the decision. She had been unable to complete her next book after *Death and Life,* in part because she spent so much time fighting the Lower Manhattan Expressway. But there was one reason bigger than all the others. Ned and Jim were approaching draft age, and there was no way Jacobs would allow them to be shipped to Southeast Asia to fight a war she didn't believe in.

As if begging her to stay, the neighborhood residents put on special events in her honor and held fund-raisers for her legal defense. "As you know, Jane was arrested at the so-called hearing on the Lower Manhattan Expressway," read a notice for a June 3 cocktail party benefit for the Jane Jacobs Legal Defense Fund at the Village Gate on Bleecker Street, from the West Village Committee, which by that time was using handsome stationery with a Village streetscape at the top. "The case involves not only Jane's personal freedom but issues of free speech and the community right to assert its views . . . Any excess funds will be used to fight the Lower Manhattan Expressway."

Jacobs was a guest of honor at a banner raising outside the Church of the Most Holy Crucifix a month after the Seward Park hearing. The banner, hung across Broome Street from the home of an elderly Italian immigrant to the loft of a youthful artist, read, "No Expressway Through Our Homes." It was created by the people of nearby Cooper Square, site of a neighborhood affordable housing project that the city wanted to turn over to SoHo residents evicted by Lomex. "By joining together we can defeat the expressway," which will "destroy our homes, our businesses and our jobs," La Mountain proclaimed at the ceremony. "The city must see the wisdom of our stand, and the folly of theirs."

La Mountain's wish was about to come true. Mayor Lindsay wasn't thinking in terms of wisdom or folly, but he did see that Jacobs's arrest had permanently tarnished the Lower Manhattan Expressway as a project pushed by heartless bureaucrats who would go to any lengths to subdue public opposition. Infrastructure and economic development remained as important as ever, but the public-relations damage was irreversible. In the months following Jacobs's arrest, the mayor reverted to his original position—that Lomex was an unworkable and ill-conceived proposal. On

July 16, 1969, Lindsay declared that the project was dead "for all time," and he swore the black line from the Holland Tunnel to the Manhattan and Williamsburg bridges would be erased on official city maps forever.

~~~~~

Moses continued to lobby for the project, but Jacobs's arrest marked the beginning of his final fall from power. In 1968, Governor Nelson Rockefeller called for a reorganization of the vaunted Triborough Bridge and Tunnel Authority, into a new Metropolitan Transportation Authority that would administer not just the bridges, tunnels, and roadways but also the subways and commuter rail systems of New York. Moses supported the idea, thinking he would continue to be on the board, and would likely be named to a new offshoot authority to build the Rye–Oyster Bay crossing as well. But instead Rockefeller demoted Moses to a position as a consultant to the new Metropolitan Transportation Authority, though he allowed him to keep his Randall's Island offices and even retain his secretaries and chauffeurs. From then on Moses's letters to reporters and city council members and business groups were on MTA stationery that listed the board members up top and "Robert Moses, Consultant" below.

Moses continued to tap away at the typewriter on Randall's Island, dashing off memos urging reconsideration of the project to whoever would listen. In August 1970 he sent a package to the New York *Daily News,* including a newspaper clip of a fatal crash where a car ran into a building on Houston Street. The "rookeries and rabbit warrens" of the neighborhood, he said, were a safety hazard that would be solved by Lomex:

> We tried repeatedly to explain these tenements to the public when we urged the Lower Manhattan Expressway. We pointed out the worst of the slum buildings in this area and specifically those within and near the expressway in these rotten conditions. Triborough designed and set aside some ten million dollars to build low rental housing with play facilities for the people to be moved. The opposition was led by the local assemblyman, DeSalvio, and supported by Mrs. Jane Jacobs and her chums, who pictured this as a lovely and integrated neighborhood. We got official approval and then lost it. Our ten million [was] given to the city to help save the

subway fare and disappeared. The Lower Manhattan project was pushed around from 1941 to date—nothing new in city history. Now the entire subject must be reconsidered.

But Lomex was no more. Rockefeller killed the project for good in 1971 by dropping it from the list of proposals eligible for federal interstate highway funds. Two years later, Rockefeller also shelved Moses's last great megaproject, the bridge across Long Island Sound, acknowledging the power of the citizen activism that Jacobs had spearheaded. Large-scale projects that Moses had proposed would never again succeed without public scrutiny and consent. "It is clear that the people want to take a more careful look at decisions which affect the face of their land," Rockefeller said. With no Lomex, no Mid-Manhattan, no Cross Brooklyn, and no Rye–Oyster Bay crossing, the great highway network remained unfinished. Moses lingered on as a consultant at the Metropolitan Transportation Authority, but the Moses era was over. His brand of megaproject, with no mechanism or regard for citizen approval, was rendered obsolete. The insurrection was unloosed. His remarkable run as New York's master builder had come to an end.

Separate Ways

Happy to have left the rancor of New York behind, Jane Jacobs settled into a cozy redbrick house in a quiet neighborhood on the west side of Toronto in the late summer of 1968. She continued to collect newspaper clippings on the denouement of the Lower Manhattan Expressway battle. She had made a deal with the prosecutor to disentangle herself from charges from the Seward Park High School meeting, pleading guilty to a single charge of disorderly conduct and agreeing to pay $150 in damages to the stenotype owner—though Jacobs maintained she never touched the machine and never saw it damaged. But she had moved on. It would be many years before she would set foot back in New York.

While Jacobs started her new life in Toronto, her fight against the Lower Manhattan Expressway inspired a series of citizen rebellions against highway construction in city neighborhoods across the United States. These "freeway revolts" were led by residents, and sometimes environmental organizations, that pressured politicians to quit building interstates in thickly settled areas, using many of the same tactics that Jacobs had in her campaigns, including filing lawsuits and harnessing the power of the media. In Boston, Governor Francis Sargent abandoned plans for a highway known as the Inner Belt, a bypass for the north-south

OPPOSITE: Jane Jacobs after she moved to Toronto, with her books. *Maggie Steber*

interstate through downtown that would have run through the heart of several densely populated neighborhoods, and an additional spur known as the Southwest Expressway; the funds for the roadways were diverted to expanding the public transit system. In San Francisco, the freeway revolt not only killed the freeway proposals through the city center but galvanized community groups determined to have a say in all public works and development projects from then on. By 1971, highway construction was being stopped in its tracks in Baltimore, Milwaukee, New Orleans, and Philadelphia. In the years that followed, I-291 and Route 7 in Connecticut, three routes designed by Moses himself in Portland, Oregon, the Somerset Highway in Princeton, New Jersey, and other roadway proposals in Seattle, Detroit, Memphis, Washington, D.C., and Baltimore were all abandoned. A new breed of politicians staked their careers on siding with the anti-freeway movement.

Jacobs herself helped lead a similar rebellion not long after arriving in Toronto. City planners there were promoting a downtown bypass called the Spadina Expressway, which would have run straight through her neighborhood. Like Moses, the officials in Toronto were committed to the project—the first stage had already been rushed into construction—but they seemed to listen, somehow more genuinely than Moses and his colleagues had, to Jacobs and the other neighbors who objected. Jacobs's reputation may have had something to do with this; city officials knew that this was a woman capable of stopping a highway. Spadina was dropped in 1971, and shortly thereafter Jacobs helped plant grass and shrubs on the flattened earth that had been cleared for the roadway.

In New York, the neighborhoods in the path of the Lower Manhattan Expressway flourished. At the corner of Chrystie and Broome streets at Sara Delano Roosevelt Park, deep underground, the eighty-foot foundation for the project was all that remained. Through the 1980s, all along Broome Street, one of the most remarkable urban success stories of the twentieth century began to take shape: SoHo, with its bistros, art galleries, designer shops, and unfinished loft space that over the years would sell for $1,800 a square foot. No new highway would be built in Manhattan after 1968, not even Westway, a proposal to submerge the West Side Highway along the Hudson River from midtown to lower Manhattan, with open space and residential and commercial development on its surface.

Beginning in the 1980s, the movement that Jacobs had set in motion with her victory over Lomex went a step further. Not satisfied with stopping construction of new freeways, planners and community activists sought to tear down the most intrusive roadways that had been pushed through in the Moses era. Boston replaced the Central Artery, a hulking elevated structure through the heart of downtown based on the Lomex model, with the $16 billion Big Dig—a mile-long tunnel with thirty acres of green space and civic buildings on top. While the project itself went over budget and had structural problems, real estate values have soared since its completion in 2007, as downtown neighborhoods split apart by the highway were reunited. Other cities have dismantled inner-city expressways without replacing them at all. The Embarcadero viaduct along the waterfront in San Francisco, damaged in the 1989 earthquake, was hauled away to make way for a surface boulevard with a trolley line. Portland, Oregon, erased a freeway through its downtown. Milwaukee, Denver, Baltimore, and Buffalo all dismantled major city roadways. In Seattle, the People's Waterfront Coalition, led by a young activist named Cary Moon who said she modeled herself after Jacobs, has for years campaigned to tear down the Alaskan Way Viaduct along that city's waterfront—a double-decked structure at the base of a steep hill that is also in danger of collapsing in an earthquake—and replace it with a surface boulevard with transit. And in New York, neighborhood groups have clamored for the demolition of two Moses roadways—the Bruckner and Sheridan expressways—to be replaced by parks, a simple surface road with bike paths and sidewalks, affordable housing, and eco-friendly businesses.

Jacobs's then-radical argument against the Lower Manhattan Expressway—that building new highways just invites more traffic that quickly fills the lanes to capacity—is now widely accepted, and known as the phenomenon of "induced demand." Transportation planning in the United States is slowly but surely coming around to this view—that the country has built enough new highways, not only in cities but in the countryside. More politicians are seeking to shift federal funding to transit, streetcars, and high-speed rail, for a more balanced transportation system. Light-rail systems are now being expanded in some unlikely places: Dallas, Phoenix, Minneapolis, and Denver.

Even in Los Angeles, Mayor Antonio Villaraigosa has given up on bumper-to-bumper freeways and started exploring whether well-designed surface boulevards could handle both local traffic and commuters. In other places, a more dramatic step has signaled the end of the automobile era in cities. London's mayor, Ken Livingstone, imposed a $16 charge for private cars entering the city center, enforced by a system of transponders and cameras; city officials say chronic gridlock is a thing of the past. New York's mayor, Michael Bloomberg, proposed a similar plan, to charge drivers $9 to enter Manhattan below Eighty-sixth Street.

~~~~

I n Toronto, Jacobs was finally able to complete the book delayed by her citizen activism in New York, *The Economy of Cities.* "I resent," Jane said, "the time I've had to spend on these civic battles. The new book was begun two years later than it should have been because of [the Lower Manhattan Expressway] and the urban renewal fight in [the] West Village. It's a terrible imposition when the city threatens its citizens in such a way that they can't finish their work."

The Economy of Cities was published in 1969 as the Lomex plan was being shelved. The books that followed—*Cities and the Wealth of Nations* (1984), *Systems of Survival* (1992), *The Nature of Economies* (2000), the last a conversation over coffee by five fictional characters—all focused on how cities function as economies. Jacobs had begun to see links between the order of the natural world and man-made systems, and how dynamic order emerged spontaneously from many individual decisions. Her belief that planning required flexibility and a light touch was bolstered by a growing fascination with chaos theory and fractals, and a theory of systems that put a premium on diversity over uniformity. She pursued these sophisticated ideas while remaining outside any kind of traditional academic setting.

Jacobs returned to the United States to plug the new books, right up to her last—the foreboding *Dark Age Ahead* (2004), a prediction that North American culture would deteriorate and implode, in part brought on by a burst housing bubble. She also wrote a book on the Quebec secession movement and, finally, chronicled the life of her great-aunt Hannah Breece, who taught on the islands off the Alaskan coast, in *A Schoolteacher in Old Alaska.* None of the books were blockbusters like *The Death and Life of Great American Cities,* and Jacobs began to chafe when the questions inexorably led back to her days among the bohemians in Greenwich Village, fighting the New York battles—as if she were a rock singer constantly being asked to play an old hit.

Yet the book's influence was undeniable for a new generation of citizen activists, students—who viewed her as a kind of folk hero—and city planners. Activists in cities across the United States modeled themselves after Jacobs, acting as watchdogs over local government and demanding to be heard on everything from street-corner wastebaskets to the shadows cast by proposed skyscrapers. *The Death and Life of Great American Cities* became a standard text at colleges and universities, architecture and planning schools, and a generation of planners, architects, and elected officials based their careers on the principles of urbanism Jacobs set forth in the book.

A roommate at Yale gave Alexander Garvin, a prominent planner and designer in New York City today, a copy of *The Death and Life of Great American Cities* around Christmastime in 1961. "It changed my life," he said. "There's nobody that I know in the business of cities who hasn't been inspired by her," said Susan Zielinski, a transportation planner. "It was not only us kindred spirits. She held up at every level, including among a lot of people at Harvard who she challenged."

The Harvard professor James Stockard recalled how he got a call from a young man who had gone through the Loeb Fellowship at Harvard's Graduate School of Design, saying the mayor of Salt Lake City wanted him to be chief planner. He was worried, as he had no formal training in urban planning. "Do you own a copy of *Death and Life*?" Stockard asked him, and the answer was yes. "That's all you need to know."

Though the planning profession balked initially, the Jacobs principles are now the foundation of its professional guidelines. The American Planning Association, or APA, the earlier version of which recoiled at Jacobs, now has as its goals "safe, attractive, and healthy neighborhoods, affordable housing, and accessible, efficient, and environmentally friendly transportation." Urban renewal and top-down redevelopment schemes are viewed as the shameful past; the APA's motto is "making great communities happen." The Congress for the New Urbanism, a group of architects and planners who argue for traditional town planning and compact, mixed-use neighborhoods, often cites Jacobs as an inspiration for the group's efforts to reform zoning and combat sprawl. The principles of the related "smart growth" movement echo Jacobs's call to redevelop buildings and establish lively, transit-accessible, and pedestrian-friendly places. Developers, as well, have embraced the Jacobs principles with a vengeance, as any glance at an issue of *Urban Land* magazine, a publication of the Urban

Land Institute, will attest. Even corporate home builders are beginning to shift from single-family-home subdivisions to more urban environments; Toll Brothers has turned to projects in Manhattan and Hoboken, New Jersey, and other builders, such as Pulte Homes, have thrown investments into denser developments.

The business of development in the United States has changed completely as a result of Jacobs's work. Builders and local government officials alike defer to the concerns of the neighborhood, involving the community in every step of the process. They offer "community benefit agreements," including parks, affordable housing, day-care centers, and other amenities. They live in fear of being viewed as riding roughshod over citizens.

In the 1990s, planners at municipal housing authorities and at the federal Department of Housing and Urban Development came around to Jacobs's view that big public housing projects weren't working. Some, like the Robert Taylor complex in Chicago and Pruitt-Igoe in St. Louis, have been torn down and replaced by Greenwich Village–style streetscapes of smaller individual homes with front porches. Cities are revisiting the landscapes of 1950s- and 1960s-style urban renewal and working on plans to fill in windswept plazas with more activity. The Jacobs theory promoting "eyes on the street"—the creation of safe, active neighborhoods with plenty of opportunities for people to monitor goings-on—has become not only a standard in urban design but accepted practice in crime fighting and community policing. Historic preservation and "adaptive reuse"—turning old buildings such as factories into condominiums or office space—became a bedrock policy in American cities. Everything from the design of workplaces to social media—the online networks of Facebook, YouTube, and open-source software—owes a debt to Jacobs and her original analysis of how decentralized, diverse, and ground-up systems function best.

~~~~~

Robert Moses, meanwhile, has been inexorably cast in the role of villain. After losing the Lomex battle, he was relegated to the sidelines in New York City politics and planning, retaining only the title of consultant for the new Metropolitan Transportation Authority. His urban renewal, highway, and housing programs had failed to stem the decline of the city, which veered into bankruptcy. In 1975, Mayor Abraham Beame, stared down by banks who refused to lend the city any more money, had to ask the federal government for a bailout; President Gerald Ford rebuffed the request, prompting the infamous New York *Daily News* headline "Ford to City: Drop Dead." The arson fires raged in the South Bronx. While the suburbs boomed, New York City's poor, immigrants, and people of color faced crumbling services and rising crime as the last vestiges of a once-thriving manufacturing economy disappeared. This was the fate of the city that Moses so desperately sought to avoid.

At a ceremony at Lincoln Center for the opening of Fordham University's Manhattan campus in 1970, Moses, then eighty-one, was honored with a bust plaque engraved with the words "Robert Moses: Friend of Fordham, Master Builder." His eyes welled up in tears. But the glory days were over. The biography that would destroy his reputation was in the works. Robert A. Caro, a young reporter on the Long Island newspaper *Newsday,* had become curious about Moses after covering the 1964 World's Fair and began researching a book on him. The resulting project took Caro seven years to complete.

The Power Broker: Robert Moses and the Fall of New York was a devastating prosecutorial brief, detailing an obsession with power, ruthless evictions of the poor and people of color, manipulations of the legal and legislative process, misuse of eminent domain, cronyism, patronage, corruption, and insider contractor and developer deals. Coming out in 1974, right at the time of Watergate, *The Power Broker* inspired legions of journalists and politicians to root out backroom deals and secret financial negotiations. Robert Moses became the classic case study for the abuse of power.

Jane Jacobs was an important source for the book, but she is not mentioned once in its pages. Though there was an entire chapter on Jacobs in the original manuscript, it had to be cut, along with others on the New York Port Authority and the City Planning Commission and detail on the departure of the Brooklyn Dodgers, because the doorstop-size book had grown too large by hundreds of pages.

Not until the publisher sent Jacobs the bound page proofs of *The Power Broker* did she realize the full weight of the nemesis she had battled.

"Bob is reading one of them while I am reading the other. We lie in bed at night, propped up under the reading light with our twin volumes and Jimmy says the sight is hilarious," she wrote to her mother.

Well, we always knew Moses was an awful man, doing awful things, but even so this book is a shocking revelation. He was much worse than we had even imagined. I am beginning to think he was not quite sane. The things he did—the corruption, the brutality, the sheer seizure and misuse of power—make Watergate seem rather tame. I think the big difference is, the press did not expose Moses, in fact (particularly the *New York Times*) aided and abetted him in every way, so that he got away with his outrages and kept building upon them further for thirty years before there was any public exposure of what his victims, of course, knew only too well . . .

Exposure is the only defense of the people against such tyranny and lawlessness. I wonder whether it teaches any lessons for the future. Doubtful, but I hope so.

Moses, of course, was unable to stop the publication of *The Power Broker*, and instead issued rebuttals of selected charges. It was obvious, he said, that his opponents were coming out of the woodwork to vilify him. In a response to Caro, Moses seems to have Jacobs in mind: "The current fiction is that any overnight ersatz bagel and lox and boardwalk merchant, any down-to-earth commentator or barfly, any busy housewife who gets her expertise from newspaper, television, radio, and telephone is ipso facto endowed to plan in detail a huge metropolitan arterial complex good for a century," he said. "Anyone in public works is bound to be a target for charges of arbitrary administration and power broking leveled by critics who never had responsibility for building anything . . . I raise my stein to the builder who can remove ghettos without moving people as I hail the chef who can make omelets without breaking eggs."

After the failure of the Lomex project, his demotion, and the publication of *The Power Broker*, Moses spent his final years in virtual exile. He and his second wife maintained the residence at Gracie Terrace in Manhattan, but spent much more time in Babylon. Their Long Island home was close to Robert Moses State Park and to the harbor on Great South Bay, where there is a clear view of the Robert Moses Causeway leading to Fire Island. To be closer to the ocean, Moses rented cottages at Oak Beach and Gilgo Beach nearby.

"He loved it down here," a neighbor said. "He could see his bridge and his park from here. He was still alive and had something to remember."

On the afternoon of July 28, 1981, at the cottage at Gilgo Beach, Moses felt chest pains and was taken to the Good Samaritan Hospital in West Islip, Long Island. He died of heart failure the next day, at the age of ninety-two. Remarkably, the man who had spent hundreds of millions of dollars on public construction projects in New York State had less than $50,000 in assets when he died. His pursuit of power and eagerness to get things clearly did not include the goal of building his own personal wealth.

For a man so determined to see things go his way, Moses would be appalled that his approach to urban planning is now seen as the model of how not to build a city. His entire career, built on energy, ambition, and single-minded pursuit of power, has been repudiated. Since his death, American cities have spent most of their time trying to correct the mistakes of the Moses era; even his great triumph, Lincoln Center, is today undergoing a much-needed rehabilitation in order to better accommodate pedestrians.

In recent years, however, the Moses legacy has been reconsidered. It was Herbert Kaufman, a political science scholar, who in 1975 first suggested that the Caro critique was overblown, though his claim garnered little attention. Alex Krieger, a professor at Harvard's Graduate School of Design, lectured in 2000 that while history has taken a dim view of Moses's tactics, cities everywhere are in need of reliable infrastructure—and with citizens continually blocking cities' efforts, it was difficult to get even the most necessary projects passed. In 2006, the *New York Times* architecture critic Nicolai Ouroussoff suggested that the planning profession had become obsessed with fine-grained, tree-lined blocks, at the expense of the things that actually make cities function. "Today, the pendulum of opinion has swung so far in favor of Ms. Jacobs that it has distorted the public's understanding of urban planning. As we mourn her death, we may want to mourn a bit for Mr. Moses as well," he wrote. Moses's vision, he said, however flawed, represented "an America that still believed a healthy government would provide the infrastructure— roads, parks, bridges—that binds us into a nation. Ms. Jacobs, at her best, was fighting to preserve the more delicate bonds that tie us to a community. A city, to survive and flourish, needs both perspectives."

Among government, business, and civic leaders in New York who have been frustrated by what they see as paralysis, there has even been talk of the need for a new Robert Moses, to supply basic infrastructure and the big projects needed to propel the city as a competitive economic center for the twenty-first century. Projects on the scale of those of Moses could not take place today, as the kind of thoughtful citizen involvement Jacobs envisioned has evolved into mere NIMBYism—the protest of "not in my backyard." Citizen opposition now brings even modest projects to a grinding halt. The proposed rehabilitation of an abandoned factory building, a housing complex on a vacant parcel, the development of a parking lot near a transit station, the slightest modification of a structure deemed historically significant—all evaporate before the all-powerful neighborhood residents, who seek conditions to stay exactly as they are and reward politicians who agree with them. To some, New York risks becoming a city preserved and unchanged, as if under glass. In Boston, Mayor Thomas Menino complained that citizen veto power had made some neighborhoods go "BANANAs—build absolutely nothing anywhere near anything."

In the winter of 2007, Columbia University, the Museum of the City of New York, and the Queens Museum of Art put on Robert Moses and the Modern City, a series of exhibits reevaluating the Moses legacy. The basis for the exhibits was to remind visitors of Moses's less sinister motivations—his determination to save the city, and his dedication to its health. Contributing scholars went so far as to say that the Cross Bronx Expressway wasn't so devastating, and couldn't be blamed for being the direct cause of the decline of the South Bronx.

The retrospective on Moses's efforts in public housing also underscored something that Jacobs never fully addressed: gentrification. Her prescription for "unslumming" run-down areas and the improvements in the West Village were not easily duplicated on a broad scale, and in many cases what she called "oversuccess"—or gentrification—took over. Her goal was to incorporate affordable housing into existing neighborhoods, without warehousing the poor in giant towers, but urban neighborhoods have become so wildly popular that only the wealthy—and predominantly white—can afford to live there. Parts of New York, Boston, Chicago, and San Francisco have become every bit as exclusive as wealthy suburban enclaves, if not more so. Cafés and art galleries have replaced hardware stores and Laundromats.

The gentrification saga repeats itself over and over: first come artists seeking undiscovered and affordable digs, then architects and designers, then the young professionals, and then the celebrities and retiring baby boomers. When the Jacobses paid $7,000 for 555 Hudson Street in 1947, they were pioneers helping to save a neighborhood from being designated a slum. Today, the process has been honed by young urbanites and savvy developers, who transform forlorn blocks into ritzy enclaves seemingly in a matter of weeks. In contrast to the bagpiper or the friendly shopkeeper in Jacobs's time, today fashion designers, actors, supermodels, and NFL quarterbacks prowl the streets of Greenwich Village.

Jacobs anticipated gentrification in her efforts to build the West Village Houses, a project that presaged today's neighborhood-based community development approach. The "windbreaks" against rapidly rising real estate values she envisioned are today embodied in policies such as "inclusionary zoning," where local governments require that new residential development be 10 or 15 percent affordable. Another innovation is the community land trust, where a nonprofit organization buys land and sells homes based only on the cost of the structure, exclusive of the plots they sit on; buyers are restricted from making a big profit if they sell, which has the effect of keeping the affordability perpetual. If Jacobs were building the West Village Houses today, chances are she would have tried to make the project a community land trust.

Jacobs was convinced the city was the best possible place for people to live, and in many ways gentrification proved her right. She argued that the problem was a matter of supply and demand—that there weren't enough urban neighborhoods, and if they were as ubiquitous as suburban sprawl, they wouldn't be such a precious commodity, and prices would come down.

On this point, Moses and Jacobs actually agreed: cities needed to be flooded with as much new housing as possible, made available to the broadest range of incomes as possible. They disagreed on the form that housing should take, but Moses was, in the end, trying to rebuild the city so more people could live and work there. He appreciated the mix of uses that Jacobs advocated, and spoke harshly of the "dormitories" of the suburbs. Some of his housing projects—Kips Bay, Chatham Towers, Lenox Terrace, even, some would say, Washington Square Village—have endured today as successful urban places. His beaches, parks, and public pools remain important elements of what makes New York City livable. His methods, and the failures of the worst towers-in-the-park redevelopments, have overshadowed the legacy of effective city building.

Moses was, as well, a product of his time. Many other cities were engaged just as enthusiastically—and in some cases more destructively—in urban renewal and highway building. After World War II, accommodating the car seemed like the sensible course for urban planners everywhere. The environmental and energy challenges of the twenty-first century are very different. Had Moses been in charge of building the world's greatest transit system, he would be cheered today no matter how many people he had uprooted.

~~~~

Toward the end of her life, Jacobs was constantly asked to accept honorary degrees, but always refused—even after forty-five minutes of urging and cajoling by the president of Harvard. She did accept the Thomas Jefferson Foundation Medal in Architecture, awarded at the University of Virginia, in 1996. "I accepted it because it wasn't an honorary degree, so it's not a credential," she said. Her father, the first in the family to attend college, was a UVA alumnus. At the reception, Jane and Bob were photographed sitting on a bench, with a cane at their side.

Bob died of lung cancer a year later at the age of seventy-nine. Without her lifelong partner, Jacobs lived alone in Toronto, agreeing to the occasional interview but never authorizing a biography.

In her last years in Toronto, Jacobs tended to her garden and found more time to enjoy cooking and baking, delighting in such concoctions as a loaf of bread in the shape of a turkey, adventurous entrées such as wild boar, and crab-apple, pecan, and pumpkin pies. She cultivated sweet peas and tomato plants in the backyard and watched as the crocuses poked up in the spring, alongside her mail-house orders of bulbs and herbs, with black squirrels racing all around. She began to compost the needles of Christmas trees—hers and her neighbors'—after learning of the practice from her daughter, Mary, who had moved to British Columbia. Jacobs's son Jim, an inventor and physicist, married and settled in Toronto. Her second son, Ned, married and moved to Vancouver, where he is an activist in urban redevelopment like his mother, and a musician.

Jacobs had removed some interior walls on the first floor of the Toronto house so the living room, dining room, and kitchen formed one big space, just as at 555 Hudson Street. The walls, lined with books, were painted in the bright colors of the early 1970s; she kept a Native American breastplate by the bay window, and the dining room tablecloth was an aboriginal print, with a big globe-shaped paper chandelier overhead. Family photographs and drawings by her daughter were all around. A stranger watching her emerge from the front porch of the ivy-covered brick row house would see just another retiree on her way to the farmers' market.

She was selective in her public appearances, but always drew big crowds. At a forum held by Boston College Law School in 2000, Jacobs took questions from the audience, some of whom spoke with such care and awe to suggest they were addressing the pope. "I know a lot of planners and people who I challenged did take it personally as if I were just having fun kicking them," she said when asked about her battles. Cities on the whole, she added, were "doing much, much better. Cities are beginning to heal themselves . . . [to] get back their old pizzazz." The audience hung on every word.

Those gathered at Boston College, where Jacobs's papers are archived, had good reason to pay attention to what she said about how cities work. Through the 1980s and 1990s, America had rediscovered the charm and utility of its cities. Young professionals and retiring baby boomers had flocked to urban neighborhoods, enjoying the density and activity and mix of amenities that Jacobs espoused. As the twentieth century came to a close, cities across the country sought to replicate Greenwich Village and SoHo in old districts of warehouses and brownstones, from LoDo in Denver to Belltown in Seattle to the Mission in San Francisco and the South End in Boston.

City living is increasingly recognized for its health benefits, another idea that Jacobs introduced. When city officials balked at the lack of elevators in the West Village Houses, Jacobs responded by suggesting that it was great exercise to use the stairs. One resident said walking up five flights every day kept her seventy-seven-year-old husband fit and trim and "great in bed." Studies have shown that urban dwellers who walk or bike and take transit, instead of sitting behind the wheel of a car for every errand and commute to work, aren't as heavy as their suburban counterparts.

The value of local businesses and a local economy, a bedrock theme in *The Death and Life of Great American Cities,* is also at a premium. The local food movement emphasizes the availability of locally produced food that does not travel thousands of miles to big supermarkets and restaurants. "Locavore" was the word of the year for the *New Oxford American Dictionary* in 2007, and many cities have "buy local" programs supporting small, family-run businesses in their downtowns to help them compete against suburban shopping malls and chain stores. As gasoline prices increase, the notion of a self-contained neighborhood, with the needs of life within a few blocks, has grown in appeal.

Cities are also increasingly seen as an answer to the challenge of climate change. They are dense and have transit; if their buildings can become more energy efficient, they represent the potential for the greenest form of human settlement, and compared with suburban sprawl can help reduce greenhouse gas emissions. Manhattanites, on a per capita basis, consume less energy than anywhere else in the country. In the context of the planetary emergency cited by Al Gore in *An Inconvenient Truth*, cities play a major role—and Jacobs provided the owner's manual for how they function best.

On April 25, 2006, Jacobs was taken to a Toronto hospital after suffering what appeared to be a stroke. She died two weeks shy of turning ninety, having struggled with health problems all the previous year.

After that sad spring day in Toronto, with Jacobs no longer able to veto them, the honors came bursting forth. Some of them would surely have made her chuckle. At the Silverleaf Tavern on Thirty-eighth Street in Manhattan, bartenders christened a drink called the Jane Jacobs—a blend of Hendrick's gin, elder-flower syrup, a dash of orange bitters, and sparkling wine. On May 24, 2006, a dozen women gathered under the arch at Washington Square Park in a knitting circle in her honor, and every year on the anniversary of her death others gather at the White Horse Tavern to celebrate her work on behalf of the West Village. At the Congress for the New Urbanism's annual convention in 2006, two thousand people gathered for a moment of silence in her memory.

New York City's mayor, Michael Bloomberg, proclaimed June 28, 2006, as Jane Jacobs Day. In Toronto, organizers started the annual Jane Jacobs Walk through the most cozy, tight-knit neighborhoods of the city. The American Planning Association issued the National Planning Excellence Award for Innovation in Neighborhood Planning in honor of Jane Jacobs. The Jane Jacobs Medal, awarded by the Rockefeller Foundation and the Municipal Art Society, recognizes "visionary work in building a more diverse, dynamic and equitable city through creative uses of the urban environment . . . whose accomplishments represent Jacobsean principles and practices in action in New York City." The first recipients were the organizers of a farmers' market and an effort to recycle waste from waste transfer stations in the Bronx.

The local community board in Greenwich Village accepted petitions to call the stretch of Hudson Street from Eleventh Street to Perry Street Jane Jacobs Way, and to rename Bleecker Playground Jane Jacobs Park. While the street sign was uncontroversial, the latter proposal has met resistance from some modern-day mothers—in perhaps an even better preservation of her legacy—who worry that children will be confused if the name is changed.

The girl from Scranton stood up to Moses and challenged the status quo. Now virtually all those engaged in city building follow her rules. Her triumphs are engraved in the protocols followed by developers, city officials, and advocacy and grassroots organizations, and copies of *The Death and Life of Great American Cities* sit on the shelves of the planning offices at city halls across the country.

The morning after Jane Jacobs died, the owner of the Art of Cooking, the housewares store occupying 555 Hudson Street in Greenwich Village, went to unlock the door and open for business. She found bouquets of lilies and daisies at the doorstep, and an unsigned note: "From this house, in 1961, a housewife changed the world."

ACKNOWLEDGMENTS

Many threads come together to make a book: people and sources and inspiration and, in this case, the city itself—with all its complexity and beauty—which is finally, I believe, taking its rightful place at the top of the American and global agendas.

Richard Abate was the first to see that this epic battle over the future of the city had not yet been told with Jane Jacobs and Robert Moses sharing a stage. His guidance was invaluable to tell this story from start to finish in a work of narrative nonfiction. Tim Bartlett at Random House, ably assisted by Lindsey Schwoeri, who kept me organized, did what good editors do: he took the manuscript and made it better.

I have special gratitude for the Lincoln Institute of Land Policy; its president and chief executive, Gregory K. Ingram; board chair Kathryn J. Lincoln; Armando Carbonell, senior fellow and chair of the Department of Planning and Urban Form; and all the people of this great organization, which has supported my writing and research on urbanism. Because it is an institution concerned with cities and land use, it is perhaps unsurprising that it would have connections to this work: the Lincoln Institute gave an award to Lewis Mumford, and Jane Jacobs was among those providing praise; the institute's work in community land trusts is grounded in a foundation of neighborhood stewardship that Jacobs established. Outside my office is a gallery featuring Raymond Moley, and signed photographs to him of Nixon and FDR; Moley was an adviser to David C. Lincoln and helped bring about the founding of the Lincoln Institute, and, as I discovered, he was the very same man who knew Robert Moses and wrote the foreword to *Public Works: A Dangerous Trade.*

I read *The Power Broker* as a student at the Columbia University Graduate School of Journalism and, like many journalists, was awestruck by Robert Caro's standard-setting biographical research, sourcing, and eye for narrative detail. More than twenty years later, Columbia's Kenneth T. Jackson and Hilary Ballon artfully revived a consideration of the master builder, and sparked an important civic dialogue, with the Moses exhibitions at the Museum of the City of New York, Columbia University, and the Queens Museum of Art. The scholars who contributed to the exhibitions and *Robert Moses and the Modern City* revealed new perspectives and untold stories, notably Robert Fishman, professor at the University of Michigan, who identified the battles of Washington Square Park and the Lower Manhattan Expressway as particular turning points. Laura Rosen at the Metropolitan Transportation Authority Special Archives was a kind and indispensable guide through Moses's remarkable career as head of the Triborough Bridge and Tunnel Authority.

Jane Jacobs never cooperated with biographers. Her sons, Jim and Ned, were protective but extremely gracious in answering my questions. Scholarship on her life and work is led by Christopher Klemek and Peter Laurence, the latter especially generous in meeting with me to discuss her early career. I owe thanks to Justine Hyland, David Horn, and Robert O'Neill at the John J. Burns Library at Boston College, guardians of the Jane Jacobs Papers; the New-York Historical Society; the *Villager,* the *Village Voice,* the *Boston Globe,* and the *New York Times;* Carol Greitzer, Ed Koch, Roberta Brandes Gratz, Albert LaFarge, Jason Epstein, Nathan Glazer, Carol Gayle, Elizabeth Werbe, Lex Lalli, and Matt Postal, who led the lively walking tours through Greenwich Village and SoHo as part of the Municipal Art Society's exhibition on Jane Jacobs; James Stockard, Sally Young, and the inestimable network that is the Loeb Fellowship, and Alex Krieger and Mary Daniels at Harvard University's Graduate School of Design; Eugenie Birch at the University of Pennsylvania; Robert Yaro and Alex Marshall at the Regional Plan Association; David Goldberg at Smart Growth America and Transportation for America; Steve Filmanowicz and John Norquist at the Congress for the New Urbanism; and Sarah Henry, Charles McKinney, Bill Shutkin, Kennedy Smith, and Ken Greenberg. I am also indebted to my friends John and Stacey Fraser, Tim and Mimi Love, Chris Lutes, Brian McGrory, Mitchell Zuckoff and Suzanne Kreiter, John King, Hamilton Hackney, Paul Quinlan, Brad Frazee, Steve Moynahan, James Burke, Josh Rabinowitz, Kate Zernike, and Phil Huffman; and my supportive family, Mary Alice Flint, Julia Flint, Melissa and Chris Cappella, Martha Flint, George and Emily Flint, and Jack and Gloria Cassidy.

And finally, my wife, Tina Ann Cassidy, a fellow journalist and author, who went through the manuscript and encouraged me at every turn, putting up with late nights at the keyboard and trips to New York on the Acela, and giving me the time to write this book after she gave birth, at home, to our son Harrison, who with his brothers, George and Hunter, now has her engaged in an ongoing test of patience. This book would not be possible without her.

ANTHONY FLINT
Boston

Introduction: Anarchy and Order

xiii "The city is like an insane asylum": Leticia Kent, "Persecution of the City Performed by Its Inmates," *Village Voice,* April 18, 1968.

xiv "I don't think so either": Jane Jacobs, deposition on Seward Park High School hearing, April 30, 1968, as cited in Max Allen, ed., *Ideas That Matter* (Toronto: Ginger Press, 1997).

xiv "We want Jane!": L. D. Ashton, "L.M.E. Fight Still On," *Villager,* April 18, 1968.

One: The Girl from Scranton

4   Arriving at her Brooklyn apartment: Jane Jacobs, interview with James Howard Kunstler, *Metropolis,* March 2000.

4   her assignments in Scranton: Jane Jacobs, autobiography for *Architect's Journal,* Nov. 22, 1961, as excerpted in Max Allen, ed., *Ideas That Matter* (Toronto: Ginger Press, 1997), p. 3.

7   On one outing: Jane Butzner, "Caution: Men Working," *Cue,* May 17, 1940.

8   She began to range: Jane Jacobs Papers, MS02-13, box 8, John J. Burns Library, Boston College.

8   She often went up: Jonathan Karp, "Jane Jacobs Doesn't Live Here Anymore," *At Random* (Winter 1993), as excerpted in Allen, *Ideas That Matter.*

8   From a young age: Ibid.

9   "Fortunately, my [high school] grades": Jacobs, autobiography.

9   Though her work: Peter Laurence, "Jane Jacobs Before *Death and Life,*" *Journal of the Society of Architectural Historians* (March 2007), p. 8.

10 "They hired me": Mark Feeney, "City Sage," *Boston Globe,* Nov. 14, 1993.

10 Shortly after that appearance: "Miss Butzner's Story in Iron Age Brought Nationwide Publicity," *Scrantonian,* Sept. 26, 1943.

12 "Cupid really shot that arrow": Feeney, "City Sage."

12 She won third prize: Jacobs Papers, MS02-13, box 8, folder 1.

13 she made up imaginary friends: Douglas Martin, "Jane Jacobs, Social Critic Who Redefined and Championed Cities, Is Dead at 89," *New York Times,* April 26, 2006, citing interview in *Azure,* 1997.

13 Another imaginary friend: Ibid.

14 At a time when: Jacobs Papers, MS02-13, box 2, folder 1.

15 She ended up doing the most work: "Amerika for the Russians," *Time,* March 4, 1946.

18 Haskell admired her gumption: Laurence, "Jane Jacobs Before *Death and Life,*" p. 10.

18 "I was utterly baffled at first": Jacobs, autobiography, p. 4.

18 "I had no credentials": Albert Amateau, "Jane Jacobs Comes Back to the Village She Saved," *Villager,* May 12, 2004.

19 Two years into Jane's tenure: Laurence, "Jane Jacobs Before *Death and Life,*" p. 10.

19 "First he took me": Paul Goldberger, "Tribute to Jane Jacobs," speech at the Greenwich Village Society for Historic Preservation, Oct. 3, 2006, www.paulgoldberger.com.

20 He emphasized the need: Doug Sanders, "Urban Icon," *Globe and Mail* (Toronto), Oct. 11, 1997.

20 Back in the offices: Alice Alexiou, *Jane Jacobs: Urban Visionary* (New Brunswick, N.J.: Rutgers University Press, 2006), p. 42.

22 She even described: Laurence, "Jane Jacobs Before *Death and Life,*" p. 12.

23 "I can remember": Lucile Preuss, "Jane Jacobs' Way of Life Fits Her Preaching," *Milwaukee Journal,* July 8, 1962.

23 "By showing me East Harlem": Jane Jacobs, *The Death and Life of Great American Cities* (New York: Random House, 1961).

25 "Sometimes you learn more": Jane Jacobs, "The Missing Link in City Redevelopment," talk before the April Conference on Urban Design at Harvard University, as excerpted in Allen, *Ideas That Matter.*

25 One man applauding: Mumford to Jacobs, May 3, 1958, in Allen, *Ideas That Matter,* p. 95.

26 A reporter for the *Harvard Crimson:* "Urban Designers Stress Need for Public Relations," *Harvard Crimson,* April 11, 1956.

27 "These projects": "Downtown Is for People," in William H. Whyte Jr., ed., *The Exploding Metropolis* (Berkeley: University of California Press, 1993).

27 "Look at what your girl did": Peter Laurence, "The Death and Life of Urban Design: Jane Jacobs, the Rockefeller Foundation, and the New Research in Urbanism, 1955–1965," *Journal of Urban Design* 11, no. 2 (June 2006), pp. 145–72.

27 She thanked him: Albert LaFarge, interview with author, Albert LaFarge Literary Agency, Jan. 31, 2008.

27 "This cultural superblock": Jacobs, "Downtown Is for People."

28 "My God, who was this crazy dame?": William H. Whyte Jr., "C. D. Jackson Meets Jane Jacobs," preface to the paperback edition of *Exploding Metropolis*.

Two: The Master Builder

32 "hanging highway in the sky": Brochure published by Socony-Vacuum Oil Inc. (Standard Oil of New York), Robert Moses and the Modern City, exhibit at the Museum of the City of New York, Jan.–May 2007, Hilary Ballon and Kenneth T. Jackson, curators.

32 "The Triborough is not just a bridge": The Crossings of Metro NYC, Eastern Roads, www.nycroads.com/crossings/triborough/.

35 "He was always": Robert Caro, *The Power Broker: Robert Moses and the Fall of New York* (New York: Knopf, 1974).

35 he would be praised: Ibid., p. 556.

36 From an early age: Ibid.

36 While Emanuel Moses: Ibid., p. 30.

37 Handsome and charming, Moses: Ibid., p. 36.

37 One Yale friend: Ibid., p. 41.

37 "To-morrow!": Caro, *Power Broker*, p. 40.

37 He came up with an idea: Ibid, p. 41.

38 "The Oxford education": Ibid., p. 49.

41 "Bob Moses": Cleveland Rogers, "Robert Moses," *Atlantic Monthly*, Feb. 1939.

41 "You want to give the people": Raymond Moley, 27 *Masters of Politics* (Westport, Conn.: Greenwood Press, 1949); Cleveland Rogers, *Robert Moses: Builder for Democracy* (New York: Holt, 1952), p. 33.

43 "If we want your land": Caro, *Power Broker*, p. 183.

43 "There will be squawking": George DeWan, "How Planner Robert Moses Transformed Long Island for the 20th Century and Beyond," *Newsday*, www.newsday.com/community/guide/lihistory.

43 When one member: Ibid.

43 "We were bested": "A Few Rich Golfers Accused of Blocking Plan for State Park," *New York Times*, Jan. 8, 1925, p. 1.

44 Moses began to view controversy: Robert Fishman, "Revolt of the Urbs," in Hilary Ballon and Kenneth T. Jackson, eds., *Robert Moses and the Modern City* (New York: W. W. Norton, 2007).

44 The man who transformed Paris: Robert Moses, *Public Works: A Dangerous Trade* (New York: McGraw-Hill, 1970).

44 "Once you sink that first stake": Caro, *Power Broker*, p. 218.

46 When Jones Beach: Robert Moses, "Hordes from the City," *Saturday Evening Post,* Oct. 31, 1931.
48 notice and replace them: Caro, *Power Broker,* p. 602.
48 The achievements: "Moses and His Parks," *New York Times,* Sept. 13, 1934.
50 He had a lively private correspondence: Moses, *Public Works.*
51 "Cities are created": Ibid., p. 308.
52 "You can draw any kind": Caro, *Power Broker,* p. 849.
54 New York over the next twelve years: Hilary Ballon, "Robert Moses and Urban Renewal," in Ballon and Jackson, *Robert Moses and the Modern City.*
55 He instructed a staffer: Ibid.
55 "Five minutes from Wall Street": "Robert Moses and the Superblock Solution," part of Robert Moses and the Modern City, exhibit at Columbia University, Jan.–May 2007, Hilary Ballon and Kenneth T. Jackson, curators.
57 the *Bob:* Caro, *Power Broker,* p. 159.
57 In the meeting: *Brooklyn Dodgers: The Ghosts of Flatbush,* HBO documentary series, 2007.

Three: The Battle of Washington Square Park

63 the fountain gave off: Willa Cather, *Coming, Aphrodite!* (New York: Penguin, 1999).
65 "Moses' temple to urination": Jane Jacobs, interview with Leticia Kent, oral history project for the Greenwich Village Historical Society, Jane Jacobs Papers, MS02-13, John J. Burns Library, Boston College.
65 "I have heard with alarm": Jacobs to Wagner and Jack, June 1, 1955, Shirley Hayes Papers, box 4, folder 5, New-York Historical Society.
66 Before the Dutch arrived: Nick Paumgarten, "The Mannahatta Project," *New Yorker,* Oct. 1, 2007.
66 Only after African slaves: Emily Kies Folpe, *It Happened on Washington Square* (Baltimore: Johns Hopkins University Press, 2002).
67 Despite their protests: Ibid., p. 64.
70 Poetry readings: Luther S. Harris, *Around Washington Square* (Baltimore: Johns Hopkins University Press, 2003), p. 180.
70 Independent journals: Greenwich Village Society for Historic Preservation, www.gvshp.org/.
72 "You will be glad to hear": Folpe, *It Happened on Washington Square,* p. 282.
73 "It seems a shame": "Moses Scores Foes on Washington Square," *New York Times,* June 11, 1940, p. 27.
74 "I realize that in the process": Moses to Charles C. Burlingham, Jan. 17, 1950, La Guardia and Wagner Archives, box 99, La Guardia Community College/CUNY, as cited in Harris, *Around Washington Square,* p. 244.
75 "Thanks for your good work": Jacobs to Hayes, tear-off campaign petition to the Washington Square Park Committee, April 30, 1955, Hayes Papers, box 4, folder 11.

76 "There is no justification": Shirley Hayes, "You Can Help Save Washington Square Park," flyer, Hayes Papers, box 3, folder 3.

76 "A few women got together": Douglas Martin, "Shirley Hayes, 89; Won Victory over Road," *New York Times,* May 11, 2002.

77 Her early involvement: Robert Fishman, "Revolt of the Urbs," in Hilary Ballon and Kenneth T. Jackson, eds., *Robert Moses and the Modern City* (New York: W. W. Norton, 2007).

77 Jacobs helped drop off: "De Sapio Supports Study on Village," *New York Times,* Dec. 20, 1957, p. 29.

79 "We weren't trying to embrace": Jacobs, interview with Kent.

79 The developers there: *Village Voice,* Jan. 1, 1958.

80 Years earlier: Lewis Mumford, "The Sky Line: The Dead Past and the Dead Present," *New Yorker,* March 23, 1940.

80 "The attack on Washington Square": "Lewis Mumford, City Planning Expert and Author Urges Washington Square Park Closed to Traffic," press release issued by the Joint Emergency Committee to Close Washington Square to Traffic, March 1958, Hayes Papers, box 5, folder 1.

81 "The public was told": Robert Moses, *Public Works: A Dangerous Trade* (New York: McGraw-Hill, 1970), p. 454.

81 "I consider it would be far better": Eleanor Roosevelt, "My Day," *New York Post,* March 23, 1958.

81 "little parks and squares": Norman Vincent Peale, letter to the editor, *New York Times,* April 17, 1958, p. 30.

81 "Rebellion is brewing": "Village Seen as Bunker Hill of City," *Villager,* July 3, 1958.

81 Abrams turned the speech: Charles Abrams, "Washington Square and the Revolt of the Urbs," *Village Voice,* July 2, 1958.

82 "We were doing our own planning": Carol Greitzer, interview with author, Sept. 2007.

83 Passannante, Bob Jacobs said: Jacobs, interview with Kent.

84 "It is our view": Dan Wolf, "The Park," *Village Voice,* Nov. 9, 1955.

84 When a Moses aide: Dan Wolf, "Those People Down There," *Village Voice,* May 30, 1956.

84 Jacobs deployed kids: Jacobs, interview with Kent.

85 "She would bring the three children": Jane Jacobs tribute, DVD by Liza Bear, June 2006.

85 One day when she was shopping: "Jane and Ned Jacobs," photographic feature in *Esquire,* July 1965.

85 "There is something to be said": Clayton Knowles, "Moses Hints at Advance to Rear in Battle of Washington Square," *New York Times,* May 19, 1958, p. 27.

86 Moses stepped up the rhetoric: Charles G. Bennett, "2-Lane Roadway in 'Village' Gains," *New York Times,* July 17, 1958, p. 29.

86 Wearing his trademark dark glasses: Charles G. Bennett, " 'Village' Protesters Led by De Sapio," *New York Times,* Sept. 19, 1958, p. 1.

87   That fall, Moses addressed the Board of Estimate: Jane Jacobs, interview with James Howard Kunstler, *Metropolis,* Sept. 6, 2000.

87   Pink parasols: "Crowd Hails Square Ribbon Tying," *Villager,* Nov. 6, 1958.

89   The fountain basin: Jane Jacobs, *The Death and Life of Great American Cities* (New York: Random House, 1961), p. 105.

89   The residents around the park: Angela Taylor, "Little Ones Get Hurt, Older Ones Are Bored," *New York Times,* Oct. 10, 1966, p. 70.

91   "What I would like to do": Jacobs to Gilpatric, Rockefeller Foundation, July 1, 1958, Jane Jacobs Papers, MS1995-29, box 13, folder 13, John J. Burns Library, Boston College.

91   "You sort of fell in love": "Jane Jacobs," *Asbury Park Press,* April 27, 2007.

Four: Urban Renewal in Greenwich Village

97   There was Mr. Slube: Jane Jacobs, *The Death and Life of Great American Cities* (New York: Random House, 1961), p. 50.

98   "These real estate grabbers": Eric Larrabee, "In Print: Jane Jacobs," *Horizon* 4, no. 6 (July 1962), p. 50.

98   "Be patient": Priscilla Chapman, "Survey of the City's Neighborhoods: The West Village," *New York Herald Tribune,* July 30, 1963.

99   Jacobs was paging through: John Sibley, "Two Blighted Downtown Areas Are Chosen for Urban Renewal," *New York Times,* Feb. 21, 1961, p. 37.

101 "He is a strong man": "James Felt, Former Chairman of City Planning Agency, Dies," *New York Times,* March 5, 1971.

101 Everything had its place: Christopher Klemek, "Urbanism as Reform: Modernist Planning and the Crisis of Urban Liberalism in Europe and North America, 1945–1975" (Ph.D. diss., University of Pennsylvania, 2004), chap. 4.

102 "When those needs": Peter B. Flint, "J. Clarence Davies Jr. Dies at 64; Realty Executive and Civic Leader," *New York Times,* Feb. 3, 1977, p. 36. ˙

102 When Moses saw: Robert Caro, *The Power Broker: Robert Moses and the Fall of New York* (New York: Knopf, 1974).

103 "I thought he would be ours": Ibid.

103 As Jacobs tucked him into bed: Jane Jacobs, interview with Leticia Kent, oral history project for the Greenwich Village Historical Society, Jane Jacobs Papers, MS02-13, John J. Burns Library, Boston College.

103 Also in 1960: Photo caption, 1960, Jacobs Papers.

104 Jane went to the White Horse Tavern: Jacobs, interview with Kent.

104 Prior to the meeting: Sam Pope Brewer, "Angry 'Villagers' to Fight Project," *New York Times,* Feb. 27, 1961, p. 29.

105 "It always began": Albert Amateau, "Jane Jacobs Comes Back to the Village She Saved," *Villager,* May 12, 2004.

105 The study: Jane Jacobs tribute, DVD by Liza Bear, June 2006.

105 "The aim of the committee": Brewer, "Angry 'Villagers' to Fight Project," p. 29.

106   "The scythe of progress": Charles Grutzner, "Stevens Expands Lincoln Sq. Plans," *New York Times,* Oct. 27, 1956.

106   "We cannot rebuild": Videotape of Lincoln Center dedication ceremony, Metropolitan Transportation Authority Special Archives.

107   "The bulldozer approach": "Wagner Opposes 'Village' Change," *New York Times,* Aug. 18, 1961, p. 23.

107   The city had: Jacobs, interview with Kent.

108   The Committee to Save the West Village: Ibid.

108   On many nights: Alice Alexiou, *Jane Jacobs: Urban Visionary* (New Brunswick, N.J.: Rutgers University Press, 2006), p. 102.

108   Leaflets could be dropped off: Jacobs, interview with Kent.

109   "We understood": Ibid.

109   Eisner confirmed: Amateau, "Jane Jacobs Comes Back to the Village She Saved."

109   "I urge you to vote": Sam Pope Brewer, " 'Villagers' Seek to Halt Renewal," *New York Times,* March 4, 1961, p. 11.

110   "They brought this proposal": Ibid.

110   "We couldn't go two steps": Priscilla Chapman, "City Critic in Favor of Old Neighborhoods," *New York Herald Tribune,* March 4, 1961.

110   A *New York Times* reporter: John Sibley, " 'Village' Housing a Complex Issue," *New York Times,* March 23, 1961, p. 35.

111   It was standard practice: Jane Jacobs, interview with James Howard Kunstler, *Metropolis,* March 2001.

111   When the SoHo housing project: Sam Pope Brewer, "Project Foe Hits 'Village' Group," *New York Times,* March 14, 1961, p. 26.

112   She told reporters: Ibid.

112   In March 1961: Sam Pope Brewer, "Citizens Housing Group Backs 'Village' Urban Renewal Study," *New York Times,* March 28, 1961, p. 33.

112   The commentators included: "Civic Groups Score 'Village' Project," *New York Times,* March 28, 1961, p. 40.

113   "I think it should be": Mayor Wagner Papers, as cited in Klemek, "Urbanism as Reform," chap. 4.

113   They wore slogans: Walter D. Litell, "Embattled Villagers Defend Home," *New York Herald Tribune,* March 28, 1961.

113   An Associated Press photographer: Jacobs, interview with Kent.

113   "People who get marked": Jacobs, *Death and Life of Great American Cities,* p. 5.

113   "We are prepared": Richard J. H. Johnston, " 'Village' Group Wins Court Stay," *New York Times,* March 28, 1961, p. 34.

114   Wagner laughed: Ibid.

114   After the hearing: John Sibley, "New Housing Idea to Get Test Here," *New York Times,* May 23, 1961.

114   At a hearing in May: John Sibley, "Planners Hailed on New Approach," *New York Times,* May 25, 1961, p. 37.

114   The petition demanded: John Sibley, "Ouster of Davies and Felt Sought," *New York Times*, June 8, 1961.

115   Still, the mayor's: "Wagner Opposes 'Village' Change," *New York Times*, Aug. 18, 1961, p. 23.

115   On the eve of the vote: Charles G. Bennett, "Mayor Abandons 'Village' Project," *New York Times*, Sept. 7, 1961, p. 31.

115   Felt wrote in a report: Edith Evans Asbury, "Plan Board Votes 'Village' Project; Crowd in Uproar," *New York Times*, Oct. 19, 1961, p. 1.

116   the mayor suggested: Ibid.

116   On October 18, 1961: "Villagers Near-Riot Jars City Planning Commission," *New York Herald Tribune*, Oct. 19, 1961.

117   "You are not an elected official!": Ibid.

118   "We had been ladies and gentlemen": Edith Evans Asbury, "Deceit Charged in 'Village' Plan," *New York Times*, Oct. 20, 1961, p. 68.

119   Flipping through her saved correspondence: Jacobs, interview with Kent.

119   Surrounded by angry residents: Walter D. Litell, "West Villagers Still on Warpath," *New York Herald Tribune*, Oct. 20, 1961.

120   "It's the same old story": Asbury, "Plan Board Votes 'Village' Project," p. 1.

120   "For the past ten years": Edith Evans Asbury, " 'Village' Project Backed in Fight," *New York Times*, Oct. 21, 1961, p. 24.

120   there was still work to do: Edith Evans Asbury, "Board Ends Plan for West Village," *New York Times*, Oct. 25, 1961, p. 39.

121   first full profile of Jacobs: Brooks Atkinson, "Critic at Large: Jane Jacobs, Author of Book on Cities, Makes the Most of Living in One," *New York Times*, Nov. 10, 1961.

123   "The economic rationale": Jacobs, *Death and Life of Great American Cities*, pp. 5–7.

123   "Intricate minglings": Ibid., p. 222.

124   "a brashly impressive tour de force": Lloyd Rodwin, "Neighbors Are Needed," *New York Times Book Review*, Nov. 5, 1961.

124   In the book: Jacobs, *Death and Life of Great American Cities*, p. 90.

125   letter to Bennett Cerf: Moses to Cerf, Jacobs Papers, box 07-2670.

126   "Mrs. Jacobs has presented": Dennis O'Harrow, "Jacobean Revival," American Society of Planning Officials newsletter, Feb. 1962.

126   "In asking for comment": Mumford to Wensberg, Jacobs Papers, box 13, folder 11.

126   In a scathing review: Lewis Mumford, "Mother Jacobs' Home Remedies," *New Yorker*, Dec. 1, 1962.

126   It was as if: Written comments on newsletter, Jacobs Papers, box 07-2670.

126   "She describes her folksy": Roger Starr, "Adventures in Mooritania," Citizens Housing and Planning Council of New York Inc. newsletter, June 1962.

127   The free economy: "Plans Against People," Review and Outlook, *Wall Street Journal*, Oct. 19, 1961.

127   She inscribed a copy: Copy of *The Death and Life of Great American Cities* owned by Kennedy Smith.

128 She pronounced the project: James V. Cunningham, "Jane Jacobs Visits Pittsburgh," *New City,* Sept. 15, 1962.

128 "You must have heard": William Allan, "City Planning Critic Gets Roasting Reply," *Pittsburgh Press,* Feb. 22, 1962.

128 On a tour of Philadelphia: Frederick Pillsbury, "I Like Philadelphia," *Sunday Bulletin Magazine,* June 24, 1962.

129 "Madonna misericordia": Jane Kramer, "All the Ranks and Rungs of Jacobs' Ladder," *Village Voice,* Dec. 20, 1962.

129 "We don't live in no slum": Roger Starr, *The Living End: The City and Its Critics* (New York: Coward-McCann, 1966), p. 103.

129 "I like attention paid": Adele Freedman, "Jane Jacobs," *Globe and Mail* (Toronto), June 9, 1984.

130 "Our sympathy goes out": Charles G. Bennett, "City Gives Up Plan for West Village," *New York Times,* Feb. 1, 1962, p. 30.

130 "I'm talking about": "Writer Sees Blacklist on Negro Home Loans," *Philadelphia Inquirer,* Oct. 23, 1962.

131 a radical idea from the start: Alexander Burnham, " 'Village' Group Designs Housing to Preserve Character of the Area," *New York Times,* May 6, 1963, p. 1.

132 "Not a single person": West Village Houses brochure, Jacobs Papers.

132 "It appears": Burnham, " 'Village' Group Designs Housing to Preserve Character of Area," p. 1.

133 "We are really not against": Jerome Zukowsky, "Villagers Want 5-Tier Walkups to 'Save' Area," *New York Herald Tribune,* May 6, 1963.

133 issued a statement: Burnham, " 'Village' Group Designs Housing to Preserve Character of Area," p. 1.

133 William Zeckendorf: "Zeckendorf Is Back with Old Dreams and a Dowager's Money," *House and Home,* March 1968, as cited in Max Allen, ed., *Ideas That Matter* (Toronto: Ginger Press, 1997).

134 Paul Goldberger: Paul Goldberger, "Low-Rise, Low-Key Housing Concept Gives Banality a Test in West Village," *New York Times,* Sept. 28, 1974, p. 31.

135 ran another profile: "Crusader on Housing," *New York Times,* May 6, 1963.

Five: The Lower Manhattan Expressway

137 "The Triborough Bridge": Robert Moses, speech at the fifth anniversary of the opening of the Triborough Bridge, as cited in Robert Moses and the Modern City, exhibit at the Museum of the City of New York, Jan.–May 2007, Hilary Ballon and Kenneth T. Jackson, curators.

138 "Greater convenience, greater happiness": Interstate Highway System, Dwight D. Eisenhower Presidential Library & Museum, www.eisenhower.archives.gov.

140 For years, many New Yorkers: Hilary Ballon and Kenneth T. Jackson, eds., *Robert Moses and the Modern City* (New York: W. W. Norton, 2007).

144   The Associated Fur Manufacturers: Morris Kaplan, "Industry Opposes Midtown Artery," *New York Times*, Aug. 1, 1957, p. 26.

144   Midtown was going to suffer: Robert Moses and the Modern City, exhibit at the Museum of the City of New York.

145   "The route of the proposed expressway": Triborough Bridge and Tunnel Authority and New York City Port Authority, *Joint Study of Arterial Facilities* (1955).

148   Scattered merchants: Charles G. Bennett, "Residents Assail Downtown Route," *New York Times*, Dec. 10, 1959, p. 44.

148   "Not to be overlooked": Editorial, *New York Times*, Nov. 16, 1959.

149   Together with fellow Democratic state senator: Douglas Dales, "Bill Attacks Plans for Expressway," *New York Times*, Jan. 15, 1960.

149   He encouraged the editorial writers: Editorial, *New York Times*, Nov. 7, 1960.

149   It would be pure folly: Joseph C. Ingraham, "Moses Warns City on Expressway," *New York Times*, Aug. 24, 1960, p. 31.

149   "There is no point": Charles G. Bennett, "Expressway Plea by Moses Ignored," *New York Times*, Aug. 25, 1960, p. 31.

150   "No hasty action": Charles G. Bennett, "Crosstown Road Deemed Far Off," *New York Times*, Nov. 1, 1960, p. 41.

150   The report by Relocation and Management Associates: Charles G. Bennett, "City Withholding Expressway Data," *New York Times*, Jan. 3, 1961.

150   Moses railed against any hint: "City to Complete Road Begun in '39," *New York Times*, Jan. 16, 1961.

150   Mayor Wagner had dropped: Joseph C. Ingraham, "Expressway Gets Mayor's Support," *New York Times*, Feb. 13, 1962, p. 29.

150   "Where can I go?": John F. Murphy, "Emotions Mixed on Proposed Manhattan Expressway," *New York Times*, Feb. 27, 1961, p. 29.

150   monopolized the proceedings: Charles G. Bennett, "2 Angry Groups Picket City Hall," *New York Times*, April 1, 1962, p. 35.

150   The deputy mayor even threatened: Charles G. Bennett, "Board Expedites City Expressway," *New York Times*, April 6, 1962, p. 37.

151   On one occasion: Leo Egan, "Moses Scolds City as Coy on Virtues," *New York Times*, April 22, 1960, p. 33.

151   A brighter moment came: "Mrs. Roosevelt Scores Road Plan," *New York Times*, June 19, 1962, p. 37.

152   all in opposition to Lomex: Robert B. Semple Jr., "Little Italy Wins Stunning Victory over Big Highway," *National Observer*, Dec. 24, 1962.

153   The E. V. Haughwout building: Ada Louise Huxtable, "Noted Buildings in Path of Road," *New York Times*, July 22, 1965.

154   "It's all part of a huge": *Village Voice*, Aug. 30, 1962.

155   she helped orchestrate: Alice Alexiou, *Jane Jacobs: Urban Visionary* (New Brunswick, N.J.: Rutgers University Press, 2006).

155 Bob Dylan: Roberta Brandes Gratz, *Cities Back from the Edge* (New York: Wiley, 1998), p. 298.
156 "Every delay gives added hope": "Decision on Expressway Urged; Auto Club Scores Delay by City," *New York Times,* July 9, 1962, p. 33.
156 Jacobs reminded reporters: Charles G. Bennett, "New Delay Looms for Expressway," *New York Times,* Aug. 17, 1962.
156 he was quoted saying: Edith Evans Asbury, "Downtown Group Fights Road Plan," *New York Times,* Dec. 5, 1962, p. 49.
157 "The expressway would": *Village Voice,* Aug. 30, 1962.
157 "We always have been trying": Joseph C. Ingraham, "Now, More Roads," *New York Times,* Nov. 23, 1964, p. 41.
157 One evening, La Mountain informed Jacobs: Jane Jacobs, interview with Leticia Kent, oral history project for the Greenwich Village Historical Society, Jane Jacobs Papers, MS02-13, John J. Burns Library, Boston College.
158 At the Board of Estimate hearing: Robert Moses, *Public Works: A Dangerous Trade* (New York: McGraw-Hill, 1970).
158 Jacobs planted a tree: Jason Epstein, interview with author, Sept. 2007.
158 "We won! Isn't it marvelous!": Jacobs Papers, MS02-13.
158 "You can well imagine": Ibid.
159 He promised a new: Charles G. Bennett, "Expressway Plan Revived by Moses," *New York Times,* April 11, 1963, p. 35.
159 "No matter where": Charles G. Bennett, "Planners Urged to Revive Downtown Expressway," *New York Times,* April 18, 1963.
159 "I have yet to hear": "Barnes Sails into Troubled Waters," *Village Voice,* Jan. 3, 1963. In a clip of the article, Jacobs wrote in the margin: "In my own way I helped stave off this disaster—what a bastard Barnes was!"
160 "It's before the mayor": Murray Illson, "Moses Optimistic on Expressway," *New York Times,* Jan. 24, 1964, p. 24.
160 "would turn downtown Manhattan": Edith Evans Asbury, "Showdown Nears on Expressway to Traverse Lower Manhattan," *New York Times,* June 5, 1964.
160 "The basic problem in New York": Editorial, *New York Herald Tribune,* Jan. 31, 1965.
160 proposals for a newfangled Lomex: "Renewal Proposed Along Expressway," *New York Times,* Aug. 3, 1964.
161 "We better start planning": Joseph Lelyveld, "Decision Pending on Expressway," *New York Times,* Jan. 24, 1965, p. 71.
161 "We're not going to stall": Charles G. Bennett, "Wagner Studying Expressway Data," *New York Times,* Dec. 24, 1964.
162 "Most gratifying": Clayton Knowles, "Wagner Orders Building of Manhattan Expressway," *New York Times,* May 26, 1965, p. 1.
162 "A world is being destroyed": Samuel Kaplan, "Expressway Vexes Broome Street," *New York Times,* May 27, 1965, p. 39.

162   In the summer of 1965: Ada Louise Huxtable, "Lindsay Surveys City from Copter," *New York Times,* July 24, 1965, p. 8.
162   Lindsay called Wagner's lame-duck endorsement: Martin G. Berck, "Leave Expressway Question to Next Mayor—Lindsay," *New York Herald Tribune,* July 23, 1965.
163   "We would appreciate photos": Moses to Charles Moerdler (buildings commissioner), Dec. 29, 1966, Metropolitan Transportation Authority Special Archives.
163   He urged the city transportation chief: "Moses' Prediction Angers Opponents of Manhattan Expressway," *New York Times,* June 28, 1964, p. 41.
163   made available to reporters: Moses to Arthur Palmer (transportation administrator), Sept. 28, 1966, Metropolitan Transportation Authority Special Archives.
164   "That area is our neighbor": Lelyveld, "Decision Pending on Expressway," p. 71.
165   The 139 iron-front buildings: Joyce Wadler, "Public Lives: A Polite Defender of SoHo's Cast-Iron Past," *New York Times,* May 29, 1998.
165   Gayle's practical approach: Jacobs to Gayle, Nov. 15, 1993, courtesy of Carol Gayle.
165   "dubious historical and artistic value": Moses to Palmer, Feb. 7, 1966, Metropolitan Transportation Authority Special Archives.
166   "One of the principal reasons": Madigan-Hyland Inc., "Need for the Lower Manhattan Expressway," 1965, Metropolitan Transportation Authority Special Archives, 1012-4A.
166   "What is now little more": Excerpts from opening statement of Charles F. Preusse on behalf of the Triborough Bridge and Tunnel Authority, Dec. 22, 1964, Metropolitan Transportation Authority Special Archives.
166   *This Urgent Need: This Urgent Need,* 1964, Metropolitan Transportation Authority Special Archives.
167   "Traffic is usually self-generating": Semple, "Little Italy Wins Stunning Victory over Big Highway."
167   threatened a citywide work stoppage: "Building Trades Picketers at City Hall," *Village Voice,* June 10, 1965.
168   a possible solution: Steven V. Roberts, "City Considering Proposal for 80-Foot Elevated Lower Manhattan Skyway," *New York Times,* Sept. 28, 1966, p. 37.
168   "a complete betrayal": Edith Evans Asbury, " 'Villagers' Protest 'Secret' Road Plan," *New York Times,* March 15, 1967, p. 44.
169   "probably the most dramatic breakthrough": Ronald Maiorana, "Lindsay Lists Details of Cross-Town Road Plan," *New York Times,* Oct. 3, 1967, p. 37.
169   "The underground idea": Ibid.
170   "The in-out, over-and-under proposal": Ada Louise Huxtable, "Where It Goes Nobody Knows," *New York Times,* Feb. 2, 1969, p. D32.

170 "The citizenry never wins": Clayton Knowles, "More Road Study Asked by Sutton," *New York Times,* March 29, 1967, p. 51.

170 It was critical: Mike Pearl, "Jane Jacobs Charges a 'Gag' Attempt," *New York Post,* April 18, 1968.

172 "I hate the government": Jane Jacobs and the Future of New York, exhibition at the Municipal Art Society, New York, 2007–2008.

172 heard about it just in time: Frances Goldman, interview with author, April 15, 2007.

173 At the microphone: Leticia Kent, "Persecution of the City Performed by Its Inmates," *Village Voice,* April 18, 1968.

173 time to give the "errand boys": Jacobs, interview with Kent.

174 The terrified stenotypist: Jacobs to Bess Butzner, April 11, 1968, as cited in Max Allen, ed., *Ideas That Matter* (Toronto: Ginger Press, 1997).

174 "I have been arrested again!": Ibid.

175 The events of the evening: Richard Severo, "Mrs. Jacobs's Protest Results in Riot Charge," *New York Times,* April 18, 1968, p. 49.

175 "If this is how": Ibid.

175 Jacobs was laughingly being accused: Peter Blake, "About Mayor Lindsay, Jane Jacobs, and Peter Bogardus," *New York,* May 1968.

176 "As you know, Jane was arrested": Invitation by the West Village Committee, Jacobs Papers.

176 "By joining together": Cooper Square Community Development Committee and Businessmen's Association, press release, May 10, 1968, Jacobs Papers.

177 project was dead "for all time": Maurice Carroll, "Mayor Drops Plans for Express Roads," *New York Times,* July 17, 1969, p. 1.

177 In August 1970 he sent a package: Moses to Reuben Maury of the New York *Daily News,* Aug. 31, 1970, Metropolitan Transportation Authority Special Archives.

178 "It is clear that the people": Governor Nelson A. Rockefeller, statement, June 3, 1973, State of New York Executive Chamber, as cited in Ballon and Jackson, *Robert Moses and the Modern City,* p. 241.

Epilogue: Separate Ways

181 She had made a deal: *Village Voice,* Oct. 3, 1968.

183 And in New York: "Hunts Point Campaign Comes to Manhattan," *Hunts Point Express,* Nov. 26, 2007.

183 Even in Los Angeles: Steve Hymon, "L.A. Officials Do a 180 in Traffic Planning," *Los Angeles Times,* Feb. 25, 2008.

184 "I resent": Susan Brownmiller, "Jane Jacobs, Civic Battler," *Vogue,* May 1969.

185 A roommate at Yale: David Dunlap, "All in the Planning, and Worth Preserving," *New York Times,* April 27, 2006.

185 "There's nobody that I know": Susan Zielinski, interview with author, Feb. 2008.

185 Harvard professor James Stockard: James Stockard, interview with author, Oct. 1, 2008.

185 The American Planning Association: American Planning Association Web site, www.planning.org.

186 Everything from the design: David Brooks, "A Defining Moment," *New York Times,* March 4, 2008.

187 Though there was an entire chapter: Norman Oder, "The Missing Jane Jacobs Chapter in *The Power Broker,*" Atlantic Yards Report, Oct. 9, 2007, http://atlanticyardsreport.blogspot.com/2007/10/missing-jane-jacobs-chapter -in-power.html.

187 "Bob is reading one of them": Jacobs to her mother, June 12, 1974, as cited in Max Allen, ed., *Ideas That Matter* (Toronto: Ginger Press, 1997).

188 "The current fiction": David Dunlap, "Scrutinizing the Legacy of Robert Moses," *New York Times,* May 11, 1987 p. B1.

188 "He loved it down here": Carol Paquette, "Showcasing the Career of Robert Moses," *New York Times,* Oct. 1, 1995.

189 It was Herbert Kaufman: Herbert Kaufman, "Robert Moses: Charismatic Bureaucrat," *Political Science Quarterly* 90, no. 3 (Autumn 1975), pp. 521–38.

189 "Today, the pendulum of opinion": Nicolai Ouroussoff, "Outgrowing Jane Jacobs and Her New York," *New York Times,* April 30, 2006.

190 "BANANAs": Anthony Flint, "Menino Urges Business Leaders to Become More Involved," *Boston Globe,* Feb. 4, 1999, p. 24.

192 "I accepted it because": Jane Jacobs, caption in Allen, *Ideas That Matter,* p. 150.

192 Without her lifelong partner: Mark Feeney, "City Sage," *Boston Globe,* Nov. 14, 1993.

192 Jacobs had removed some interior walls: Jane Jacobs, interview with James Howard Kunstler, *Metropolis,* March 2001.

193 "I know a lot of planners": "Jane Jacobs and the New Urban Ecology," Boston College, Nov. 18, 2000, transcript, Jane Jacobs Papers, MS02-13, box 9, folder 2, John J. Burns Library, Boston College.

193 One resident said: Albert Amateau, "Jane Jacobs Comes Back to the Village She Saved," *Villager,* May 12, 2004.

194 On May 24, 2006: Patrick Arden, "Knitters Protest Park Project Knotted Up in Court," *Metro,* May 24, 2006.

194 The Jane Jacobs Medal: Rockefeller Foundation, www.rockfound.org.

195 While the street sign: "Let the Jane Jacobs Tributes Continue," Gothamist, gothamist.com, June 9, 2006.

195 "From this house": Dunlap, "All in the Planning, and Worth Preserving."

Page numbers in *italics* refer to photographs.

A

ABOUT THE AUTHOR

ANTHONY FLINT has been a journalist for twenty-five years, primarily at the *Boston Globe*, where he covered planning and development, architecture and urban design, and housing and transportation. He is now at the Lincoln Institute of Land Policy, a think tank in Cambridge, Massachusetts. He was a Loeb fellow at Harvard University in 2000–2001, a visiting scholar at the Graduate School of Design at Harvard while writing his first book, *This Land: The Battle Over Sprawl and the Future of America* (2006), and a policy adviser in the Massachusetts state government agency coordinating housing, transportation, energy, and the environment. A graduate of Middlebury College and the Columbia University Graduate School of Journalism, he lives in Boston with his wife and three sons.

ABOUT THE TYPE

This book was set in Fairfield, the first typeface from the hand of the distinguished American artist and engraver Rudolph Ruzicka (1883–1978). Ruzicka was born in Bohemia and came to America in 1894. He set up his own shop, devoted to wood engraving and printing, in New York in 1913 after a varied career working as a wood engraver, in photoengraving and banknote printing plants, and as an art director and freelance artist. He designed and illustrated many books, and was the creator of a considerable list of individual prints—wood engravings, line engravings on copper, and aquatints.